# ACCORDING TO ROGER

## My Journey Into Bible Truth

### Second Edition

# ACCORDING TO ROGER

My Journey into Bible Truth
*Philippine Copyright 2009*

By;
Roger Walkwitz

**2nd Edition**

All Rights Reserved.

ISBN 13: 978-1463699741
ISBN 10: 1463699743

# ACCORDING TO ROGER

## My Journey Into Bible Truth
### Second Edition

Roger  W. Walkwitz
Asia Pacific Messianic Fellowship
2751 SE 150th Ave, Morriston, FL 32668, USA
Roger@Walkwitz.com
www.Walkwitz.com/Roger

*"If you love Me, keep My Commandments!"* John 14:15

Listen to Our Story Dramatized!
Go to: www.unshackeled.org
Click on: Listen Online
Click on: Archives 2008
Click on: Programs 3007 & 8
Enjoy! Now read the book
and fill in the details!!

# CONTENTS

i

ii

# FOREWORD

The first time I heard Roger Walkwitz refer to Jesus as Yeshua, I was surprised. From the time I first met him when he married my sister, Naomi, until I wrote his testimony for "Unshackled!" fifty years later, I had witnessed a man completely dedicated to the Most High God and the study of His Word, the Holy Bible. Now he called Him Yeshua. Why?

The Lord Jesus Christ is the name most followers of Jesus use, and so did Roger for decades. But his understanding of the Bible grew as he studied God's Word. And study he did. My husband was a fighter pilot in Vietnam, taking R & R, when he visited Roger and Naomi in Banaue, Philippines. He enthused about Roger's clever invention, described in this book, that brought water to their home above the rice terraces. And, he added, Roger was translating the Bible into the Ifugao language.

We visited them in Hawaii in 1969, taking our sons. We didn't know Jesus then, but we saw Jesus in them. And no wonder: Roger was always studying the Bible.

In 1972 I fled Malaysia to their world in Baguio, Philippines as my marriage fell apart. Roger and Naomi prayed for us. They were the only Christians I knew, the only Bible I read. I envied the peace they had, but it was nine years before I was born into God's Kingdom. My husband and I remarried, thanks to the faithfulness of God and the prayers of saints.

Like Roger, my first exposure to a Messianic Jew was a shock. I didn't know there were Jews who believed in Jesus as Messiah. That man, like Roger, was a Bible to me, pointing to the scriptures. But Roger was way out in front, digging deeper into Bible truth. By then, 1982, he knew the importance of Israel in God's plan and was teaching others the prophesies of the Old Testament.

When I began writing radio dramas for "Unshackled!" testimonies came in from Messianic Jews, followers of Yeshua. Roger and Naomi were retired from missionary service in the Philippines and reaching out to Jews, especially in the Far East. This year they shared their testimony as an "Unshackled!" radio drama. Writing the script, I learned the source of Roger's unwavering dedication to the Bible, his love for the Lord.

This book reveals a couple's commitment to the Lord and His Truth. No matter where you are in your walk with Him, I invite you to read and be challenged to make your own discovery of Bible Truth.

Kennetha Gaebler
Colorado Springs, CO
October 2008

# INTRODUCTION

For many years, my wonderful Bible students in the Philippines have asked me, "Sir, please write down your teachings in a book for us." My reply has always been: that takes too much time and I do not have that kind of time. It would take isolation of a sort, away from distractions and interruptions, to allow Yeshua to write that book in my mind first. Then I can sit down and type it out.

However, it seems that now, at the beginning of 2008, that that time has come. Why now? The Pacific Garden Mission in Chicago had asked for Our Story to dramatize on their long running radio drama "Unshackled!" This will be an opportunity for the Lord to use our Testimony of His Love and Faithfulness to reach out to many people worldwide. Therefore, it is with great pleasure that I put down in writing Our Story. My mind is filled with things to say, people and events to refer to, praises to our Messiah Yeshua for all He has done to fulfill His Promises! It has been a wonderful journey, walking with Him, watching Him work through me and others to accomplish His goals.

**ACCORDING TO ROGER,** then, is my story, my journey into Bible Truth and the necessary practice of that Truth in everyday life. In no way do I claim infallibility for any of my conclusions, as infallibility is not possible for any human being. However, being an honest scientist, I am fully convinced of my conclusions with no known errors. Even then, there are many things I do not understand or cannot explain. If , after examining my conclusions any reader might have evidence to the contrary, I would like to hear about it. Opinions and Traditions I know already. It is evidence that I seek.

Naturally, many persons and teachers have influenced my understanding of Scripture. These include my parents, Clarence & Emma Walkwitz; sister Mildred and brother Don; those at my lifelong home church, College Church in Wheaton, IL; my close friends during high school years and after; Wheaton College where I earned a BS CHEMISTRY, a professional degree; fellow faculty members at Bryan College where I taught chemistry, math, and coached track and cross country; Columbia International University where I earned an MA in Biblical Education; University of North Dakota-Summer Institute of Linguistics, where I almost earned a master's degree in linguistics; Missionary Internship at Ward Presbyterian Church in Livonia, MI; the University of Hawaii where I earned an MEd in Science Education; Jerusalem University College-Institute of Holy Land Studies where I earned a Graduate Certificate in Middle Eastern Studies; fellow missionaries in the Philippines with Far Eastern Gospel Crusade, now known as SEND International; the many Believers in Yeshua (Jesus) among the BIBAK mountain tribes people of Northern Luzon, Philippines; many keen Believers in the Philippine lowlands and other countries; excellent Messianic Jewish Bible teachers of more recent days; and the many authors of good books, some of whom I know and others I have never met personally.

However, there is one person that had a great input in early years into my approach to and understanding of Scripture, by challenging Traditions! That man was Ralph Mount, Naomi's pastor when she was young, who watched over her as a virtual orphan, making sure that she finished a degree at Bryan College. Ralph Mount was a mechanical engineer who supported himself and his family in various ways while pastoring Pleasant Valley Baptist Church in Mansfield, OH. Ordained in the American Baptist Denomination, his example was very biblical by not taking a salary from the church.

As an engineer and Bible student, the Wilderness Tabernacle was a fascination for him. He wrote his findings in a book, *The Law Prophesied*, in 1963. His book is far and above any other book on the subject that I have found, including in Israel, and his scale models superior to any other. His interest in prophecy led to writing *Babylon* in 1964, and his deep interest and love for Israel and the Jewish people led to writing *A Land Born in a Day*, also in 1964. I also continue to be keenly interested in these myself.

About the time that we left the USA (end of 1957) to serve as missionaries to the mountain tribes people of the Philippines, Ralph and Marianna Mount began traveling the USA for 14 years, teaching in more than 300 churches, Bible schools, and seminaries. His main teaching was a week long demonstrated series on The Tabernacle, with his models. After that he bought some land in Florida, subdivided it, hoping to develop a congenial Christian community, and settled down to study some more. In 1982 we bought a house and lot in his subdivision for future retirement, and in which our son and daughter-in-law, Ray & Carolyn, lived until we did "retire" about 10 years later.

Naomi, my wife of 52 years, naturally has had a big influence on my life, beliefs, and practices as we debate issues, interpretations, and applications of Scripture. She also produced (with my help!) three stalwart sons: Ray, Randy, and Ron. She also did the majority of their home schooling up to eighth grade. Ray with Carolyn, Joshua, and Ben went to be with Yeshua as the result of a fiery plane crash in the Bahamas on March 22, 1998. Randy with Janie, Jake, and Sam live in Glendale, Arizona, while Ron is still single as of this writing and lives next to us in Morriston, Florida. We are a small family but a precious one, thanks to the graciousness of our Lord!

However, my greatest Teacher has been and is the Spirit of God. He has opened my understanding time and again, just like Yeshua promised! The conclusions reached are still my own as guided by the Spirit, but as stated above, I do not claim infallibility and cannot blame the Spirit for any potential mistakes. However, at this point I am sure of my conclusions with no doubts. In my explanation of Scriptures, it will be necessary to cite a few Hebrew and Greek words. These will be written in English letters, not in Hebrew and Greek. For emphasis I may underline or **bold type** certain words or phrases, as this is a teaching book, not just an autobiography or storybook.

As this book unfolds, may God's glory shine in the Truths He has taught me, and may it be an instrument in His hands to guide others in their **Journey Into Bible Truth and Practice**.

Roger W. Walkwitz
2751 SE 150th Ave.
Morriston, FL 32668, USA
March 22, 2009

# CHAPTER ONE

## In The Beginning, God Created the Heavens and the Earth

Whether it was hot or cold, sunshine or rain, day or night, I do not know, except that a birth certificate says that on September 14, 1929, Clarence and Emma Walkwitz had a baby boy named Roger William Walkwitz at a hospital in Mt. Clemens, Michigan. What I do know is that six weeks later, the Stock Market crashed and the Great Depression began. Was there a connection between the two? What I also know is that Emma Walkwitz lost a small fortune, an inheritance from her prosperous Iowa farmer father, in the Stock Market crash. Dad was a giver, Mom was a saver, and so we barely survived the lean years of the Great Depression, like many others.

My boyhood was lived all over the USA. My earliest memory was living in St. Petersburg, Florida, where my younger brother, Don, was born in 1933. My older sister, Mildred, was born in Denver, Colorado, in 1926. Dad was a civil engineer, the superintendent on the job to make sure the contractor followed all the specifications on large building projects. As each building was completed, Dad was transferred to another state and another project. My elementary school years were in Kansas, Minnesota, Michigan, and Ohio. As a result, no friendships, not even contacts, remain from those years.

During those early years, our family attended quite regularly either a Congregational or Presbyterian church. Mom was raised Lutheran; Dad, a Presbyterian. But neither knew anything about salvation in Jesus Christ. I remember going to DVBS (Daily Vacation Bible School) in Ohio and memorizing some verses. But like my parents, I did not know I needed to be born-from-above. We were just urged to be good, to keep the Ten Commandments and the Beatitudes. In Zanesville, Ohio, I attended the communicants class for 12-year-olds, preparatory for church membership, and memorized much of the Westminster Catechism. When Dad was being transferred to the Chicago area in 1941, I had to go ahead of the class and face the Elder Board alone so I could pass before we moved. I then became a member of the Central Presbyterian Church of Zanesville, Ohio. This was in December 1941.

After I had answered all their questions satisfactorily, the Elders asked me what I thought I wanted to do with my life. My answer? I have to chuckle at that today — was it prophetic? I told them that I thought I would like to be a preacher! They all thought that was so wonderful, that this dear 12-year-old boy was dedicating his life to be a preacher! What I did not tell them was that I thought being a preacher looked like a pretty soft, easy job, which, for the churches we had been in, was probably the case. So early on, I formed some opinions of the clergy class that would be significant as time went on.

The pastor at this Presbyterian Church in Ohio had gone to Princeton Seminary. When he learned that Dad was thinking of relocating to Wheaton, Illinois, near Chicago, he said that we ought to look up his seminary classmate there, Evan Welsh, the pastor of College Church in Wheaton. We moved to Wheaton a week before Pearl Harbor, December 1941. College Church was independent. We were more comfortable with mainline denominations, so we went to the Presbyterian Church in Wheaton. We did not find a warm welcome there, so after a few weeks, we decided to check out College Church.

At College Church we did find a warm welcome and a new style of service and message content. Before long we learned that being good was not enough. We had to be "born again" — we had to make a public profession of faith in Jesus Christ! So over the next few years, each of our family of five did just that. Dad was 48, Mom 46; both began eagerly studying the Word, by radio and correspondence courses from Moody Bible Institute in Chicago, in addition to the classes at College Church. Prophecy taught Sunday afternoons by a retired foreign missionary really motivated Dad and Mom to dig into the Scriptures.

After struggling with the Lord for some time, I made my public profession of faith in Jesus Christ in February 1943, at age 13, during some special evangelistic meetings at College Church with Torrey Johnson preaching. Only one other professed that night, a pretty 11-year-old girl. I thought, "Lord, do you have something in mind for the two of us together?" Apparently not, as she married a doctor and went to Africa as a missionary, while I was later called to the Philippines.

Discipling has rarely been what it ought to be. I just continued on with the programs of the church with no special follow up. However, I was hungry to really know the Bible, so I read daily, starting from Genesis 1. **"In the beginning, God created the heavens and the earth."** That was plain and simple. God created everything just like He said, in 6 days of 24 hours each. Evolution is a lie, a big hoax of the devil! This Truth was to be foundational forever, through all my scientific study and teaching, especially as I was writing my thesis/paper on evolution for my M.Ed. in Science Education at the University of Hawaii in 1969. The faculty committee of three were all evolutionists, but they gave me an "A" because I had proved my point, that teaching high school biology without considering all aspects of origins was not scientific! "Evolution only" showed prejudice.

I found that Genesis 3 illustrates salvation quite well. God's grace reached out to Adam and Eve, offering opportunity for confession of sin and the exercise of their faith to accept God's forgiveness, and the provision of clothing made from the skin of a sacrificed lamb. "Without the shedding of blood, there is no payment for sin." It was God's initiative, which is always the case. Adam and Eve were forgiven, but the temporal result of their sin was tough to bear. Furthermore, they now had a sinful human nature, which they passed on to their children and on to every human being.

God's Promise to Abram in Genesis 12:3 made a lifelong impact on my life. Combined with being passed from Isaac and Jacob, the Promise became, **I will bless those who bless Israel and the Jews, and I will curse those who despise Israel and the Jews.** I thought, Lord, that is very clear to me. I will always be a blessing to Israel and the

Jews wherever I find them. If they are a blessing back to me, fine. If not, then that is their problem, not mine. Over the years we have had many Jewish Israeli friends, and we have stayed in their homes in Israel, with very, very few "who did not want to be blessed" by our friendship.

Bible teaching and evangelism are best done by starting with Genesis. A foundation of ultimate Truth needs to be laid as to who God is and who we are, and the relationship between the two, before an intelligent, valid decision can be made to surrender one's life and to put one's complete trust in the LORD Jesus Christ (*YHVH Yeshua HaMashiach*). Our part lies in evangelism, teaching and prayer. God still has His part -- enlightening the mind and heart to His Truth by His Spirit.

# CHAPTER 2

# Wheaton Community High School, Class of 1947

Junior High, grades 7 and 8, were rather nondescript, as I continued to read my Bible and to grow spiritually and socially, slowly overcoming my shyness and making a few friends. During these two years, I had a newspaper route and a grocery store job to earn spending money. World War II was at its height. Food and gasoline were rationed.

As a freshman in Wheaton Community High School (WCHS), I decided to take Latin. It turned out to be a good choice. I not only learned grammar, but the Latin Club banquet on March 15, 1944, the "Ides of March," also proved to be a significant day for my future. All freshman boys taking Latin were to be the "slaves," the servers at the banquet. While waiting in the lower hall after school let out until it was time to set up for the evening banquet in the cafeteria, I stood around watching the track team practice up and down the hallways and stairs. It was cold and snowing outside.

Soon Herbert Hodges, the track coach, came over to me and said, "Walkwitz, why don't you come out for track?" "Shucks, I can't run," I replied, which was true. I was not an athlete in any sense of the word. I was a skinny scholar type, but Coach Hodges encouraged me. I told him that my Dad had told me that I almost died of a weak heart when I was about 2 years old, so how could I be a runner? "Get a physical from a doctor and come on out," Coach Hodges said.

I did get the physical. The doctor said that I should work up slowly and that should strengthen my heart. So I joined the track team. The perk was that I was now excused from PE, which I did not like, and given a study hall instead. When the weather cleared a bit, we would run around the paved circle in front of the school, while the track was still soggy wet. I was the laughing stock of the track team since I could not run quietly on my toes, but went flat-footed plop plop. Everyone could hear me coming. I learned to laugh at myself too, and we had good times together.

This was essential physical development for the pioneer missionary work Yeshua had in mind for me in the mountains of the Philippines. A strong heart and body would be absolutely essential. Cross-country running was added the next year, which was good for the heart, lungs and muscles. I was able to earn a varsity letter in both cross-country and track for my junior and senior years.

A requirement for my senior English class was for everyone to write a speech that would be suitable for giving at graduation time. "My Future in Chemistry" seemed to grab the interest of the selection committee, so I was one of five who would have to memorize and give his speech. The main speaker was Dr. Preston Bradley, a very liberal preacher from Chicago. Without telling anyone, I decided to add a very short testimony for Jesus at the end of my speech, as I was growing in my boldness and confidence to speak out for my Lord. I had to give an alternative to what Dr. Bradley probably would say about God.

Spiritual growth from my daily Bible reading and study was augmented by activities of the high school youth group at College Church. It was newly formed and named Hyacks, an acronym formed from <u>high</u> school and <u>aca</u>demy, as those attending came from Wheaton Academy, a private Christian school, as well as the public high school. Lifelong friends were formed there, some of them being missionary kids. Because of the war, many missionaries were not able to return to their foreign fields. Many settled in Wheaton, so I observed how they lived. Some were jobless, as all they knew to do was teaching and preaching. Apparently, they did not have a secular profession or capability to earn a living otherwise, which was not right in my thinking. With so many men in the military, surely there would be plenty of jobs available so they would not be dependent on others for money.

It was good for me to learn about missionary life from the viewpoint of the missionary kids or MKs as we call them. As yet, I had no inkling that Yeshua would call me to become a missionary. In fact, I resisted all the emotional appeals at Missionary Conferences to volunteer or "commit my life for full-time service." That was not mine to choose. In fact, my life already belonged to the Lord and I intended to serve Him fulltime, whatever the details were. It was up to Him to direct my life for His purposes. I was willing for anything, but it was up to Him to call me specifically so that there would be no mistake. Missions is a Calling — not a profession, not a job, not an alternative to working at home. College Church had annual Missions Conferences, so I learned a lot during those years, and again, formed my own opinion about missionaries, preachers, and clergy. I preferred not to become one of them. I would serve my Lord and support myself.

I also learned a lot from my Scofield Reference Edition of the KJV Bible. God says in Revelation 2:6, "But this thou hast, that thou hatest the deeds of the Nicolaitanes, which I also hate." The footnote says, "From *nikao,* 'to conquer,' and *laos,* 'the people,' or 'laity.' There is no ancient authority for a *sect* of the Nicolaitanes. If the word is symbolic it refers to the earliest form of the notion of a priestly order, or 'clergy,' which later divided an equal brotherhood (Mt. 23:8) into 'priests' and 'laity.' What in Ephesus was 'deeds' (2:6) had become in Pergamos a 'doctrine' (Rev 2:15)."

The 1967 New Scofield Reference Edition completely changed this footnote to cover up the evidence, trying to use the writings of some later "church fathers" as justification, and trying to equate Balaamism with Nicolaitanism, which are very different. Church history is clear that the original footnote is correct, that the equal brotherhood prescribed by Jesus was changed into a clergy class and a laity class, to the detriment of the church.

Therefore, I never intended to become a clergyman. Although I much later accepted ordination as a proof of my ministry because of outside critics against me, I never assumed that status or used its titles. BIBAK Bible Fellowship was established on a non-professional, non-clergy foundation, with leadership by duly recognized Elders and Deacons, all of whom are self-supporting in their various jobs and professions. We intend to maintain the equal brotherhood that Jesus prescribed. There is strength in obeying the Lord and not giving in to Tradition that is not biblical.

During the last two years of high school, two missionary kids became special friends. Jack Fitzwilliam was repatriated with his mother, Jennie, from a concentration camp in China under the Japanese army. His father died of typhus in China when Jack was away at school. They were China Inland Mission folks, and Jack's school was in Chefoo, China. (How many wonderful stories of Chefoo I heard!) Jack also arrived in Wheaton with a British accent, which was an amusement to all of us. Jack was interested in science and was also a classmate at WCHS. Jack played on the soccer team.

Harold Cook was a missionary kid from Venezuela, South America, and the Orinoco River Mission. Harold's health turned bad as a small boy so that he could not survive in the tropics anymore. The family moved to California where his Dad taught, until he was offered a job teaching at the Moody Bible Institute in Chicago. The Cook family moved into a house just a block from ours. Harold was interested in science as well, and was one year behind Jack and me at WCHS. Harold was also a runner on the track team.

Together, the three of us formed the Trio Science Laboratories. In the basement of the Walkwitz residence, we had a chemistry lab, an electronics lab, and a photography darkroom where we could develop and print black and white film and photos. We also worked together painting houses and hanging wallpaper. We were "Inferior and Exferior Decorators." Being very kindhearted businessmen, we met expenses but did not earn very much. Every elderly family in town needed a bargain, and we gave them plenty.

# CHAPTER 3

## Christian Service Brigade and Wheaton College Class of 1951

College Church had weeklong summer Family Bible Camps at campgrounds in the area. These were lots of fun and challenging to our commitment to our Lord. By high school graduation, I had become very active, along with my friends. Some at College Church were concerned as to how to direct this activism and energy into useful ways.

One evening a representative of the Church Education Committee arrived at our house when Jack, Harold, and I were busy in our basement laboratories. They had a proposal to make. They would like us to take over the leadership of the Stockade section of the Christian Service Brigade program at the church. This was for boys 8-11 yrs old, and met on Friday evenings.

Oh, boy, what to do now? That would mess up our weekends. Besides, Jack and I had a job cleaning an office Friday evenings. Also, did we want to be tied down to such a regular ministry, every Friday? The girls would just have to fit in to our schedule...

According to Roger

Reluctantly we agreed. We were ashamed to say "No," as we felt capable of doing anything - maybe even this - although we knew the Lord had to do His work in and through us, if anything worthwhile would come of it. We were not willing to just spend time "baby sitting" or playing games. This had to be spiritually productive. And it proved to be, as we followed the lives of many of these boys as they entered adulthood and found their God-given place in society. The three of us led the Stockade for three years. Then the Battalion, for boys 12-18 years, needed a leader. So I took over that myself during my senior year at college, which allowed no time for anything extra.

As usual at this stage in life, and in the setting of a Christian college, taking Bible classes each semester in addition to our chosen major, a lot of questions come up with decisions to be made. During these four years, I remember only one direct statement from any faculty member that has stayed with me. It was in our junior year doctrine course, taught by Carl Armerding. The question of Creation and Evolution came up. Dr. Armerding stated that he did not know how many, if any, of the Wheaton faculty believed in literal Creation of 6 days of 24 hours each, but he did believe it. He was a chemistry major, and had been a foreign missionary, Bible teacher and pastor at times. His position encouraged me in my position, formed when I first read Genesis.

About 20 years later, I was helping out at Faith Academy, the school for missionary kids in the Philippines, by teaching chemistry and a few other subjects. The biology teacher was also a Wheaton grad of some years after my class. I asked her about her position on Creation. I was not too surprised at her answer. She said that she was taught Theistic Evolution at Wheaton College! However, when she went on to graduate school, she worked through the evidence and came up with the same conclusion as I did: God created everything in 6 literal days of 24 hours each, just as the Bible says; that evolution is a total lie, a hoax of the devil, as is also Theistic evolution. It is impossible to reconcile Creation with Evolution.

Creation is foundational Truth and therefore of great interest to me and my fellow teacher at Faith Academy. Therefore, I decided to write to the Board of Trustees of Wheaton College about it. In my letter I stated what Carl Armerding had said, what my fellow teacher at Faith Academy said, and what my own position and concern were. I also asked how many Wheaton faculty did believe in literal Creation. The replies I got were very sad; and yet, what was I to expect?

The Chairman of the Board of Trustees of Wheaton College at the time wrote to imply that it didn't make much of a difference, as we had more important things to deal with. The Vice-Chairman of the Board wrote that he totally agreed with me, but where could he find competent science teachers that agreed with literal Creation? The third reply was from the President. His letter "rode the fence" as a compromise, trying to justify a non-commitment to literal Creation or Evolution. No one told me if any faculty members at Wheaton did believe in literal Creation.

Wheaton College has been on the skids, on the downward slope, for many years. As a result of this, I lost most of my interest in the college. Once the foundations are eroded, the rest of the structure is going to fall, and it is falling. I attend class reunions when possible, but that is about all.

Some years after this, we were home on furlough, living in

Wheaton. All three of our sons had a year or more at Wheaton College. All three would tell me, "Dad, you would not believe what they are teaching us at Wheaton College!" We had taught them good foundational Bible Truth, so when they heard teachings off this foundation, they could spot it well and were not fooled or impressed. Students go to Wheaton to be grounded in the Bible, but instead are taught compromises with the world system.

My final year at Wheaton was a tough one. With full responsibility for the Battalion of CSB at the church, Illinois National Guard meetings and work, my study time and grades suffered. I missed graduating with honors by just a hair. I had no time for girls, so I graduated a bachelor without a girlfriend. Without any clear direction from the Lord otherwise, I graduated with a major in professional chemistry with a minor in secondary education. Teaching chemistry in a high school seemed like a way to earn and serve the Lord among teenagers. Quality teachers can have a big influence in young lives, as Coach Hodges initially did in my decision to go out for track. My home could be a haven for high school kids on weekends in whatever city I found a job, if the Lord provided the right wife. This all seemed great, except for a few things.

# CHAPTER 4

## Illinois National Guard and William Jennings Bryan College

As soon as my college graduation ceremony was over, with Billy Graham speaking at the outdoor stadium of my Wheaton High School, and with no time to even say "Goodbye" to any special classmates, I had to hurry to Wisconsin to help direct the summer Family Bible Camp of College Church. This was always a blessing, with families together for a week, children sleeping in dorms of their age group. After that, it was back to painting houses with Jack and Harold.

Before my senior year at college, I joined the Illinois National Guard. The Korean War was on. Wheaton College did not have an ROTC (Reserve Officer Training Corps) unit at the time. My Dad was a Lieutenant in the army in WW I. My neighbor was in the Guard. I was a patriot; I joined. With little training, I soon became a corporal, with the job of being Battalion Sergeant Major, since I was in Headquarters Co.

## According to Roger

In the summer of 1951, a race riot occurred in Cicero, Illinois. We were called up to patrol the streets. For this I received my one and only "campaign ribbon," as there was nothing exciting during my later two years in the regular army.

Something that bothered me quite a bit at the time was that many students at Wheaton College were shifting to theological studies in order to get a draft deferment. Clergy were not subject to the draft. These guys did not want to go into the military. No doubt some were sincere, believing they had a Call of the Lord for ministerial or missionary work, but I had my doubts. I had no respect for Draft Dodgers, especially if they were dubious clergy aspirants!

But there was one outstanding exception, Dr. Robert G. Rayburn, pastor of College Church during some of my high school and college years. Dr. Bob had volunteered as a chaplain in the army during WWII. During the Korean War, he was called up, since he had stayed in the Reserves. He was sent to Korea along with several other replacement chaplains. Upon arrival, the head chaplain in Korea asked these men if anyone would volunteer to be the chaplain for a paratroop battalion. He could not assign any of them to this dangerous job unless the chaplain volunteered. After a long silence, Bob volunteered.

As soon as Bob got to his outfit, the sergeant assigned to Bob told him to stick with him, as they were going to jump into combat the following day! Bob was shown what to do. He had never jumped with a parachute before. Yeshua watched over Bob and protected him. Bob had the respect of the men and had a wonderful ministry to them from the Word of God. Dr. Bob also earned the respect of us young men back home in Wheaton.

## Illinois National Guard and William J. Bryan College

With the country and world the way it was, I decided not to even look for a teaching job after graduation. I could not guarantee any school that I would be around to finish the school year, as there were always rumors that our Guard Division would be called up for active duty. This could have been an uneasy situation, but for me, it was peaceful. The Lord had to work out whatever He wanted me to do. Lessons in faith, trusting the Promises of the Lord, were very real for me since I gave my life to Him at 13 years. I had nothing to worry about. "Trust and obey, for there is no other way..."

One day in the middle of the summer of 1951, one of my chemistry teachers, Dr. Green, showed up at the house we were painting with another gentleman. Dwight Ryther, Dean at Bryan College in Tennessee, was looking for a chemistry teacher. Talk about a job interview in painter's overalls! Dr. Green said that with my professional chemistry degree, I could easily do the job. I could get my PhD later on. I informed Dean Ryther of my draft status if I left Illinois and the Illinois National Guard. He would be taking a risk if I should take the job. Dean Ryther was a retired Colonel, so he had a little experience in these matters.

Now what? I was planning to teach in high school! I wasn't even thinking of a PhD in professional chemistry like my other four classmates. OK, I will look over the catalog and forms and decide later. I read the catalog. Bryan College was small and had just started a track and cross-country program. Maybe I could assist the coach! Furthermore, Bryan College stood for literal Creation, 6 days of 24 hours each day, just like Genesis says. I liked that! I filled out the papers and sent them in, with a note that I would like to assist the track coach since I had earned a varsity letter at Wheaton College.

# According to Roger

Soon I had a reply. "You are accepted to the faculty of Bryan College to teach chemistry and math, and you are the coach!" The previous one had left the college. Wow! This sounded great, better than I expected. On campus during the reception of the faculty by the Board of Trustees, Dean Ryther introduced me as one who never asked what his salary would be. I had never thought of that! This was a ministry with and for the Lord! Money was not the objective, although I was sure I would be paid something. It did not matter to me how much. I was single, had a car, ate in the school dining room, and rented a room from the school. After all the deductions, there was a little pocket money left.

The class schedule that year was Tuesday through Saturday. This was to make it possible for students who had weekend preaching opportunities to get back and prepare for classes on Tuesday, and also for students to go out around the county to teach released-time Bible classes in the public schools. Although a Christian liberal arts college, Bryan was interested in practical evangelism and Gospel outreach. Since cross-country in the fall and track in the springtime were the only intercollegiate sports, having classes on Saturday was not a serious problem.

Since I had a heart for this type of outreach and had a car, I volunteered to take a group of students on Mondays. I was given five students, two guys and three young ladies, a car-full for my 1939 Mercury Sedan. Naomi Hildebrand was the prettiest of the three girls, but we did not "connect" that year. We went to two elementary schools. I taught grade 6; the others taught the other grades. Naomi also did hospital visitation. To earn, Naomi was a dining room waitress and together with another girl, was the janitor for my chemistry room and laboratory. Ralph Mount paid whatever she could not earn.

## Illinois National Guard and William J. Bryan College

In February, I got a letter from Uncle Sam. Roger William Walkwitz was to report to the Induction Center for his physical exam prior to being inducted into the Armed Forces of the United States of America! Now wasn't that nice. Uncle Sam needed me, and so did Bryan College, at least until the end of the semester. I went ahead and took the physical, of course. A couple months later, I received my induction notice to report to the Wheaton office of the Draft Board on a certain date, so they could meet their quota. With so many student clergy exemptions, we regular guys had to make up the Wheaton quota.

Dean Ryther and I went down to the local draft board in Dayton, Tennessee, to see what could be done. They offered to ask Wheaton for a change of induction site to Dayton. By the time the paperwork is processed, school should be over. No letter arrived in Dayton; school was over; and I was on my way home to Wheaton. Karen Fitzwilliam, the first child of Jack and Alice, was born June 10, 1952 — a cause for celebration for my best friends. So I became an "uncle." After two weddings, that of a Bryan faculty friend and of Bob & Peggy Jo Carlson on June 14, and visiting around, I went to the Wheaton Draft Board and requested a change of induction from Dayton, Tennessee, back to Wheaton, since I was now at home.

The clerk was not happy with me. She said the paperwork was late and that I was AWOL (Absent Without Leave). She gave me a one-way ticket to the Chicago Induction Center for the next day, June 20, 1952! So I went home, packed a few items in a bag, said goodbye to my Mom the next morning and was off to the army. My Dad was away on a job, but both came to Ft. Sheridan, north of Chicago, to see me the next Sunday. Within a week, we were processed and sent down to Ft. Breckenridge, Kentucky, for five months of basic combat training with the 101$^{st}$ Airborne Division. No, we did not train as paratroopers! That was an option later. The usual basic training was only two months. We were heading to Korea, to be ready for actual combat. It was tough training but I handled it just fine, because I knew absolutely that I was in the right place at the right time, in the center of God's will for me. In the future I could proudly say that I had served my country well, doing all that had been asked of me.

# CHAPTER 5

## In The United States Army, From Private to Sergeant in Two Years

In 1952, inductees into the US Army had either a 2-month basic training for support functions or a 5-month basic training for front line combat. I was put in the 5-month program, maybe because I was AWOL, but more likely, because that was where Yeshua wanted me to be. I did not question things that were out of my control, because they were in His control! Military life was rough. Religion was tolerated, Chaplains were provided; but actually, religion was an irritant to the usual military life style. I faced military life with a positive attitude, joyful in the LORD with no intention to compromise just to be "one of the gang." Instead, I could be a loner and live my life my own way, as much as possible, to please my LORD and hope that He could use me as a witness for Him.

Combat training was tough physically; but as an athlete, I could handle it just fine. I also enjoyed learning to fire all kinds of small weapons. In high school, I had joined the

American Legion Rifle Club and had learned how to shoot a rifle. In the army, I had no problem earning my Expert Rifleman badge. We trained as combat infantry, so we did not get involved with tanks and big stuff. On the 4th of July, training was suspended with time off, except for a couple of us who were put on KP (kitchen police). I remember being given a large tub of shrimp to clean for lunch! I had no complaint about "army chow," but having shrimp was only this one time.

When the five months were finished, all of the 350 or so men in our outfit were sent to Korea, except for me. The war was still on. I lived in a holding barracks for a week before my orders came through. I was assigned to Petroleum Laboratory Tech School in Ft. Wadsworth on Staten Island, New York, for the next five months. That was nice. I would still be going "overseas," at least onto an island. My assignment was probably because I had been teaching college chemistry and that training ought to be utilized. But to me, it was again of the LORD as He watched over me. The men in this Petroleum Lab Tech School had had only the 2-month basic training. A couple of them were Jewish, the first Jewish men that I met.

One Friday afternoon as classes were ending, one of the Jewish men asked me if I would like to go with him to the Synagogue that evening. We would take the ferryboat across the bay over to Manhattan where the Synagogue was. I said, "Sure!" as this would be the first time ever to be in a Jewish Synagogue. I was not impressed by the service. Many men were in the back talking, while the rabbi was up front, sitting down giving his teaching. They all wore black, so I guess it was an Orthodox Synagogue. I knew very little about Judaism at that time. At least I learned why Jesus and Paul sat down when they taught in the synagogues. That was the style, which I sometimes adopted later.

When the Lab Tech School was finished, I was assigned to Ft. McArthur, in San Pedro, California to the 950th Petroleum Laboratory. I had my car, so I drove all across the USA, stopping at home and other places on the way. TPA (Travel by Private Automobile) was at $0.06 per mile, with leave time to make the trip.

We were six men in all: one Lieutenant, one Sergeant and four of us privates. Three of us were Lab Techs and one was a driver. Our job was to check all the petroleum products purchased by all the US military installations in the entire southwest of the USA, to ensure they met specifications. Only when we gave our approval would the supplier be paid. Of the three of us Lab Techs, two had degrees in chemistry, Dick Rowton and myself, and the third was a high school grad, Marlyn Schaubert, a farm boy from North Dakota.

Every three months, the Pentagon would send us a large carton of numbered petroleum product samples. The same samples were sent to all the Petroleum Labs all over the world, wherever US military would purchase supplies. We were to test all these, tell what they were and give the exact specifications of each. This was a challenge for us. So we each did the tests separately, and then compared results. If there was any variation, we would run the tests again before submitting our results. Guess what? We were rated the No. 1 Lab in the world during my year in California! Was it worth it? You bet!

When I first arrived at Ft. McArthur, in San Pedro, California, and reported for duty at the 950th Lab, Lt. Kispert asked me, "Walkwitz, do you know how to type?" "Yes, sir." I said. "Good, you will also be the Company Clerk." Having been the Company Clerk as well as Battalion Sergeant Major in the Illinois Guard, I had a good idea of what there was to do. So I soon caught up with the paper work that was waiting and started looking at the ARs, the Army Regulations. I found that I could put us three up for promotion every three months, the maximum! That did not mean that it would be approved, of course, but why not try?

We got our promotion right away, probably because of our rating as the No. 1 Lab the first time we submitted our report (and every time after that!). As soon as we got that promotion, I wrote up the request for another promotion. Soon we got that, and the Lieutenant also got his for Captain. He was very pleased with his men. By the time the year was up, we three had gone from E-2 to E-5, a Sergeant with three stripes on top and one curved underneath. Also, the officer did nothing to rate his promotion, except for the work we had done.

Once a month, soldiers were allowed a 3-day pass for a long weekend. We were caught up in our work, so we asked for, and got, a 3-day pass for the last three days of April and the first three days of May, a 6-day "weekend." The other two were now married, so the five of us drove in my car up to visit Yosemite and other national parks, camping out with equipment checked out from Special Services. Both couples were clean-cut people, non-smokers, but not born-from-above that I could detect. We have kept in touch and have visited both in their home places in Texas and North Dakota.

Thinking ahead, I decided to apply to the University of

Tennessee for acceptance into the Graduate School toward a PhD in Chemistry when I got out of the army in June 1954. To my pleasure, I was accepted and offered a scholarship. Wonderful! So eventually, I would go back to teaching and coaching in college, maybe at Bryan College, maybe somewhere else by the time I finished. I found that I enjoyed the combination very much. And besides, I would have my GI Bill along with the scholarship. The LORD was so good to me, especially since it was His idea in the first place for me to major in professional chemistry and He brought the job at Bryan to me. I did not look for that job.

We usually had weekends off, so I would be out visiting some friends from Wheaton and attending church somewhere, meeting new friends. Army friends could not understand how I could find so many people to visit in the Los Angeles area. But it was simple: the Christian connection and Wheaton connection! One Sunday evening, I was in a church in the Los Angeles area. The Wycliffe Bible Translators mission was just entering the Philippines and told of the need for Bible translations in the many tribal languages. In my heart, the LORD started convincing me that my days in chemistry were basically over and that He had a new job for me to do: teaching the Bible to mountain tribal people in the northern Philippines, including translating it if needed.

"Father, this is not fair!" I prayed. "You led me to take chemistry; You provided the teaching job; You provided the scholarship at UT, and now - all of this is to be thrown away for something entirely different?" To me, this was going to the end of the world. Growing up in Wheaton with missionaries and missionary kids (MKs) all around, with a couple of MKs as my special friends, I knew plenty about missions.

According to Roger

I had told the LORD long ago that I was willing to do anything that He asked me to do, but that it was up to Him to make the Call very clear so that there would be no mistake. The Call to teach at Bryan College had been very clear. The Call to the army was unavoidable! The Call to teach Bible to mountain tribal people in the Philippines was also now clear, unavoidable, if I wanted to continue walking in step with God. "Can two walk together unless they be agreed?" asked God in Amos 3. I learned early from the Scripture that it is always best to obey the Boss; so I said "Yes," I would do it, but I was not happy about it.

What was I going to do with the scholarship from UT? What additional training would I need? What a mess it was, but I was at peace with it. When no one was in the barracks, I knelt down by my bunk with the letter from UT before me and asked what to do. The answer was simple. I wrote a letter back and thanked UT very much for the acceptance and scholarship, but explained that I had "a prior commitment" so that I could not accept their offer at this time. They would never understand my "prior commitment" to the LORD, so I did not bother to explain it. Also, I said "at this time," as I secretly hoped that some mission would reject me, and then I would be free to apply again.

Knowing that I would need linguistic training, I applied with the Summer Institute of Linguistics (SIL), the teaching arm of the Wycliffe Bible Translators, for acceptance in their 1954 summer program at the University of North Dakota, the branch that trained for the Far East. I was accepted. Also about that time, I received a letter from the Dean at Bryan College offering me again my teaching and coaching position for the school year 1954-55 since he knew I would be discharged in June.

So, what was I to do? After consideration and prayer, I wrote back that I would be happy to accept the position again, but for only one year, as I intended to go to graduate school or seminary to get more Bible training for my new, potential missionary career. Would I get ordained as a clergyman? No way! That was not for me. I would always be just "Roger" to everyone, without any titles. Of course, at Bryan College I would be Mr. Walkwitz or Coach!

The summer went fine at the University of North Dakota with my linguistics study. It was quite interesting. My analytical scientific training enabled me to do quite well in the analysis of a new language. First, I would have to write it down phonetically, as I would be dealing with languages that were spoken but were not written yet. Learning to speak a new language, however, was to be more difficult for me. After the summer, I drove back home to Wheaton, Illinois, packed up and drove on down to Dayton, Tenenesse, to begin my year of teaching and coaching again at Bryan College.

# CHAPTER 6

## Bryan College, CBC/CIU, SIL, Naomi Hildebrand & Our Wedding!

Bryan College had changed a bit since my last time teaching there. Classes now were Mondays through Fridays, so the Bible teaching outreach into the county was done at other times. Therefore, I did not have a group of students to take to the elementary schools. Classes were going well, the cross-country team was running fine and I was enjoying campus life again. How I would miss it after that year. Yet I was committed to the plan that Yeshua had for me and I needed to think ahead, not backward

Bryan College had a Christmas banquet for faculty and students, couples or singles. Being a bachelor, I had the opportunity to ask someone to be my date. I was not thinking at all of a life partner yet! That would be way down the road, as I had a lot of preparation to do first. Looking over those young ladies still available, I decided to ask Naomi Hildebrand, that prettier girl who was in my group my first year when we taught Bible in two county elementary schools.

Naomi had come as a freshman my first year of teaching, from Mansfield, Ohio. Now she was a senior, majoring in English. The Christmas banquet was enjoyable. Afterwards, couples were strolling around the campus and main building. As Naomi and I strolled along, I noticed a sprig of mistletoe over the doorway of one of the rooms. Being the mischievous type, as we walked under the doorway, I stopped and gave her a little kiss. Or was it a little hug and a little kiss? Anyway, I knew she liked it. Men always know!

Naomi was a bit rebellious her first year at Bryan. However, one lady speaker at the annual Missions Conference at the College that year had been a missionary to the pygmies of Africa. Her message touched Naomi's heart, and so she gave her life to the Lord to be a missionary to the pygmies of Africa. That settled her down to the college business at hand. After all, her pastor had sent her to Bryan College to make something of herself. It was not wise to fool around, and now she had a goal and objective in life.

Naomi also worked to help with expenses. One job was being a waitress, since the college operated then on a dining room rather than a cafeteria set-up, except for breakfast. As a single faculty member, I ate all my meals at the dining hall and was assigned to head a certain table. Naomi was assigned to wait on our table. Some of the runners on the track or cross-country teams usually filled up my table. We had great times together. Some of the guys still relate the tricks they played on me. I don't remember any girls brave enough to sit with us.

In the spring, I decided to go to Columbia Bible College as they reportedly had a good missions training program in their Graduate School and Seminary. The school is now called the Columbia International University, or CIU. Columbia, South Carolina, was not too far away. I had not been to the campus before, so I decided to drive over one weekend to check it out, as I had a friend there that I could stay with. Naomi and two other girls wanted to go along, as they had interests there also. They stayed in the dorm. We all liked the campus. Naomi and I enrolled.

Summer came. I went home to Wheaton to paint houses for the summer to earn some cash, as salary at Bryan was minimal and for only the school year, not 12 months. I had my GI Bill to pay most of my expenses at CBC in the fall. I lived in a house with a bunch of grad school guys, some of them GIs like myself. With the goal of finishing an MA in Bible Education, with a major in missions in one year instead of the usual two, I did not allow myself time for much else but study. My SIL credit from the summer of 1954 transferred. I was planning to take the second summer of SIL after the year at CBC, which would also transfer, so it was possible. Writing the thesis along with classes would also be a challenge. What topic should I select?

Of course I would get married some day and probably have children. What would I do about their schooling when living in remote areas to reach the tribal people? Several close friends were products of MK schools of the CIM (China Inland Mission). I did not like the policy of the CIM, which had children sent away to a boarding school for first grade and onward. No! I would keep my children at home, and pioneer home schooling. Parents should be the dominant influence on their own children. "The Academic Education of Missionary Children" was the topic approved. Later on, Wheaton College library used it extensively and finally asked to make a copy for themselves.

Naomi was busy with her classes but had no plan to get a degree. She was also quite frustrated with the very restrictive rules at CBC. We occasionally had some limited fellowship since we already knew each other. I did not have time to get acquainted with any new girls. I applied for the second summer of SIL at the University of North Dakota and after that, checked to see if I could find any mission board that would interest me.

Naomi's pastor agreed to help her a bit more for the summer; so Naomi was able to go to SIL also. As the school year ended, I did have my thesis finished, ready for the committee to review. It was OK except for a few paragraphs that needed re-writing, so I could not graduate with the class of '56. I would do the final typing myself and submit it later. The computer had not been even invented then! I had to stay several days longer to get some requirements done. Naomi stayed and worked a bit so she could hitch a ride home to Mansfield, Ohio.

There were no Interstate Highways in those days, so it was a long trip. We drove straight through, as we could not stay overnight anywhere. We arrived early morning at Naomi's Aunt Maye's farmhouse. I was tired so I slept a bit. Later in the day I met her pastor, Ralph Mount. He was a mechanical engineer, a self-supporting pastor. But now he was running a goat dairy, selling goat milk on a route of customers and making some goat cheese. His idea was to learn a lot about goats for further Bible understanding. He was a very good practical Bible teacher.

We left after a few days for North Dakota, with a stop in Wheaton to re-pack and for Naomi to meet my Mom. We arrived OK, checked in and registered. Classes began the next morning. After a couple of weeks, we decided to apply with Far Eastern Gospel Crusade for missionary service to the tribes in the Philippines. We both got fairly quick replies from the headquarters in Minneapolis. I was accepted; Naomi was turned down as a bad risk because of her background. Well, maybe that settled it — the Lord was telling me not to marry her.

However, I did not think she would be a bad risk. She wanted to be a missionary to the pygmies of Africa. She seemed to have good qualities, was a wholesome girl, who had a tough time early in life, but not because of her fault. Slowly I was getting the picture. Maybe this match might be OK, and maybe it was time to marry. After all, I was running out of dining halls and dormitories! Since the mission rejected Naomi, was this an indication that I should not marry her, or was she a quality person who was misunderstood by others and needed a break? I was heading to Detroit for Missionary Internship with FEGC, either with or without her.

A day or two prayerfully considering the future was imperative. It was not an easy decision to make — the second biggest decision of my life after deciding to respond to Yeshua as my LORD and Savior. This decision could make my life or break it. It could not be based on emotional love. I did not believe in divorce. It was the Lord's decision that I needed to know. I could love anyone that the Lord gave to me. Was Naomi God's gift to me and I could not see it that clearly? Was the decision of the mission correct, based on the references that they had received? They had never met her. Were those who gave references prejudiced, based on their perception of life and the Bible?

I thought of asking the mission to accept her and we could come as singles. Then she would have a chance to prove herself different from how she was perceived by those who gave references, and we could be married "in good standing." However, time was moving on quickly. I did not want to delay getting to the Philippines and wanted to "get to work." I am a 24/7 person, not a 40-hour per week person. Time and opportunities were not to be wasted. And what if the mission refused to accept her? Then what? I had to decide, and now. What was the Lord saying? How I wish He would write His decision on a piece of paper!

By faith, I decided to trust the Lord and go ahead to marry Naomi. If any problems developed, she would have to change according to my standards, under my "tender loving care," since God gave me the responsibility of leadership in my family. It was her duty to love and obey. And it was God's written intention to bring us both into conformity to His will and His image as we continue to obey His Word. No matter what background we start with in life, if our hearts are submitted to Him, He will bring about change, for good.

We went for a ride in the evening and parked somewhere. She was a country girl and liked country music so I said, "Honey, don't you think it's about time that you and me got hitched?" No, I did not say just that, but whatever I said, Naomi gladly accepted! The next day, I wrote the mission and told them that Naomi and I were getting married and that they would have to accept us both. They reluctantly agreed, and several times advised me not to marry her. She was a bad risk. We set the date for September 8, that being 1956. On the way from North Dakota, we joined the Mission Conference going on near Minneapolis for a few days, met the director and many others. Our interview was short.

Naomi's bad background was like this: she was born second in a family of six girls and one boy. Ralph Mount used to come by to pick up the older children for Sunday school. Her father died of alcoholism when she was not yet a teenager. Early on, Naomi's Mom would send her and her younger sister to the tavern to get their father and bring him home. Known as the Sunshine Sisters, they would sing and collect the coins that were tossed their way, and bring their father home. After he died, things at home deteriorated. Her mother treated her badly, called her a religious fanatic and would not let her go to Sunday School anymore. She ran away and phoned her grandmother to come to get her.

The custody situation went to court. Her grandmother testified on Naomi's behalf. Naomi was to live in foster homes and have no contact with her family until she was 18. Some of the foster homes were bad, so the Mounts let her stay with them for a while as they had two daughters her age. When Mrs. Mount had to have a serious operation, Naomi went to live with an old lady from the church, a widow who never had any children. Everyone called her "Aunt Maye." Naomi had stayed with her years earlier to help on the small farm, but when she got homesick, she alternated with her younger sister. On her little farm, Aunt Maye had a few cows, which Naomi milked each morning before catching the bus for school. The church was right next to the farm. Naomi was active with the young people in singing groups, quiz teams, and other activities. During high school, at about 16 years, she put her trust in Jesus Christ, making a public profession at a city-wide evangelistic campaign.

In her senior year at Rural Union High School, one Saturday night after Senior Play practice, she dated a guy with a car and with another couple. As they were driving along a country road, classmates in another car challenged them to race, a game called "chicken" to see who would flinch when passing. They crashed and rolled over and over for about a hundred yards. Aside from going hysterical, Naomi was not hurt. There were no seat belts in those days. The sheriff brought her home to Aunt Maye, who had been staying up, waiting.

The news was broadcast on the local radio with their names; so at church the next morning, Naomi was reminded that by the grace of God she was alive and well. Ralph Mount challenged her to do something with her life. The choice was to let her marry some local farm boy or go away to college. Ralph encouraged her to go away to Bryan College as a working student; he would pay whatever expenses she could not earn. He was working as a mechanical engineer at Westinghouse and pastored their small Baptist church outside of town. He had always refused to accept a salary from the church.

Back in Minnesota, after our short interview with the leaders of Far Eastern Gospel Crusade, we drove home to Wheaton. Naomi stayed a couple days and then I took her into Chicago to get the bus for Mansfield and to prepare for the wedding. We had sent out Invitations while still in North Dakota and recruited our wedding party. Life was on a roll and there was no stopping it, even if there were objections from the mission! There was a certain amount of apprehension at how fast events were going, but I had peace from the Lord that this would all work out OK. We were both clean-cut, wholesome kids eager to serve our Lord, so we decided to put the past behind and look forward to the future together.

## Bryan College, CBC/CIU, SIL, Naomi Hildebrand
## & Our Wedding

The wedding was on Saturday evening, September 8, 1956, at the Pleasant Valley Baptist Church, outside Mansfield, Ohio. Ralph Mount officiated the ceremony. His wife took care of the reception. My best man was Jack Fitzwilliam, my high school friend and MK from the CIM school in Chefoo, China. My brother Don was in the army in Germany; my other high school friend, Harold Cook, was in the army in Korea. So neither one could come for our wedding. Naomi's matron-of-honor was classmate Janice Thornton. Others in this select group were Bob Carlson, Chuck Thornton, Ed Amstutz, Shirley Jurliss, Mildred Walkwitz, Betty Winne, Dave Salstrom (soloist) and Myron Sawyer (organist). Thanks, Gang! You were the best!

This select wedding party fanned out in the area Saturday morning to find some flowers, as we had no money to buy any. Naomi borrowed her wedding gown and bridesmaids' gowns from a recently-married classmate at Bryan. I had told my men to bring their 35mm cameras and I would supply the film and flash bulbs, as we could not afford a photographer. At home in Wheaton we had a darkroom with my two buddies, so we would develop the B&W film and print the pictures ourselves. Ever worked in a darkroom with a girl, and got any work done? Whoever looked at an expensive album after the first year anyway? During the reception, a man slipped me a $100 bill! Now we could have a honeymoon! He was a Christian factory owner who employed Naomi and other Christian students during the summer. God is so good!

After a couple of weeks, we reported to Gull Lake Bible Conference grounds in Michigan for our orientation to Missionary Internship and our church assignment. We were assigned to intern at Ward Memorial Presbyterian Church in Detroit. The previous pastor had been our pastor at College Church in Wheaton when we first went there in 1942, while the new one had some ideas for expansion and needed some cheap "quality help" with a good track record.

# CHAPTER 7

## Missionary Internship and Far Eastern Gospel Crusade

Ward Memorial Presbyterian Church folks gave us a warm welcome and a furnished upstairs apartment in Detroit, Michigan. It had a separate coal-fired furnace in the basement, which was my job to keep going in the wintertime. Our responsibilities were to be the sponsors for the post-high school young peoples' group and a younger grade school group; work all day Monday on the pastor's library filing magazine articles; and do house to house visitation the rest of the week in Livonia, a nearby town where the new church would be located.

On Sundays, the group forming the new church met in an elementary school in Livonia where the pastor, Dr. Bartlett Hess, would conduct an early service. I taught the adult Bible study in the school while he would return to Detroit for the service in the main church. At the main church Sunday evening, we had the YP (Young People) group and Naomi also had a younger group, followed by the evening service. Naomi was Baptist, I was Independent and of course the pastor was Presbyterian. However, we did not have any theological discussions that I remember.

Each year the church had a Missionary Conference. I was responsible to disciple those who might respond to the call for missions. Having some good friends and sources, I put together a packet of booklets for each one. I remember the pastor and the speaker, the head of Missionary Internship, R.E. Thompson, being quite impressed that I had put together such an excellent packet, with some booklets even they were not aware of. Why should they have been surprised? After all, we were "quality people" with a good track record!

More seriously, I had been to many Missionary Conferences in Wheaton and knew quite a bit about the whole enterprise, from missionary friends and MKs, and from the Bible. I knew that missionary work was a Calling from the Lord, not another type of job or an alternative to earning a living at home. Paul and Barnabas were called by the Lord to go out to new areas. They did not choose to do this, and it was not a job to them. I also thought that being a missionary did not make one first class, or any better than anyone else that stays at home. I hoped to deal with these issues with those who responded, for their own sake.

What did we learn through these eight months of Missionary Internship? Not much that would help us in tribal work. Dr. Hess did tell me that my adult class Sunday morning in Livonia was very pleased with my Bible teaching. Well, thank you Lord for insights into Your Word and the understanding to be able to pass them on to others. Somewhere along the line, I had learned that "To understand something thoroughly, Teach it to others." I enjoyed teaching. I think the two years teaching at Bryan College gave me the experience and confidence necessary to be a relaxed teacher.

Halfway through the Internship, we were officially welcomed as Approved Candidates for FEGC. Now it was our job to represent ourselves to churches and friends in order to raise our financial support, which was $240/month at that time. We got $200 and the rest went to the mission operations, both home and field. Ken Taylor, of Living Bible fame, was the chairman at the time of the Missions Committee of my home church, College Church in Wheaton. While we were in Internship, he wrote us that they had heard that we were going to the mission field and that the Church would be taking on some of our support. Wonderful! With some meetings here and there, and working to earn in between meetings, we were set to go to the Philippines in about six months. We were advised that Naomi should not get pregnant until she had been on the field for some time, because of the many adjustments we would need to make. Somehow Naomi got pregnant anyway. That meant that we had to fly, as taking a ship was too risky. Here are excerpts from Naomi's diary about our trip:

"Thurs Dec 19, 1957. *We left Wheaton at 10 am for Chicago airport* (Naomi is 4 months pregnant. We flew on a DC-6 propeller plane, her first flight.) *Stayed overnight in LA with friends. Flew to Hawaii the next morning. I've enjoyed the flight so much from the very start! We stayed at the Edgewater Hotel in Waikiki – on the ocean and it was just gorgeous!*

//Sat Dec 21. *For supper we went to a Japanese*

*restaurant and for $1.45 we ate all we could of all different kinds of food!*

*//Mon Dec 23. A friend took us to the airport. We left at 10:45 pm for Tokyo. There were very few on the plane, so we took several seats and stretched out* (Boeing Stratocruiser, 4-engine propeller. No jets yet.) *We arrived at Wake Island before dawn for refueling, and arrived at Tokyo about noon on Wed Dec 25. Jack & Alice Fitzwilliam and family met us. We had dinner. Got to their darling little home about 4 p.m. We went to bed early as we had been up a long time.*

*//Thu Dec 26. Fitz's had Christmas dinner for us and about a dozen more missionaries.*

*//Fri Dec 27. Six of us went to Hakoni for the night. It took about 4 hrs to get there, over terrible narrow roads (driving on the left side). Supper consisted of sukiaki – ugh is all I can say! The men played billiards, Rog won. All but me took an ofero (hot tub). Rog looked like a pickled beet!*

*//Tue Jan 31. Today we went into Tokyo to shop and see the big city. We took the train again – they really pack the people in! Rog got me a beautiful pearl ring, a Mikimoto solitaire for $15. I love him so – he's so sweet. We stayed up till midnight to see in 1958! Then, sleep!!*

*//Fri Jan 17. Had a big Japanese dinner, and then went to the airport. Plane delayed until 1 am! Took 9 hrs to get to Hong Kong.* (We stayed one week in HK to see various missions and sightseeing.)

*//Sat Jan 25. The plane to Manila took 2 1/2hrs.*

*We got off and to our amazement there wasn't anyone there to meet us!* (The Terminal building was a Quonset hut.) *We tried phoning but gave up and took a taxi (had the foresight to bargain a price first! Cost 8 pesos or $4). Took over an hour to get there* (mission headquarters). *Everyone was surprised and shocked to see us here!* (Two letters had not been picked up at the post office. However, we were welcomed with many meals and fellowships while staying at the guesthouse.)

We were soon set-up in a ground floor apartment in Caloocan City, part of Metro Manila. Missionaries took us on orientation trips to the different areas where FEGC had church planting projects going on. We also began studying *Tagalog*, the so-called national language of the Philippines. That was a mistake. We should have studied *Ilocano*, which was the trade language of the northern part of Luzon Island where the mountain tribal areas were. The mountain people did not like Tagalog, the language of lowlanders that had been exploiting them for many years. There are eight major languages and nearly a hundred other languages in the country, many needing Bible translations, and many yet unwritten.

One orientation trip was up north to Banaue, Ifugao Province, where FEGC had a church- planting ministry and the Good News Clinic, which later became a hospital. Naomi did not go on this trip since her pregnancy was well along the way, and the trip was difficult on very rough roads and riding truck-type buses. We had not really felt at home in the Manila area and among the Tagalog-speaking people; but when I got to Banaue, I felt right at home! This was the place the Lord wanted us to be, absolutely!

How soon could we move up there? The clinic was closed as Dr. Jim Irvine and his family were on home service. It would be better if Naomi had her first child at a hospital in Manila. Raymond Donald Walkwitz was born by C-section June 5, 1958. He would not come naturally after nearly 24 hours of labor. It was good that we stayed in Manila for this first delivery. It cost us 3-months' salary! Thankfully, we had some savings. We had no medical insurance then, which we were not in favor of, anyway. We took good care of ourselves, ate healthy and did not run to the doctor for every little thing like some others. Later, when medical insurance was required, we paid in over $80,000 for insurance that we did not use.

A few years earlier, FEGC had started a small elementary school for their MKs. Other missions wanted to send their children, too. That would not work, so FEGC offered to turn over their school equipment and two teachers if the others would work together to establish a school for all MKs. This turned out to be Faith Academy. It started in June 1957 with grades 1-8. Ninth grade was to start in June 1958. I was drafted to teach 9th grade, all subjects, while continuing Tagalog study nearly fulltime, while Naomi took care of Ray and also studied Tagalog. We finished the school year, packed up and moved north to Banaue, Ifugao, Mountain Province, for most of the next nine years!

# CHAPTER 8

## Banaue, Ifugao,
## Mountain Province, Philippines
## 1959-62

Russ Honeywell, a missionary from Manila, loaned us his VW van to bring us and some of our things to Banaue. The bulky things would come by truck. I had made an earlier trip to check out the house that the missionaries there had picked out for us. The mission finds all housing, with our approval, and pays all rents from a central fund to which we contribute. This house was a few miles out of town, in a village where we could learn the Ifugao (EE-fu-gao) language more easily.

In town, several languages were spoken, including English. We picked up our mail at the post office in town, and bought some food supplies there. A standing order of fruits and vegetables came on the bus from Baguio (BAA-gi-o) City each week, a 9-hour trip of only 110 miles! Chinese merchants came once in a while with canned goods and 5-gallon cans of kerosene for our pressure lanterns. We kept well-stocked, as typhoons could block roads for weeks at a time.

We drove up the rocky mountain road with Ray, our 1 year-old son, in the borrowed VW van. When Naomi got to the house, she cried. This was not what she had expected! It did not help that she was several months pregnant again. It was only a small one-bedroom shack with no facilities, with a small kitchen and living room — three rooms total. We were really camping out! There was an outhouse about 50 feet away. Drinking water was fetched at a spring, a 5-minute walk down the mountain, where laundry was also done by hand. There were no telephones or electricity in the whole province! We were really isolated with no vehicle.

For water for the galvanized iron kitchen sink, I put a 55-gallon drum under a downspout and with a hose, brought rain water inside. We took sponge baths there at night. Light was from a kerosene pressure lantern. We were thankful to have a local girl come daily to help us with fetching water, doing laundry, cleaning, and helping with learning Ifugao language. After several months, we did buy a small motorcycle, and I ordered from Japan a pump organ for Naomi to play. She had taught herself to play a bit, so this was a diversion for her.

We had brought a kerosene-burning stove with us, since the missionaries said there was no propane available in the mountains. The kerosene fumes made Naomi nauseated in Manila, so we bought a propane stove anyway and arranged with the Dangwa Bus Company to bring to us from Baguio tanks of propane gas. Dangwa was the only bus company serving Banaue, with one trip a day. In fact, Dangwa served most of the whole mountain region. We were the only ones in the area to have such a luxury. We also brought with us an old kerosene-burning Servel refrigerator. Another luxury! It weighed a ton and was too heavy to carry. So we and others rolled it end over end to get to the top of the hill upon which our house stood. After letting it sit upright for 24 hours, we lit the burner and it worked just fine.

We had a tremendous view from our house. To the East was the famous bowl of the Banaue rice terraces, the most extensive in the world; and to the West were the rice fields of the village of Gohang (GO-haang). Sometimes clouds in the valley would come up the mountain with an easy East wind and go right through our house and on to Gohang in the West. George and Mary Namulngo (na-MUL-ngo) lived in Nunchitar (nun-chi-TAR), Gohang. Every little clump of houses had a name. Ours was Hiwang (HI-waang), Gohang. George and Mary were the first Believers in Jesus in their area, and were now leading a fledgling congregation. George contracted tuberculosis from being forced by the Japanese to work underground in a mine during the war. Since the Good News Clinic was several miles away, I gave him his injections.

George was my language teacher. He would help me write out Bible teachings that I could give, reading them of course. But his real passion was to get the Book of John, the Gospel that opened his heart to the Truth, translated into his language. Of the few missionaries that came there before us, some had some linguistic training, including a Bible translator. But none of them would help George. So when he asked me, of course I was very happy to help him. He had finished Grade 7 before the war when they had some good American teachers. So he knew English quite well. He was also musical; so we translated or wrote about 100 hymns and songs. It was my linguistic analytical ability that helped in these endeavors, but I never did learn to speak the Ifugao language.

Market Day in Banaue was on Saturday. Vendors had a regular circuit of selling their wares in a different town each day of the week. People would flock to the town to see what they needed to buy. Some men got drunk and staggered home during the afternoon. Sometimes we would have Gospel meetings mid-morning in the town during Market Day, with Naomi and I singing duets and the preaching done by local Believers. The missionaries that lived in town, Bill and Daisy Baskett, also decided to have a Q&A Bible Study session at their house from noon until 2 PM every Market Day, with me as the "answer man." This would attract a lot of the young people, of which there were plenty.

Only one question that I distinctly remember was this, "Sir, when I read my Bible, I see that the people are meeting on Saturday. Why do we meet on Sunday?" I replied that the church changed it to Sunday to commemorate the Resurrection of Jesus. This was the reason that I had been taught. I knew that was not a very good answer or reason, but it was not until years later that the truth dawned on me that the Ten Commandments were written by God Himself, on tablets of stone with His own finger. So how can the church or anyone dare change what God wrote? I also learned that anti-Semitism had a lot to do with the change, which came nearly 300 years after Jesus!

As time went on, I was shocked to discover the changes in the Bible that the Roman Catholic Church had made, and was more disturbed that Protestant and Evangelical churches were continuing some of these illegal changes! Why? Traditions or not, we were going to change things back to the originals, but that would be years later when God opened my eyes to all these that were never taught to me before.

There were half a dozen fledgling congregations or Bible study groups developing in the area around Banaue. Local leaders were very young in the Faith and young in years. To meet this need, we started the Ifugao Bible Institute, meeting most of Saturday when those who had jobs could attend. The Philippine Constitution provided for released-time Bible classes in the local elementary schools during class time. We decided to take advantage of this to give our students some practical experience and to bring the Bible to the children. Teaching children is the best way to gain experience, as they interact genuinely. We had 20 students. We assigned them in 10 schools in teams of two.

Naomi assisted in the Oteo (o-TI-o) School and I assisted in the Gohang School. The head teacher in each one was an ardent Roman Catholic, as were many of the educated Ifugaos. Pagan animists were the majority of the population. The Belgian Fathers was the Catholic order that functioned in this province. Two Belgian priests were in charge. They had an elementary and high school in Banaue with many nuns teaching. The priests had told the students that if they ever saw Walkwitz's motorcycle parked somewhere, they should push it over the edge to the field below. It was amazing for us to learn first hand of the hatred that religious bigots have toward others, especially the clergy!

Trouble soon broke out. Naomi and I, along with our student teachers, were accused before the authorities of mistreating and forcing school children to attend our Bible classes. In reality, the Belgian priests could not handle the competition of these Evangelical missionaries teaching the Bible in the schools and around the area to the adults. So they manufactured this case in an attempt to have us thrown out of the country. The head teachers were complicit with their most trusted students from Roman Catholic families.

In the court case, the elementary students were the star witnesses, who told many horrible things that Naomi and I had supposedly done to them. After all of them had testified, the investigator began to probe deeper. Their testimonies had all been memorized, coached by the teachers and the priests. When they had nothing more to say, the actual truth came out. Yes, the priests and their teachers had told them what to say. And yes, none of them had been mistreated by us or by our student teachers. Also, yes, they were learning a lot from the Bible teaching and were enjoying it very much. And they wanted us to continue.

The conclusion of the court was that there was no basis for the charge against us at all. The Catholic attempt to have us expelled from the Philippines backfired. One priest was sent back to Belgium and the other was reassigned to rest in their headquarters in Baguio. Filipino priests replaced them. The head teachers were now afraid for their jobs as they might be fired. They probably would have been if we had filed a counter case against them; but we had no intention of doing that. But in this fear, the rumor went around that they would try to poison our sons, so local Believers warned us to not let our sons accept any candy or food from anyone. In reality, the head teachers were pagan animists, with only a veneer of Roman Catholicism and no knowledge of the Bible. We maintained kindness to them and everyone around, as we were Ambassadors of Jesus the Messiah and hoped that the Spirit would touch their hearts with conviction.

However, Naomi did develop ulcers under the stress of the whole thing.

At the FEGC Philippine Field Annual Conference in 1961, I was elected to be the Chairman for the Conference in June 1962. Therefore, we had to extend our 4-year term by an additional five months. That worked out well because third son, Ronald Arthur Walkwitz was born in Manila, again by C-section, on April 10, 1962. For second son, Naomi came down from the mountains to our Guest House in Manila when she was about seven months pregnant to await the planned C-section birth, while I went back and forth a bit to maintain our ministry up north. Randall Edward Walkwitz was born November 14, 1959.

After six weeks recovering from the C-section with Randy, Naomi thought it was time to consider returning to Banaue. The roads were rough; it was too hard a trip for her in this condition. There was a small airport, about three-fourths of the way to Banaue. I phoned Philippine Airlines to see if they would make a "whistle stop" for us in Bagabag (Ba-GA-bag) on their way north to their regular stops. They said they would, dependent on the pilot and the conditions when he arrived there. We prayed for good conditions! It was a beautiful day. The pilot buzzed the airport to get the carabao off the runway, circled around and landed. We got off with our two little boys and two shopping bags of stuff. The other passengers wondered who these people were and why we were stopping here. The airplane was an old DC-3. We were very happy to be this far along on our journey home.

The missionary family that lived in Banaue, Bill and Daisy Baskett, had three teenage sons who rode motorcycles, Dave, Billy, and Don. While in Manila, we arranged to have two of them come to Bagabag airport, bringing my motorcycle. They were waiting for us. The two left on their cycle, and we four got on ours with our two shopping bags. Quite a fit. Ray rode on the gas tank in front, baby Randy behind me and Naomi at the rear. Somehow we held the shopping bags somewhere. Taking it slowly on the gravel road, we made it home in a few hours. It was slower than usual, with a stop now and then for Naomi to rest and move around. Naomi was homesick her first two years, but by now, she was a real trooper, enjoying the challenges of life in the mountains. Now there were four of us in this little shack on top of the mountain.

After one year on top of the mountain, we moved down the mountainside into a 2-storey 3-bedroom house, with a larger kitchen and a living room. Our fellow missionary who had lived there had gone on furlough and then transferred to another location. We still had an outhouse, but had exchanged our kerosene refrigerator for one that ran on propane. The kerosene tank caught fire once, but thankfully, I was able to blow it out. These were too dangerous.

One day, I noticed a spring up the mountainside, somewhat behind and some distance from our house. I got a piece of pipe and pushed it in the outlet. A nice flow of clean water came out. Great! I bought enough ¾-inch galvanized iron pipe to bring the water into our house. First, I built a reservoir, a 2-foot cube, to maintain pressure. Then borrowing pipe wrenches, pipe cutter and threader, I brought the water inside our house, with a faucet outside, for those who passed by on the trail to get a drink. The pagan neighbors around told everyone that we would soon die, because two Japanese soldiers had been buried in the area where the spring was.

After three weeks of healthful living, a young boy came up from the village below to ask if they could attach a pipe and bring the water down to their village. I answered, "Of course you can. But you must not let the water run. Turn off the faucet when not using it; otherwise the reservoir would run out and pressure would be erratic." They soon learned the nice things of civilization. I also put in a hot shower, using an instant hot water heater that operated on propane. Later on, I would have a septic tank built, a 6-foot cube with two compartments, and put in a flush toilet. Oh my, what luxury it was, and an example of cleanliness and sanitation to the people.

Remember our Internship church, Ward Memorial Presbyterian in Detroit, Michigan? One day, we got a message that Bart and Margaret Hess were in the Philippines. They were doing some teaching for various Presbyterian churches in the country, and later, were coming to Banaue to visit us. Great! They arrived late morning the day before Thanksgiving 1961. We had lunch and then I ferried them one by one on the back of my motorcycle to see places and people. They had not ridden on cycles before, but were game for the experience, as there was no other choice. They also handled the outhouse OK, but especially enjoyed the hot shower and sleeping between clean sheets for a change.

The next day was American Thanksgiving Day, but the Hesses had to be back in Baguio City that evening for a wrap-up meeting with Filipino pastors. The only bus left shortly after dawn, so I went early on my cycle to the Good News Clinic to leave it there and catch the bus before it got to town, and then to our house to be sure we had seats. I had arranged for one of our neighbors, a strong Bible student, to carry their and our bags down the hill to the roadside to await the bus, and help with our two little boys. While waiting, Bart and Margaret asked him many questions about us and our work. They told us later that the sum total was that the people knew that we loved them and loved the Lord, and therefore, they were open to our message from the Bible. Thank you, Lord!

# CHAPTER 9

## Our First Furlough
## or Home Service as it is now called

As soon as the mission annual conference was over in June 1962, I passed on to the vice-chairman, Bill Arvan, the details to take care of and our family flew off to the USA. Now we were a family of five! Ray was just 4, Randy was 2 ½, and Ron was 2 months. Our plane landed in San Francisco on our way to Chicago, and Wheaton. Naomi's first culture shock back at the US was the pay toilets at the San Francisco Airport. We had no coins! And she needed a toilet badly. I think there was one that was free at the end, which she eventually found and used. The next culture shock was when Ray saw his first black person, a really black man, and it frightened him. Filipinos are a light brown or tan, and that was what he was used to.

Arriving in Wheaton was exciting, as we had three little boys to show off to everyone, especially to grandparents Clarence and Emma Walkwitz! That was not too bad for a 4 ½- year term on the field, but that was the end of childbearing. Naomi's uterus was too thin for any more babies, so her tubes were tied when Ron was born. Better to be safe than sorry.

The first order of business back home was to buy a car. There was a nice used Cadillac with lots of room for $550. It would have been great. However, we thought a status car might not go over well with people who supported us. So we bought a used Plymouth station wagon for $750. That was a mistake. As the year went on, we had to put in another transmission and spend for some other repairs. Moral: next time buy Cadillac! Buy Quality! But would I have had the nerve to buck the perceived missionary poverty image? We were entirely dependent on donors to supply our needs, if we wanted to stay missionaries, and they had their opinions about missionaries. Again, we put our trust in the Lord and tried not to offend those who seemed interested in us. But we were not going to debase ourselves just to please certain kinds of people who had actually sent used tea bags to us overseas and well-used house slippers with bunion holes cut out.

My parents were very happy to see our boys and play with them as best they could. Dad had retired and they were ready to sell out and move to Florida, to a warmer climate. They had waited for us to return to see if I wanted to buy the homestead from them, as our base. As I thought it over, there would be problems of renting it out when we were overseas, and finding someone who would watch over it and take care of it, collect the rent and pay the taxes, etc. If we used it for each furlough, we would need to rent it furnished so we had furniture when we came home. Would we always return to Wheaton for extended periods so that we would need such a home base? We probably would, since our sons would need to be in good schools. However, when on the field, we intended to home school them until high school.

Another factor was my simple **trust** in the Lord. Should

# Our First Furlough

I get bogged down with such things when the Lord had said, and I had taken it to heart, *"No man that wars entangles himself with the affairs of this life, that he may please Him who has chosen him to be a soldier."* 2 Timothy 2:4. I was very much aware since being in the army in 1953 that I was **chosen** to be His soldier in the Philippines. To be distracted with concerns about owning and renting a house in Wheaton might be a bother to me while halfway around the world. I needed to be focused on my soldiering, my work with Him. So I told my parents, "thanks but no thanks. Go ahead and sell it and move to Florida. We would be traveling to give our reports and to raise additional support, since costs always go up. And we were not tied down to a school schedule for our sons yet."

Looking back over the years, I realized that I really hurt myself financially by being unaware of and uninvolved in financial things for many years. My sister, Mildred, eventually sold the house for my parents for $18,000. She got a good commission so that she was able to buy a duplex for herself, renting out one part for income. About 25 years later, our house sold for close to $400,000! Just think what I could have gained! My parents gave me $2000 from the sale of the house to buy a four-wheel drive International Harvester Scout to take back to Banaue.

I have always saved some money and put it into time deposits. But I never thought of the stock market, bonds or such things, because being overseas, I could not keep track of the market. I thought they would be a distraction in my work. But I do not regret that decision, because the Lord has taken good care of us all these years, He has given us good health and that has minimized expenses. He has honored my commitment to be His soldier, focused on Him alone. After all, my favorite song for years has been, "This world is not my home, I'm just a-passin' through; My treasures are laid up somewhere beyond the blue…"

For the winter, we went to Florida! Being tropical folks by now, we wanted to avoid any winter weather, if possible. My parents were now living in Tampa, Florida. They had learned of homes for missionaries in St. Petersburg, Florida, called the D&D Missionary Homes, and inquired and made a reservation for us. We stayed there for a few months and then headed for California, visiting potential donors and friends along the way. We also had heard of missionary housing in Glendale, California, so we stayed there for a couple of months to have time to contact other potential donors.

About that time, the mission office asked us to return to the Detroit area to attend a 2-month special Missionary Internship program. We learned later that some of our fellow mountain missionaries had turned in a bad report about us, so we had to be observed in this program to see what was wrong with us! We had no idea what the program was, and why we had to take it. When it was finished, the director told us that they could observe no problems whatsoever. Our Internship pastor, Bart Hess, who had visited us in Banaue, also told us that things like this happen, but we should not worry about it. We had to just learn to "roll with the punches," as a boxer absorbed the punches thrown at him, was not hurt, and came back to fight again. We should keep on with our ministry, which God was blessing along with us.

An important factor needs to be considered by those not familiar with missions. Those missionaries that succeed in actually accomplishing something lasting are usually the pioneering type, strong-minded with determination and commitment, flexible in adjusting to cultures and people, and with a definite sense of a Call from the Lord. Those without these qualities may get frustrated with the challenges, and many times, quit after their first term. Then there are those that just "go with the flow", but are not very productive — not quitters, but not winners either. There are also some who want to control others, thinking they know the will of the Lord for everyone else.

So, is there politics in missions? Yes. Is there jealousy among some missionaries? Yes! The Lord was blessing our ministry, maybe because we were doing things His way, and maybe others were upset because we were not doing things their way. I am not one to be intimidated when I stick to doing the Lord's work, since He has shown me what to do and how to do it. I refused to play politics or bother others. One well-known evangelist has said that missionaries are like manure: with too many together, they stink; spread them out and they will do a world of good.

The Team concept in missions may have some merits; but putting a group of missionaries together in a locality is based on a clergy concept. The missionaries control things for too long, and spend too much time trying to work together, especially if they come from different countries and cultures. Some are intent on building their own kingdom, and so they stay in charge. My concept is to go at it alone and work myself out of a job!

My Team concept is this: working alone as far as other missionaries are concerned, and building my Team from the local people to whom I am bringing His Word. Making disciples takes time. Big programs are no substitute. Yeshua said to "Make disciples." Then, forming these disciples into a Team from the very beginning means they are in control of things from the beginning. The congregations that develop will be their responsibility, not the foreigner's. Local leadership is also recognized and developed.

This is <u>indigenous missions,</u> which I learned from experienced missionaries at Columbia Bible College and from the Bible. We have proved that it works and is how it worked in the book of Acts. It is God's way. We follow a <u>non-professional/no clergy</u> ministry concept. When we missionaries leave, there is nothing "to turn over to the nationals" since they have been responsible from the beginning. Everyone is a Volunteer.

We had to be in Michigan, Illinois and Ohio, several times for meetings and conferences during the winter months. Ron, our baby, caught pneumonia four times during the year even though we took very good care of him. A wonderful pediatrician in our Internship church took very good care of him when we were in the Detroit area. But he told us that Ron was a tropical baby and we should get on back to the Philippines. We agreed!

During one of our last road trips in Michigan toward the end of our furlough, we were rear-ended in our new Scout, with only 800 miles on it. Naomi and I had whiplash, with our eyeglasses way in the back where the boys were sleeping on the floor. A car was burning on the side of I-94 and we were being flagged down for help. But the man driving the car way behind us apparently fell asleep for just a moment and did not see our brake lights as we began to slow down. We apparently did not suffer any major injury ourselves, but the Scout had to be repaired. The Lord was watching over us, as the accident could have been much worse. The Scout got fixed and soon we were on our way, driving to Los Angeles for our trip to Manila.

# Our First Furlough

With a "clean bill of health," full support for all three sons, and our new IH Scout, we headed for California to take a ship this time to the Philippines. The US President Lines still had two passenger ships that traveled the Pacific. We could save a lot of money by taking our vehicle with us and being in Third Class down below decks. We traveled on the President Wilson. It took three weeks to make the journey, stopping in Honolulu, Yokohama, Kobe, Hong Kong and then Manila. The water was very rough between Hong Kong and Manila. The family did fine, but I proved to be a poor sailor with a queasy stomach. Better that I be a soldier on land! The food was excellent the first day (and following days!) but I lost my appetite and could not enjoy it. On Sundays, we were allowed up on First Class for the chapel service. But after it was over, we had to come back down.

# CHAPTER 10

## Second Term. Banaue
## University of Hawaii, Faith Academy
## 1963-68

Arriving in Manila with friends meeting us this time was wonderful, not like our first arrival in this new strange country with no one to meet us! One carton with Naomi's new Bible and some other important things was stolen while everything was being brought off the ship onto the pier. Otherwise, everything arrived OK. It was nice to have our own vehicle now, with four wheels instead of two, and a roof over our heads.

When we met the Field Council, they had already decided that we were to be assigned to Faith Academy! We observed that some missionaries were more concerned for their children than for the missionaries whom they expected to take care of them. We were very concerned for our children, too, but we took care of them ourselves. We did not expect others to leave their ministry to teach our kids. So we had a little problem here.

Certainly I could teach high school kids. They loved me because I loved them, and I did a good job of teaching them, as proven before, because I taught for the Lord. On this record, the assumption was made that the Lord's place for me was to teach MKs at Faith Academy. This was especially because they needed teachers, and even more especially, because they needed someone to teach chemistry to complete the required high school curriculum.

This was their self-interest approach to placing missionaries. It did not take into consideration the Call of the Lord upon others, nor the needs and opportunities within the country. Some missionaries said they were called to serve the mission in whatever capacity needed, which was fine for them. Some of us are called to a specific ministry and the mission is a means to that end. My Call was to leave classroom teaching and bring the Bible to mountain tribes people. As in our first term, I was willing to help out, teaching on a temporary basis for the next year. But I expected the Council to honor our Call to the mountain ministry. What they needed to do was to recruit teachers who were called to teach MKs, or face doing home schooling themselves.

The school year was several months in progress already, so we proceeded on up to our house outside of Banaue, which we had kept with furniture in place. George and I resumed our Bible translation of the Gospel of John and other teachings. I met with the young emerging leaders (my Team!) to ask how things were going and how I could help them this term. Their reply surprised me but also pleased me. They said that I had spent so much time trying to learn their language and doing the translation that I had not spent enough time teaching them. They all knew

English quite well, had Bibles in English, and so wanted me to teach Bible to them in English. They, in turn, would teach their people in the Ifugao language. This was the essence of the Ifugao Bible Institute we did in the first term.

This showed to me a degree of maturity among the young leaders who understood their solemn responsibility as volunteer leaders of their congregations. They knew they needed to understand the Bible well enough so that they could teach with confidence and answer critics adequately. Wonderful! I was not good at speaking their language anyway. My analytical language skills would be enough to do the translation. From then on I taught in English. After all, there were about 100 languages in the Philippines. Schools were taught in English, at least after the first grade. Their English was sometimes *"Taglish,"* with the lowlanders mixing in a lot of *Tagalog* (ta-GA-log). The mountaineers spoke better American English.

In the meantime, I also needed to design a chemistry lab and order equipment and supplies for Faith Academy, with only $600 to work with! Semi-micro was the way to go, with small supplies and equipment. Once I was ready, I brought the data to Manila for the school to proceed. The lab was built, but not fully to my specifications for long-term usage. Instead of 2-inch thick lumber for the tabletops, they used thin plywood, which would not last long.

When there, the superintendent of Faith Academy told me of an opportunity, for teachers of science in military and international schools teaching American kids in the Far East, to go to Japan for six weeks in the summer to take graduate courses in science offered by the University of Hawaii, tuition-free. These could apply toward a Master's Degree in Science Education at the Honolulu campus later, if desired. I applied and was accepted to take an updated chemistry course. Theories do change, you know! It was a nice perk for me, a break from the mountain ministry, which I also enjoyed.

Naomi stayed in Manila in the house rented for us for the upcoming year of teaching chemistry at Faith. I was also able to bring back a lot of goodies from the PX for Naomi and the boys, since I lived and studied on a US Army base near Tokyo. Soon the school year in Manila began. It was rather routine and uneventful compared to that in the mountains, except for the fact that the University of Hawaii invited me back for a second course in Nuclear Chemistry the next summer. That was very nice. To come out to the Philippines when we did, I passed up three more years of GI Bill schooling; so now, I felt I was getting a little bit back. I had used only one year at Columbia Bible College, of the four years I qualified for from my years on active duty.

Therefore, we began to think ahead to our next furlough in 2 ½ years. Why not try for a school year in Hawaii to complete the MEd in Science Education, now that I had two summers of credits? Later, living in Banaue again, I sent to Hawaii to ask for the forms to apply for the school year 1968-69 for the science scholarship that had been offered. The secretary sent the forms by surface mail to Banaue. They arrived on the day of the deadline to receive the completed forms in Honolulu! Knowing that the Lord had put this plan in our minds, I filled out all the forms and sent them back by airmail, with a letter explaining what the secretary had done. The reply came back — so sorry, but the scholarship selections had already been made and sent out. However, I was first in line if any of the ones selected cancelled out. OK, good. Now it was up to the Lord to work it out.

Even though I had slowed down on learning the Ifugao language, I believed learning their culture and pagan animistic religion was still important. The Ifugaos worshiped a bunch of gods and their ancestors who had now become gods. It was a verbal society. Everyone knew who owned each field, and the pagan priests knew all the ancestors of an area back to *Wigan* and *Bugan*, the first Ifugaos who survived the great Flood. When the Flood came, *Wigan*, a young man, raced to the top of the highest mountain nearby. The water did not quite reach the top, so he alone survived. Bugan, a young girl, raced to the top of a different mountain and also survived the Flood. The floodwaters receded; they found each other and began the Ifugao Tribe. Legends like this abound all over the world, validating the Bible record.

Where did *Wigan* and *Bugan* come from? What happened before the Flood? No one knew any of this, so I held out my Bible and told them, "Here is the true history from the very beginning of the Creation of the earth." This was one point of entry into their lives. When asked about their gods and if there was one who created everything, they said, yes, his name is *Muntalog* (Mun-TA-log), but he does not bother us so we do not sacrifice to him. The ones that bother us, the group of *Matnongan* (Mat-NO-ngan), are the ones that we sacrifice pigs and chickens to. How do they bother you? They make us sick; they cause our houses to burn down; they cause our rice harvests to be too little; and they cause us to have accidents. Are your dead ancestors doing these things? Oh, yes, if we do not sacrifice pigs and chickens to please them.

Before young people were allowed to marry, the ancestors had to be consulted by examining the entrails of a chicken. If the omens were good, they could marry. If not,

69

they had to wait for another test a year later. For the wedding celebration, at least one pig must be sacrificed and later had to be eaten by the people attending. Before anyone in an area could harvest their rice fields, the "royal family" of the area first had to sacrifice a few pigs to the harvest gods and their ancestors in appreciation for a good harvest, or face retribution if they did not. The prayers of the pagan priests went all night long until mid-morning, as they had to pray and flatter every one of the ancestor gods. The people did not participate in the prayers. Then the pigs were killed and some blood collected. They had a few wooden idols a bit less than 2 feet tall. The priests smeared blood from the pigs on these idols. The pigs were cut in pieces, cooked, and fed to the harvesters.

George's sister-in-law, Erlinda, wanted to get married to Juan Tillay, a Believer. OK, no priest was called and no chicken was examined. The date was announced. After the village had gathered, George questioned the bride and groom, they made their vows to each other, and George pronounced them married. The Philippine government did not interfere with tribal customs.

Then the time came to kill the pig to feed the village. Everyone came. George slit the throat of the pig and let the blood run out on the ground. The people protested! They all ate blood. George used this opportunity to teach them about the Bible that the blood is for God; that blood must be shed to pay for sins; but that only the blood of Jesus could actually pay for their sins. Missiologists might call this contextualization. We just called it using practical situations, like Jesus did.

It was interesting to know all this and to be able to teach the Bible from common meeting points, like the Flood and blood sacrifices, which God also required. But for Bible translation, we had to know all this. Even more important is our choice of words and especially a name for God had to accurately represent Him! We depended on the local Believers and congregation leaders to give us the feeling behind these words, and on the Holy Spirit to give them a clear understanding of the true God. Could we use *Muntalog*, the supposed creator god? No, that would not fit, they said. What about *Matnongan*, since he or they required sacrifices just as God in the Bible, culminating in the sacrifice of Yeshua? No, none of these love us, as the God of the Bible loves us. The *Matnongan* make trouble for us. We are afraid of them.

After much deliberation, we chose *Apu Dios*, the name for God used in translations already finished in some major Philippine languages. *Apu* meant grandfather or an honorific title, and *Dios* is the Spanish name for God brought in centuries ago. There could be no mistake that *Apu Dios* is entirely different from any of the pagan gods.

At the end of January, 1966, a sixth grade girl came to our house to ask if she could work for us on Saturdays to earn money for her graduation dress. Elisa was a believer that lived fairly near, so we said yes. She had been out of school for several years, but decided that she ought to finish at least grade six. She worked very well, so we decided to let her work fulltime after graduation at the end of March. High school would cost money and she was not really interested in that. She did not like any of the men courting her either, and she was not interested in marriage. Married life was hard in Banaue; Elisa enjoyed being with us. She stayed with us while we were in the country for the next 25 years.

When our Translation Committee — George, I and several

other Believers — thought we had done the best we could, I contacted the Bible Society to see what they would think about it. They called in the SIL person in an adjacent area to help also. In his neighboring area translation, he had already been using *Matnongan* for God. He insisted that this was the native equivalent. We all objected. The men explained thoroughly why we had rejected that name.

Finally, the American Bible Society expert agreed with us. Some other suggestions were made. Then we were asked to revise the translation following the English text of the Revised Standard Version of the Bible, which the Bible Society used as their standard. I did not know any Greek at the time. I wish I had, as I knew that no English translation could do a perfect job. For sure, ours would be revised again sometime, because as initial translations are used, little nuances here and there are noticed and recorded for future printings.

With all that I have learned since that time, if I were to start out fresh in a new area to translate the Bible, I would start with Genesis. This is a foundational book, necessary to establish who God really is, before one jumps to the Gospels about Yeshua.

By the start of 1968, we had finished all revisions. The text was accepted for publication by the Bible Society, the first book of the Bible to be printed in Banaue dialect of the Ifugao language! In fact, it was the first book of any kind printed in this dialect, and it set a pattern on word spelling and usage. We were so happy and relieved. It was done. The Ifugao language had five dialects needing translations. Full New Testament translation projects were going on with the SIL in three of these at that time. Our pioneering work helped set the pattern for the use of *Apo Dios* and some other terms.

Now it was up to the Bible translators to continue. The Lord had other work for us to do.

Another exciting event happened when we were in the mountains — the Six-Day War in Israel! Remember, we had no electricity and no telephones, but we did have a short wave radio that was battery-operated, still using tubes. The high voltage batteries required were expensive, did not last very long, and could not be obtained anywhere near where we were. So I bought boxes of size D flashlight batteries and rigged up a functional power supply for the radio. We were also able to buy from town the Manila Bulletin newspaper, albeit a day later, that came up on the once-a-day bus. We wanted all the news we could get. Of course we were cheering, and praying, for Israel to be victorious.

When Jerusalem was taken on June 7, 1967, we expected the Rapture. That is what I had been taught, that when Israel takes over Jerusalem, the Rapture will occur and the anti-Christ will make himself known. The war continued, and nothing happened to us! No Rapture! I went around to check on the other Believers, and everyone was still around. OK, I thought something is wrong with this pre-Tribulation Rapture theory. This required further study and correction, or the whole Dispensational approach to Scripture had to be thrown out. Eventually, this is what we did.

As a new teen-age Believer, I had wanted to visit Israel, the Land of my Savior and Friend, someday. As Naomi and I thought it over, we decided to go through Israel on our scheduled furlough in 1968. We had worked hard and needed an exciting rest! Contradictory terms? Not for us. There is no use crossing the Pacific again. We would go the other way around and see Israel after its amazing and miraculous victory.

## According to Roger

At the end of February, 1968, we left for Manila with Elisa. She helped us until we left. Then she worked for another missionary until classes started at the Far Eastern Bible Institute and Seminary, or Febias, in Manila, where this other missionary taught. Elisa took the One-Year Basic Bible Course. She was only a sixth grade graduate, but excelled at Febias with the others who were high school graduates. She became a talented teacher of children. It was a job she combined with working for us when we returned a year later. She was also able to teach the college students in Baguio how to teach children.

# CHAPTER 11

## Second Furlough, Israel, University of Hawaii 1968-69

With the Bible Society responsible for printing the Gospel of John in the Banaue dialect of the Ifugao language, we were now ready for our delayed furlough. We gave up our house in Banaue, stored our things at the Good News Clinic, and sold our IH Scout vehicle. This was done by faith that the Lord would give us that year in Hawaii. We had reached a significant milestone in our tribal ministry, so we felt a measure of flexibility for the future.

We headed for Manila and our big trip. At that time, we could stop multiple times along the way from Manila to Detroit, Michigan, at no extra charge. Being adventurous, we decided to see a bit of the world, spending a day in Bangkok, Thailand, then on to Delhi, India and a side trip to see the Taj Mahal, then on to Israel for 17 days, our very first trip to The Holy Land! Our sons were now ten, eight, and six years old.

# According to Roger

We arrived late evening at Ben Gurion airport, went to the Travel Assistance Desk and arranged for a two-star hotel room in Tel Aviv for a couple nights. The big taxi cost $12, a lot of money in 1968! We slept in a bit. Next day, I met a Jew from England who had just arrived. England had currency controls at the time, so he could bring out only a limited amount of money. He asked if we would be willing to split the cost of a rental car for a week and tour northern Israel.

I decided that this would be safe and a good deal, since there were five of us and he was alone. He had been to Israel before, had friends here, and knew where to go. He drove first for about an hour, and I took over after that. In England they drove on the left side of the road and in Israel, on the right side. He had not fully adjusted yet. Also, he could check his map, watch signs and give directions better if I were driving. Naomi and three small boys fit in the back of this small four-door sedan.

It was a wonderful experience. We stayed in cheap places, bed and breakfast being standard, and some youth hostels. We paid our expenses; he paid his. Some of his friends told of the miracles that happened in the Six-Day War, how the Syrians fled from before the advancing Israelis. But they did not recognize the hand of God on behalf of Israel. One of these days the "blindfold" will be removed from their eyes. Our boys enjoyed climbing on the bombed out Syrian tanks and holding the weapons of Israeli soldiers that we met. We even went south to see Hebron and the Cave of Machpelah, Abraham's burying place, before we returned to Jerusalem. Our Jewish friend's time was up, but we decided to keep the car for the rest of our stay and see some more of this wonderful country.

One day, we pulled into a packing facility for oranges near Ashkelon and asked if we could buy a big box of those delicious Jaffa oranges. The man told our boys to follow him. Around back, he loaded them up with all the huge, oversized oranges they could carry! We really enjoyed all the fruit and other food, and all of our experiences in Israel. The Garden Tomb, where maybe Jesus was buried, was just around the corner of our Jerusalem hotel, across from Damascus Gate. The boys enjoyed going there several times, even by themselves, just to enjoy the peacefulness and think about Jesus. It is not safe for kids to go there alone now.

Our next stop was Istanbul, Turkey, to visit a Wheaton classmate who headed the Bible Society there. He knew of only a handful of Christians in Turkey. We did not feel very comfortable in this Muslim country. The next stop was Athens, to see the Acropolis, and then on to Rome, to see the Vatican and the catacombs. I had not studied much about Vatican City and the paganism of it all, but we saw enough in a short time. We went on to Amsterdam, but could not find any Walkwitz there (my ancestors came from Holland), then on to London for a couple of days to see Buckingham Palace, and finally, on to Detroit.

Why Detroit? We were quite sure that the Lord would give us the Scholarship to go to the University of Hawaii for the coming school year 1968-69. Therefore, we had to do our part to make it possible. That meant doing all of our Deputation in about four months, late spring and summer so that we would be finished in time to go to Hawaii. We had thought many times that traveling in a camper or motor home would be really neat. This quick mainland trip, visiting all of our supporters, would be the right time to do it. Therefore, we had contracted ahead of time to buy a ¾ ton pickup truck and put a camper body on it. That would be the most efficient way to travel. With no house to rent, we were free just to travel.

We bought the pickup in Detroit and drove to Elkhart, Indiana, to lease the camper body from the manufacturer for the four months. We finished our Deputation and were up in New York visiting with one of my cousins at their lakefront cottage. We used my brother's place in Illinois for mail and contacts. While in New York, my sister-in-law, Faith, phoned that a telegram had arrived from Hawaii, that a cancellation had occurred and that a scholarship was open for me if I still wanted to come for the year. Wow! We had done our part; now the Lord was doing His part! I quickly telegrammed back and sent a letter as well, just to be sure. Hawaii, here we come! The Lord is good, all the time!

We drove back to my brother's place in Bensenville, Illinois, settled in for a short stay, returned the camper to the Elkhart manufacturer, drove to Pontiac, Michigan, to pick up a VW hatchback from a fellow missionary to take to Hawaii, then advertised the pickup for sale. A potential buyer called. The pickup was still in the same new model year and the price was good. He asked how many miles I had on it. I replied, 10,000 in the four months we had it. He asked, "What did you do, live in it?" I said, yes, and traveled all over the US. He bought it. It was hardly broken in and in perfect shape.

We drove to California, shipped the VW and flew to Honolulu. A friend there had rented a furnished house for us, so we simply moved in. We registered the boys in the local school and I registered at the University. The owner of the house lived in the back and was very nosy, coming in when we were not home. The school was not the best either.

So we found another house up the mountainside with a beautiful view overlooking the ocean and Diamond Head. It was not furnished, so we got the essentials from the Salvation Army store. The new elementary school for the boys was a better one. They took the city bus together to Liliokalani Elementary School and back each day. They were maturing and enjoying life. Each Saturday, we relaxed at the beach, where they learned to swim. My studies at University of Hawaii, as well as the thesis that I would be required to write, were demanding a lot of time. With the two summers in Japan with UH, I could do the MEd in one crowded year.

Kalihi Union Church in Honolulu was recommended to us, as the pastor, Stan Johnson, was interested in missions. We went the first Sunday. I recognized the pastor as Ty Johnson, my sophomore big brother at Wheaton to help me in my freshman year! We met after the service. Right away, he had a job for us to be the sponsors for the post-high school young people. Ty was his nickname. We never knew his name was Stan. Later on, they took on some of our support, which required us to stop by Hawaii once in a while. This continued until we retired in 1994. How nice to be spoiled like this. Hawaii is still Naomi's favorite vacation destination.

What topic should I write my thesis on? The year would go fast, so I needed to decide soon. I had two main concerns: one, to write on something interesting and of value to me so that it would not be a waste of time; and two, to be a witness for my Lord to the faculty that would approve my thesis. It was a few years after the 100th Anniversary of the publication of Charles Darwin's book *The Origin of Species.* Evolution was being pushed everywhere.

The National Science Foundation had published a series of biology books for high schools, based on three different approaches: the Blue version (molecular approach), the Green version (environmental approach), and the Yellow version (standard approach). All of them promoted Evolution, with no mention at all of Creation or anything else. I decided to do a thorough analysis of all three versions, pointing out that this biased approach to origins — evolution only, with no mention of Creation — was not a scientific approach to the subject.

Science has to be objective, impartially examining all sides. Since no experiments could be done for either side, the conclusion would have to be a belief or speculation, a guess, not a theory. Theories in science are those that have been tested and tested with no variation observed. Therefore, both Evolution and Creation are hypotheses, not theories. The three evolutionists on my committee gave me an "A" because I had proved my point.

One committee member was the head of the biology department. In class one day, she was explaining parthenogenesis, or virgin birth. Knowing I was a Bible believer, from the talks we had before, she took great pains to explain that the birth of Jesus was an impossibility, since parthenogenesis could only produce a female, never a male. Rejoicing in the Lord, I later went to her office to thank her for the presentation and the proof that the birth of Jesus was a miracle of God, not an accident of nature. She thought she had defeated me, but the Lord had defeated her.

## Second Furlough
## Israel, University of Hawaii

Naomi also took some classes at UH, just for fun or potential use, like Teaching English as a Second Language. She also had fun selling men's Aloha shirts at Sears in Ala Moana shopping center. The year went fast. We decided to take the President Cleveland from Honolulu to Manila, with a refrigerator, gas stove, air conditioner, washer and dryer. Why these electrical appliances? Because we had promised, that if we got the scholarship from UH, we would teach one more year at Faith Academy upon our return. Since we would be living in Manila, we would need these things.

For a vehicle, I flew back to Detroit to get an IH Travelall. I drove my parents to Ames, Iowa for my Mom's 50th graduation reunion from Iowa State College, and then I went on to Los Angeles to ship the vehicle. I flew back to Honolulu, finished packing everything and boarded the ship. The people at Kalihi Union Church had never before said farewell to any of their missionaries sailing on a ship. Many came to see us off, bringing leis, the real flower necklaces. Each of us had 14 leis around our necks! They enjoyed the send-off and so did we. We felt we were special.

This time there was no passenger on board to conduct the Sunday services, except for Missionary Teacher Roger Walkwitz. I have never used the title "Reverend." Check out Psalm 111:9 KJV.

*"He sent redemption unto His people; He has commanded His covenant forever; holy and reverend is His Name."*

There were three Sundays while on board. So I had the privilege to explain the Gospel three times, up in First Class of course. However, the officer did not even allow us to have Sunday lunch in First Class after the service, even after

I had done a good deed for them. So it was down to third class again, which actually was just fine for us common people. The third Sunday was from Hong Kong to Manila. The seas were really rough, more than usual. We had to hold onto ropes along the hallways as the ship tossed. That was a rather short Sunday service for this poor sailor. However, I did finish it okay.

# CHAPTER 12

## Faith Academy and BIBAK Bible Fellowship in Baguio City 1969-72

We quickly got settled in the house rented for us, and classes began at Faith Academy. We would have liked a house closer to the school, but none were available. We had more than a half-hour drive each way at that time. Since then, population and traffic have grown considerably so that it would probably take 1½ hours today in 2008. The school year went along fairly well, with all three sons enrolled. We four traveled together each day, bringing our bag lunches. Naomi and another missionary lady, Janet McCurry, started teaching Bible lessons once a week in a Chinese school in the middle of Manila. This proved to be very interesting and challenging, as the students and teachers appreciated it.

Since we had recently visited Israel and visited one Synagogue in Tel Aviv, I decided to find out if there were any Synagogues in the Philippines. There was only one, in downtown Manila on Taft Avenue, called Bachrach Hall, for the small Jewish community. Visitors were welcome.

I took the bus to the place a bit early on Friday evening in order to visit. A somewhat elderly couple was there whose only daughter, Celia or Topsy, had arrived on her honeymoon after marrying an Israeli in Israel.

The couple invited me to their home for supper after the evening prayer service. This was amazing for me, a total stranger! This never happened in any church I had visited. I rode to their home in their one-year-old small Mercedes Benz sedan. As we gathered around the table, Mr. Tischler read from his prayer book and then sat down to pour everyone a glass of wine for the Shabbat *Kiddush* celebration. *Kiddush* means the Sanctification of the occasion, this time for the Shabbat weekend.

In my whole life, I had never had a drink of any kind of alcoholic beverage. Even when in the US Army, when sometimes beer was served free at mealtime, I refused it. It smelled like garbage to me. So when it was time to pour some wine in my glass, I said, "Please, none for me, as I am not used to it." Mr. Tischler said, "Oh, you must have some!" I knew that if I refused, that would be the end of any friendship and any witness. To have refused a sacred part of their lives would have been very offensive.

In one second, the Lord had taught me a lesson. He made wine in John 2, He drank wine but He never got drunk. "Ok," I said, "but not too much." I was afraid of any alcoholic drink; I had seen too many drunks in Chicago, especially around the Pacific Garden Mission, which took care of many alcoholics. The only cure seemed to be salvation in the Lord Jesus Christ. I had been a Believer since age thirteen. I could trust the Lord to take care of me now as I joined the Jewish people in their celebrations from that time onward.

Faith Academy and BIBAK Bible Fellowship

There was also a Saturday morning *Torah* (Pentateuch) study service at the Synagogue. I brought the whole family there one time to meet Adolf and Marian Tischler also. He said Hitler had forcibly given his name to him. They had escaped Germany and the Holocaust in 1939 and were able to come to Manila. Life was tough, but being Germans, the Japanese did not bother them too much. Adolf was the head of the Philippine branch of the Toledo Scales Company. He was a Cohen, meaning one descended from the priestly line of Israel. But his eyes were bad, making *Torah* study difficult, so he went into business. Therefore, he was one of the main leaders of the Synagogue.

They never had a rabbi whenever I visited, until much later. Adolf enjoyed talking about Scripture because he missed the teachings that a rabbi would give. But Marian always interrupted any serious conversation we had about the Bible. She was afraid Adolf would get too interested and I would try to convert him to Christianity. Adolf even told the other men at the Synagogue that I knew more about the Bible than all of them put together. This was probably true. Their services were nearly the same every time, reading the same prayers, and all of it in Hebrew. A visit to the Tischlers' home was much preferable than going to the Synagogue services. But I wanted to maintain contact with some of the men.

When the season came to celebrate Passover, the Tischlers invited Ray and me to join them. It would be my first time to experience a Passover Celebration, called the *Seder.* They knew Naomi had to stay home with the younger boys. Ray and I took the bus. I told Ray that we would have four cups of wine for the evening celebration, and that hopefully, we would not have to finish a full cup each time.

We deliberately took the bus in case we would feel a bit strange at the end of the evening. I did not want to drive. Parking was also a problem. But it all turned out well. The wine glasses were small and we were perfectly sober when the time came to go home. The Lord took care of us, and we cemented our friendship with the Tischlers and the other Jews that we met. From then on, ministry to Israelis and all Jews would take on an additional emphasis for us.

Toward the end of the school year, we were expecting to be reassigned to Banaue to continue teaching and making disciples. My Team of local men was there and it was doing fine. However, some of the missionaries that had complained about us before were still there. Apparently, we were too productive. We were working in English rather than the local dialect and the people loved us. The contrast was too much for these missionaries. They did not want us back in Banaue. One couple even said that they did not believe a person could really be born again unless he had heard the Gospel in his native language! My Team had all been born again while hearing the Gospel in English. They were now leading congregations in their native dialect and using the Ifugao Gospel of John, which had already been printed then.

The chairman of the Field Council also had his ideas. He was adamant that we should stay permanently at Faith Academy. We disagreed. The other council members did not agree with him either. I told them that either I went to the mountains to honor my Call, or I would resign after school was out. The Council met again later. The chairman was still adamant. When he could not get his way, he walked out. The vice-chairman, Cliff Bedell, took over, and the council came up with something new.

We would be assigned to Baguio (BAA-gi-o) City, the summer capital of the Philippines and a tourist destination. John Hay Air Base was also there, the R&R Base for US Military. Are we going to be on vacation? It is also one mile high, giving a moderate climate in the tropics. We sold our air conditioner in Manila  No need for it there. Baguio is also the gateway to the mountain tribal region and the center for higher education for mountain people and others.

We had also noticed that the young people who came to Baguio from Banaue to pursue high school and college education oftentimes got mixed up with the wrong crowd, messing up their lives in the process. Our ministry would be to follow up on all these young people and get them integrated into one of the evangelical churches in the city. We were limited to only this and were not allowed to start anything new.

We thought, what kind of vision is this for an active, productive missionary teacher? The mission is supposed to do 'church planting.' At least we would be working with mountain people, and could make trips back to Banaue if needed. Baguio was also a cosmopolitan city, with Filipinos from all over the islands living there, including people of different nationalities. We moved to Baguio City as soon as school was finished. We were excited to see how the Lord would work this one out. We thought this mission could turn out to be very interesting! We lived and taught in Baguio for the next 20 years!

We arrived in Baguio in June of 1970, found a house, moved in, and started visiting around. We met a retired single lady missionary, Hannah Campagna, who lived in Baguio since she found she had a more productive life there than in the USA. Hannah had a personal ministry to students.

According to Roger

We visited the BIBAK (BEE-baak) Dormitories, which had one large building for ladies and another one for men, and was limited to students from the mountain areas.

BIBAK was an acronym for the five basic tribal groups: B for the Benguets, I for the Ifugaos, B for the Bontocs; A for the Apayao people, and K for the Kalinga tribes. In these areas, there were at least nine languages spoken, plus several more dialects! However, being college students, many of them spoke very good English, better than many lowlanders. We were welcomed as "fellow mountaineers" since we had lived in Banaue for so many years.

Nothing spiritual was being done for these students. So we asked for and got permission to have Sunday evening vesper services. Together with Hannah and a few Believers we had known in Banaue, we had a joyful time singing and teaching the Bible. The joy was so contagious that more and more students joined us. As we got to know each other, we offered personal Bible studies. Naomi would go around the Ladies' Dorm and I would go around the Men's Dorm during the week, meeting with the interested ones. Several came to faith in Jesus and grew with this discipling ministry.

Usually, we did not give an invitation to respond to Jesus, as we preferred to lay a good foundation of Bible truth to which they could readily respond if the Spirit was convicting them. One Sunday evening, Hannah gave her testimony and I taught a bit. She wanted to give an invitation, so I did. Three men responded. Afterwards, we talked to and prayed with each one, and I made appointments to meet them the following day. Two of them were not really sincere and did not keep their appointments. The third was genuinely born-from-above. Joe Eming had many questions and learned rapidly. He soon cleaned up his life of drinking and smoking, on the basis of the Word that his body now was the temple of the Spirit. Two people lived in his body now, so he had to keep it clean.

Joe had an outgoing type of personality, so I took him to an area where we had outreach ministry and had him teach the Bible to the children. I had found that teaching children was the best way to train Bible teachers and preachers. Later, Joe began taking his turn in the teaching rotation at BIBAK Bible Fellowship. At school vacation times, he would go home to teach his family what he had learned. Soon each of the family members, except for two siblings, was born-from-above. The School of Tyrannus method was beginning to work! Other Believer students were emboldened to do the same, as we taught the method from Acts. More than half a dozen congregations were formed.

We also learned from some of our Banaue men who had moved to Baguio, that they were not really welcomed into the existing evangelical churches. Lowland people dominated these churches. The mountain people were subconsciously looked down upon and the mountain people could feel it. They sat in the back and could not get involved in the ministry, mostly because each church was controlled by professional clergy. Those who attended were expected to sit and enjoy the program, and contribute for the expenses.

A few miles outside of Baguio and down the mountain lived a community called Sinko. Wood carvers from Banaue lived there. Wood was hard to find anymore around Banaue, so they moved there. A missionary on vacation had helped a small group of Believers form a congregation, which was nurtured by another missionary family now based in Baguio,

Dr Jim & Helen Irvine. We went there on Sunday mornings to help out, together with some men from Baguio.

After several months, the Irvines left for the USA and we went out of town for a couple weeks. When we returned, we were told that those from Baguio who went down to Sinko on Sundays had found the meeting place padlocked. Apparently opposition had developed and the host family decided to stop the meeting. "Now what?", we wondered.

Waiting on the Lord, we remembered an important truth: birds of a feather flock together. Ethnic and language groupings work better together, as in a Chinese church, a Korean church, or a black church. A diverse group, over time, might gel together, but usually young and new Believers needed the comfort of their own kind of people. The evangelical churches in Baguio did not meet the needs of the mountaineers. This was obvious.

It was also obvious to us that the mountaineers needed a church of their own, one that they controlled, one that did things the Bible way with some things from their cultures that were neutral spiritually. They needed a church that would really disciple them and where they would really learn the Bible, instead of just sitting in the back and attending a program.

Where could we meet? We had had Bible studies and fellowship gatherings at our house, but it would be too small for a church gathering. The Irvines' place was also too small. Then Helen Irvine suggested the Baguio Health Club, which was owned by a man from Bontoc, who had also earned a Mr. Philippines title some years back. It was not used on Sunday mornings. Chairs would be needed, so we bargained to buy folding chairs that could be stacked and put out of the way, and count the cost against a very minimal rent. With only a word-of-mouth announcement, we started on the first Sunday of September, 1971. More students from the BIBAK Dorms and other adults came until the space was filled every Sunday.

Since then, every five years, BIBAK Bible Fellowship has a big celebration, praising the Lord for what He has done for them. They are still doing fine on the foundation of a non-professional ministry, with no clergy. The body works together with the leadership of their Elders and Deacons, who train new ones as they grow. Non-mountaineers cannot be full members and cannot hold office, a protection I built into their Constitution and By-Laws. However, everyone can come to learn.

Of course, I did not inform anyone in Manila of what we were doing. The restrictions put on me were ridiculous and hindered the work of the Lord. When the Manila office found out, I was blamed — first, because I had not asked for and received permission to start a church (as if that should be required of a missionary!); and second, I was told because it is a 'well-known fact' that a church cannot be started and be expected to last when built on students. Is that so I thought to myself.

Some years later, when we had grown, BIBAK was used as an example of how to do church planting! What a reversal! Does God know what He is doing, through servants who listen to His small voice in the Bible and put His plans into action? We were grateful for the Lord's confirmation that we really did follow Him and had His blessing.

As I was going through the book of Acts in my regular reading, just enjoying it and not looking for anything specific, that small voice called my attention to **Acts 19:8-10**. I had to stop and study this! This is fantastic I thought, God's way of multiplying congregations! Paul had come to Ephesus on his third journey, having stopped there briefly on his second.

> *"And he went into the synagogue, and spoke boldly for the space of three months, disputing and persuading the things concerning the kingdom of God. But when some were hardened and believed not, but spoke evil of that way before the multitude, he departed from them, and separated the disciples, disputing daily in the school of one, Tyrannus. And this continued for the space of two years; so that all they who dwelt in Asia heard the word of the Lord Jesus, both Jews and Greeks."*

How could the whole Roman province of Asia hear the Word of God in the space of two years with Paul teaching daily in one place, Ephesus? And then too, there are the seven churches of Asia listed in Revelation 2-3. Biblical Asia is actually SW Turkey today, also known as Anatolia. How did the other six get started? By researching, we found two more, Colosse and Hierapolis, making nine churches in all mentioned in the NT. What was the "secret" of how this happened?

First, how did Ephesus relate to the other eight cities? Ephesus was the center for all of Asia for education, commerce, religion, and other things. There was a flow of people from these cities in and out of Ephesus for this reason. They were coming from the interior of the province for a few days or longer to accomplish their purpose and then returning home. Some heard of this Paul, who was teaching strange things at the School of Tyrannus. Tyrannus used his school mornings and evenings. The afternoons were too hot — siesta time — so Paul used it then. He was able to make tents while teaching. People from the province came, listened, learned, and responded to the Lord. Then they went home and carried the truth of what they had learned back to their families and neighbors. Bible studies emerged. Congregations formed. As more went to Ephesus to do business and to see Paul, more and more truth was carried back home, to many cities and locations. Paul did not go to these cities. Unnamed disciples planted these churches as they were led and taught by the Holy Spirit.

So what had this to do with BIBAK? Just this: Baguio City stood in relation to the whole mountain region as Ephesus did to Asia! Baguio was the educational center, the commercial center, the cultural center, and vacation center for the mountain regions of BIBAK as well as nearby lowland provinces. Dozens, maybe hundreds of buses went in and out of Baguio City every day carrying thousands of passengers. We needed to establish a Bible Training Center in Baguio City patterned after that of Paul in Ephesus! In this way, all of the mountain region, with all of its languages, could be reached with the Good News, even without foreign missionaries!

We needed to have a place where mountaineers could come at any time to interact with us or some other Believer to learn the Bible. We needed to have regular scheduled classes for those who lived in Baguio, especially the students who had come for college. We needed to have a small dormitory for men and women for more intensive Bible training while they were in college. Could we find such a place centrally located in the city? We had to.

# According to Roger

Brent School was an Episcopal prep school in Baguio City, founded in the early 1900s. It catered to wealthier people, foreigners, military and some missionary kids whose parents lived in Baguio. Brent offered K-12. We could have used Brent for our sons' schooling, but we all much preferred home schooling for many reasons.

The son of the Headmaster was in fifth grade but could not read. Like so many other students, he had just been passed along from grade to grade. Another missionary family in Baguio was also doing home schooling; but somehow two of their young sons had not learned to read, either. Both families approached Naomi to tutor their sons, which she did, besides teaching our three sons their regular subjects! She did a good job over a period of some months, using the phonics method. Both families appreciated it very much, and I guess the boys did as well. We were given a 3-month old German Shepherd puppy as a form of thanks.

The year 1972 was significant. In June and July, it literally rained for 40 days and 40 nights. The weather station at John Hay Air Base recorded rainfall on a graph on the wall. For June and July, the graph hit the ceiling! Usually Baguio gets about 170 inches of rain per year. More than that came down during only these two months! Flooding was a serious problem in the lowlands. Filipinos dry their stored rice frequently by spreading it out on paved roads, even on main highways, when the sun is shining! If the rice is not dry, it will turn to mush when milled to remove the husk. When it is milled and allowed to sit around too long, it gets stale. Some areas were facing a measure of starvation because they could not dry their rice, since rice is the staple food. With flooded areas, trucks had a hard time bringing in supplies.

# Faith Academy and BIBAK Bible Fellowship

Ray had finished eighth grade on home schooling, with Naomi doing most of the teaching. We had decided it would be good for each of our sons to go to Faith Academy for their high school. They would need to live in the dorm, of course. School was starting in July. We were able to drive Ray to school in our IH Travelall by taking a different route to Manila. McArthur Highway, the main road between Manila and Baguio was under water for many, many miles.

It was difficult to leave him there. Ray was a shy fellow who was very kind and biblical in his behavior. He had been a Believer since he was seven years old and read his Bible every day. Those who were not so inclined made fun of him and tried to make his life unhappy. The other freshmen in the dorm were mostly this kind.

Are missionary kids angels? Hardly. Is a missionary community ideal? No! Definitely not! We were continually disappointed by events there that showed, just like much of Christianity, a lack of obedience to the commandments to love God and to love your neighbor. Pride and prejudice were evident. Considering others better than oneself was a rare trait. We just hoped that our lives would be different, be biblical, since the outworking of God's will through us depended on it.

After a few days, we decided to make our way back to Baguio together with Helen Irvine, who had taken her sons down for high school. We had left Randy and Ron in Baguio with Elisa. About two-thirds of the way back to Baguio, we encountered a flooded area. A dam had burst, flooding everything. We could not see the highway ahead of us. No vehicles were moving. We tried to recall if this portion was level or not. We decided to venture in. The water got deeper and deeper until the engine stopped. At least we said to ourselves, we were still on the highway and not in the ditch. Then, a bus came along. Thankfully we had a good towrope with us. The bus towed us for five miles to the next town. Fearing that water had entered the engine, I drained the engine oil and replaced it. We drove on after that until we came to the long bridge. It had been washed out after we had come down a few days ago! We backed up a way and found a parking place near a small store. It was late, so we slept in the car that night.

The next morning we noticed people hiking through the mountains to get around the bridge at a crossing farther up the raging river. The three of us hiked this trail. Later, Naomi and Helen caught a ride to Baguio in the back of a pickup truck and then a bus, while I returned to watch our car. Stealing is rampant everywhere in the Philippines, except in Banaue at the time we lived there. These tribal people had a pagan code of conduct that was higher than that in the Catholic lowlands. It is not the same today, however, because electricity has come, and outside people have brought in their corrupt culture with them.

After a couple days, engineers had made a makeshift bamboo bridge for people to go over the washed out bridge on foot. The son of the owners of the store where I had parked came out to meet me. He said he knew me, because he was a student in Baguio. He said that his family would watch the car for me until the bridge was repaired. He told me I could go ahead to cross the bridge and catch some transportation on the other side, just as he would be doing. After about three weeks, a temporary bridge had been made and I got the car back home. How thankful I was to the Lord for this provision based on a previous friendship.

# Faith Academy and BIBAK Bible Fellowship

Transportation problems due to the flood caused a delay in the opening of classes at Faith Academy for a week. That made life more difficult for Ray, who did not have much to do in the dorm. He also got sick, which did not help. Shortly after, we decided to go back to the States at the end of the first semester in December for a short furlough. It would seem to us that some of the personnel at Faith could not cope with the needs of all their students, or they did not see the needs at all, or they did not really care that much. They catered to their favorites, the musical students and the sports students. The ordinary students got very little attention or help. These were personnel who came specifically to teach or to be dorm parents at Faith, but Naomi & I, as well as our sons were disappointed with many of them.

The other significant event of the year was the declaration of Martial Law in September 1972, by the Ferdinand Marcos regime. The motto was, "Discipline, my friend!" as the country had always been somewhat undisciplined. For a while, life in general did improve. However, getting out of the country became very complicated, as the government did not want any of the opposition to sneak out. We had to wade through a lot of red tape and extra clearances. But finally we got our papers.

We drove down to the Manila Guest House. With all his things, Ray had taken the school bus to meet us there. We were so happy to see each other! On Friday evening we all went to the Synagogue. Afterwards we had our *Shabbat* supper with the Tischlers, and said a temporary "good-bye." We flew out on China Airlines, and enjoyed a free overnight in Taipei because of airline scheduling. We flew into California to see several friends there, and then flew on to Chicago on Christmas Day. My brother picked us up at the airport, took us for dinner, and then brought us to

Wheaton. We were pleasantly surprised that College Church had prepared their missionary house for us, complete with a refrigerator full of food!

Clarence Walkwitz
US Army 1918

Roger as a toddler 1931

Roger Walkwitz
US Army 1952

Roger Walkwitz in Army Petroleum Laboratory 1953

Roger and Naomi, first date Bryan College December 1954

Sept 8, 1956

Roger & Naomi
with Ralph Mount
Sept 8, 1956

Naomi singing Detour at Mission Conference

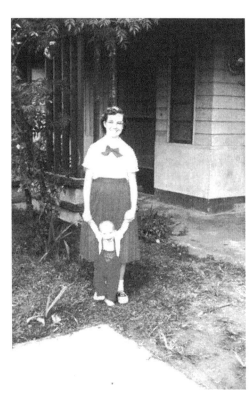

Naomi and Ray 1958
in Manila

Roger in Banaue, Ifugao 1959

Roger in Banaue with High School Club shirt 1962

Naomi & sons arrive Banaue airstrip on SIL 1967

Walkwitz Family 1962

How Walkwitz family traveled for four months in USA 1968

Our Farewell from Hawaii 1969

Roger with Mercedes
bought from Tischlers 1979

Walkwitz brass quartet 1974

# CHAPTER 13

## BIBAK Bible Fellowship and Brent School 1973-76

Our short furlough went by quickly. Ray was a freshman at Wheaton Community High School, which was also my school, and doing very well. Randy was at Franklin Junior High, and Ron was at Holmes Elementary School. Both were doing very well also. All the schools were only a good walking distance away. As usual, we told the teachers that the boys were home schooled up to some level. The boys proved to be above average for their classes. They were impatient with the long school days. There was too much time wasted. With home schooling, they were finished each day in half the time.

I did some substitute teaching in the district, but soon quit that. Usually I was given a junior high class at schools known for their disciplinary problems. The stress of that was not worth the pittance paid. A few trips were made for Missionary Conferences. We ordered a new IH Travelall from the dealer in Detroit that sold to missionaries at their cost plus $75. International Harvester vehicles were really sturdy trucks suitable for the rough roads in the Philippines. To pick it up, we as a family took the train from Chicago to Detroit. This was a new adventure for the boys. We then drove the new car all the way to California, visited our friends again, put the vehicle on a ship, and flew to Manila on Philippine Airlines.

We arrived early in the morning, and right away we took the bus to Baguio. This meant an additional 6-hour trip, making it 45 hours with no sleep for us. Everyone wanted to get home again and to see our dog, a German Shepherd and our helper, Elisa. We had kept the house. She had stayed to watch over it and to take care of many missionaries who had come to Baguio for vacation and used it. Everything was OK. School started in a few days, so back to Manila we went, taking Ray for his sophomore year, and Randy, this time for his freshman year. With two of them together in the dorm, things went much better, as they defended each other. It should not be that way among Christians, but sadly, it is in many cases.

We hoped that among our mountain people, the Lord would build a Community where love prevailed, love for Him and love for each other. We would need to model that love as we taught the Bible and lived among them. BIBAK Bible Fellowship was doing fine at the Baguio Health Club, with the leaders sharing the teaching responsibilities. They had also planned a Missions Conference to be held as soon as we got back and had our boys back in school in Manila.

Since the School of Tyrannus method focused on developing disciples who would carry the Good News far and wide, it was only natural to have a Missions Conference each year to "lift up our eyes on the fields that are ripe for harvest." We continued with Sunday evening vesper services at the BIBAK Dorms and other meetings at our house. For outreach as well as training of the new student Believers, we also started many home Bible studies during weeknights at various locations around Baguio. We believed in the on-the-job training, for real, not pretend.

About a week or two after the Brent School year started, I had a call from the school to ask if I would be willing to teach their chemistry class and one math class, which was a half load. Their chemistry teacher had suddenly left for New York, where her parents lived. Some of the Baguio-based missionaries had their children in the chemistry class which was needed for college entrance, especially for those going into the medical field. They also knew that I had taught chemistry at Faith Academy and at Bryan College.

I agreed to do so, since the class would be mornings only, and so far our ministries were mostly afternoons and evenings. As a foreigner on a pre-arranged employment visa, I could not accept any salary for myself, but I could put it into a mission fund for the building that we would eventually need for our Tyrannus Center. Sometimes, I had a lunchtime Bible study with some of my students at Brent who wanted to learn some Bible.

The new Headmaster was an American who had an adult son, Paul McGee, who came to visit for some months. He had lived on a kibbutz in Israel for a year, because his mother was Jewish! We had some good Bible studies together, together with Billy Irvine, an older MK near his age who lived in town. Soon Paul responded to the Lord and was baptized, wearing his green kibbutz-type pants and a red shirt for the blood of Yeshua! It was an interesting year, meeting a lot of people from a different stratum of society, but one year was enough. We were getting busy with BIBAK.

In the fall of 1973, I was approached by a Filipino pastor friend to go with him to a meeting of a bunch of pastors and others at the big United Church of Christ of the Philippines, or UCCP. It turned out to be an organizational meeting for a nationwide evangelistic thrust in February 1974, to be called "One Way '74." The Billy Graham Evangelistic Association was sponsoring the effort and using associate evangelistic teams. The idea was to have simultaneous weeklong meetings in every major city in the Philippines. In preparation they wanted everyone to promote home Bible studies and to prepare counselors. I was the only foreigner at this meeting. All the rest were Filipinos. Without my saying even a word, I was elected vice-chairman and the one in charge of counseling and follow-up. The chairman was the pastor of the UCCP church.

I was not interested in ecumenical activities. Besides, I was already very busy with BIBAK. I had also never been involved in any big campaign. However, I got into this by default. Apparently, I was becoming known around Baguio and respected for my type of ministry. As I meditated on the situation, I decided to go along with it to see the inside of this thing. I had not pushed myself in; others had pulled me in. Therefore, the Lord must have some reason for it.

Soon, another UCCP pastor who happened to be an Ifugao, approached me to co-teach a weekly Bible study in his area for his children and neighbors. We would alternate teaching each week. This was the directive in preparation for the campaign, so he had to do something.

OK, I said. He taught the first week. I taught the second week, but he was not there. I came the third week, and since he was not there again, I taught it. This happened for several weeks. Finally, I saw him in town and asked him why he did not come anymore. He said that it was better if I taught his children. I was not sure if he really knew the Lord at that time anyway, so I said, OK, and let it go at that. All of the children in that class, except for one, became believers and joined us in BIBAK, not in the UCCP. He let his children make their own choice.

Another foreign mission was in charge of all the preparations, meetings, and activities. They had counselors' trainings, so I urged all of our BIBAK people to participate. We knew all of our people were born again, but we were not so sure about a lot of the other church people. The instructions were that during the campaign meetings, the counselors were to be scattered all over the large auditorium. As soon as the Invitation was given, the counselors were to get up and come forward. This was a tactic to "break the ice" so to speak that thinking these were people wanting to come forward to be saved, and so would be emboldened to also come forward themselves. I was not too sure that psychology was a good idea. I depended more on the Spirit than on methods.

After initial counseling was done and cards were filled out, I asked several persons each night as to why they came forward. The answers confirmed my suspicions. Some said that Filipino hospitality required them to respond to show appreciation for the evangelistic Team coming to the Philippines and for the enjoyable program. Others came because a free Bible was given to everyone that came forward, and a Bible was expensive. Some came forward just for curiosity, to see what was going on. However, a few came that were genuinely touched by the Spirit and, with good counseling and discipling, grew as new creatures in Christ.

The One-Way '74 Campaign in Baguio made a big splash and accomplished something. I spent a lot of time and money to do my assigned part, but I would not do it again. I am convinced that the patient School of Tyrannus method is the best way to enable people to come in to the Family of the Lord. It is a whole lot cheaper too. A valid decision for the Lord needs to be based on an understanding of the basic Scriptures. So we teach first and try not to put any emotional pressure on anyone to make a decision. If the Spirit of God is not doing the convicting, then we should not try to do it.

As soon as the Campaign was over, I got a letter from my Mom that my Dad was in the hospital with leukemia. I phoned home. Mom said that everyone around them was very helpful and there was no need for me to come home. Dad had had six pints of blood, so I knew that this was the end. My parents and I had agreed that whatever happened to them, that I would stay on the job in the Philippines and not come home. It would be an unnecessary waste of money. After all, we would all eventually see each other in heaven. The Lord's work was more important than seeing a dead body in a casket.

So I did not go home, as most people would do, even though I was sure that they would have been happy to see me again, and I them. Dad died on the 10th of April, Ron's 12th birthday. My younger brother and older sister took care of all the legal and family matters. Dad was a US Army veteran from WWI, so the government provided a small marker for his grave. Mom soon moved into the Retirement Center that they had already contracted for.

The mission's Annual Conference was also in April 1974. Those were busy days! BIBAK Bible Fellowship was now becoming well known and respected in the mission field. I was elected to serve on the mission Field Council for a two-year term and was made corporate secretary. The General Director, Phil Armstrong, complimented me on the thoroughness of the minutes that I took. This began a six-year stretch of being on the Council. In this time, I could help with better understanding of my fellow missionaries and their Callings and needs because of my bad experiences with poor leadership. Then current Area Director, Frank Allen, was much better.

Being in the Field Council took some time away from Baguio, but it was good to not be around all the time. From the beginning, my objective was to work myself out of a job, not build my own kingdom. We were training others to continue the work. We helped BIBAK congregation write a decent constitution and by-laws. We made it so that only mountaineers could be full members and hold office. We also designed a unique way of recognizing their Elders and Deacons by eliminating any politics. After about a year sitting-in and observing their business meetings as associate members, we decided to resign and keep out of their way.

During this first year back in Baguio, we were surprised by a visit from the daughter of the Tischlers. I had met Topsy on my first trip to the Synagogue and at supper at her home in Manila. Her Israeli husband turned out to be a bum. They were living in the northeast of the USA. One day he just disappeared with all their money. She phoned a former boyfriend who was not too far away for help.

Charles Black was a Gentile, but they got together and got married. We entertained them and took them for a ride to show Charley the beautiful mountains and had lunch at a bus stop restaurant. We took a picture at the highest point in the Philippine highway system, 7,400 feet above sea level. We have kept in touch over the years, but I have seen no spiritual response yet. They are grandparents now. Topsy's parents have died.

The BIBAK ministry was now accepted by the mission. How could they do otherwise? It was growing. Did we need more help? Not really, but the mission thought we needed some. A German couple and a single American lady came to help. We really needed to find a building or build a building for the Tyrannus Center. We found two options. One was a large undeveloped area of at least two acres that a foreign mission owned but wanted to sell. We could build our Center there and have land for expansion or other housing. This was the best option, but we got no backing from the mission as other projects had priority. The other option was a large house on land that had been repossessed by a bank in Manila.

I went to Manila to inquire at the bank with the mission treasurer. We had very little money and the mission was really not that interested. It would need to be a mission project to be promoted in the USA, but there were other projects that had higher priority. I thought of going it alone, but did not have peace from the Lord to do that just yet. BIBAK had not grown to a level of maturity to do much on their part financially, and too much subsidy was not good for them. We needed to stick to indigenous principles as BIBAK was going to stand alone once we reached our objective of reproducing disciples, based on the 2 Timothy 2:2 principle.

Ray would be graduating from Faith in May 1976. He finally had a roommate in his junior year that bonded with him. Ray blossomed with the capabilities that he had. He was given the lead male part in the Senior Play and did an excellent job. Randy was also doing fine, joining the band, playing the cornet that I had taught him to play in Baguio. In fact, I had taught both Randy and Ron to play cornet, then taught Ray and myself to play trombone. We bought the instruments from a missionary who was going back to the States. On Sundays when all the boys were home, we played as a brass quartet to accompany the singing. We also played some singing type men's quartet songs for our annual mission conferences, such as "On the Jericho Road." Randy also joined the Faith Academy wrestling team and Ray, the cross-country team.

Ron was four years behind Ray in schooling and three years behind Randy. He did very well in his home schooling, but wanted to go to Faith for 8th grade while Ray was a senior and Randy a junior, to sort of "break in" at Faith while his big brothers were there and both doing very well. Ron is very athletic so he enjoyed participating in many sports. We decided that this might be OK, so we brought Ron to Faith for the 1975-76 school year. Naomi was now finished with home schooling! She "retired" until later when she had to help our first two grandsons with their home schooling!

In January of 1976, the owner of our rented house informed us that she wanted the house back. We moved into an apartment at Doane Rest, the missionary vacation compound built on land donated in 1932 by a Doane family in the US. This donation was done during the American time. The land was deeded to be used only for missionary vacation housing. Baguio City was the Summer Capital of the Philippines, as the government moved there

115

each summer to escape the summer heat of April and May. Missionaries also wanted to escape the heat. This was before air conditioners became available. The land was given to the Association of Baptists for World Evangelism or ABWE to administer.

After we moved in at Doane Rest, a retired American couple wanted us to watch over their house for a couple of months. It bordered the golf course at the Baguio Country Club. I did not play golf! They had two lady helpers and a gardener. We slept at this fancy house and ate our meals there, but kept our place at Doane Rest because we had lots of stuff that could not be brought to the Country Club house. We still had Elisa with us, too. She stayed at Doane Rest.

We were still looking for a suitable place for our BIBAK Tyrannus Center. Just as we were getting ready to leave Baguio for our furlough, the German couple found a place that might do. They moved in and tried to make it functional. Before we left Baguio, we arranged for Elisa to stay in the small dorm and, together with Susan, a college graduate, teach children's classes all over Baguio during the year we were away. During that year, Joe Eming and Susan got married, the first couple to be married that had come to faith in Jesus through BIBAK Bible Fellowship. Joe had graduated as a civil engineer. We were sorry we had to miss this first wedding!

Initially, a big complaint against us for starting BIBAK Bible Fellowship with college students was that a viable church could not be built with students. My reply was that this was the way the Lord led us to proceed. He will build it His own way. Just wait and see. Students graduate and get married, families develop, and stability grows. Most students will move away from the college town, but some will stay, get jobs, get married and have families, and grow to maturing leadership in the church. Be patient! And we were patient, steadfastly discipling, nurturing and teaching. God proved Himself faithful. Our critics had nothing more to say. It would have been so nice to be able to say, "I told you so!" but we didn't say it. We did not have to. They already knew we were right.

# CHAPTER 14

## Missionary Furlough Homes in Wheaton, Illinois. 1976-77

Missionary Furlough Homes Foundation in Wheaton, Illinois, had recently come into being, providing fully furnished homes or apartments for up to one year for missionaries that had children in school. We qualified because I had my home church, College Church in Wheaton. Ray was a freshman in Wheaton College; Randy, a senior at Wheaton Community High School (my school) and Ron, a freshman there too. We paid a nominal rent, based on what each mission's rent allowance was. This was a really big help and blessing!

When traveling, we enjoyed stopping here and there along the way to visit friends. From Manila, we flew to Seoul, South Korea, for a few days to see missionary friends there, and of course to do some shopping. Then we flew to Hawaii, to visit Kalihi Union Church folks. We thought this might be our last trip to Hawaii altogether as a family, so wanted to enjoy it! Then we flew to Los Angeles and rented a car for a week. While there, Ray had four wisdom teeth pulled by a dentist friend. He had also some chiropractic adjustments by a doctor friend, who had discovered that Ray had one leg longer than the other. That was not good.

Then we drove north to Redding, California, to see our medical doctor friend and family. The McCurry's had worked for some years at the Good News Clinic in Banaue. Their first three children, Kevin, Diane and John, were the same ages as our three, so we always had good times together. Dr. Bill gave us men our physicals. He removed a cyst on Ray's back, found that Randy had a heart murmur, and said that Ron and I were A-OK. They had planned to lend us their station wagon for the year, but I decided to buy it instead and leave it with Ray and Randy after we returned to the Philippines with Ron.

On the way south again, we found that the station wagon air conditioner was not working. A mechanic shop said it could not be fixed. We were not too sure about that, so later, Ray and I figured out what was wrong, bought a part for $50, and installed it. It worked just fine. We stopped by Phoenix, Arizona, as we had a supporting church there. Since we had to cross the USA to get to Wheaton, we thought it wise to visit all our supporting churches along the way. We also wanted to enjoy traveling together as a family, probably for the last time. When children start in college, you know that the empty nest is just around the corner.

We did make it to Wheaton in time for me to enjoy my Class of 1951 have its 25th Class Reunion. We soon were able to move into 107 N. President St. and get settled. Then we drove south to Hendersonville, North Carolina, to see my Mom. Tampa, Florida, proved too hot for my Dad. They chose Hendersonville because it was a bird sanctuary town. It was also in the mountains and had cooler air and beautiful scenery. My Mom, since early in her life, had always enjoyed watching birds. For some years, she was a member of the Audubon Club and had seen hundreds of different kinds of birds. She could detect their distinct calls.

Then we traveled north to Philadelphia to see some of the sites for the 200$^{th}$ Anniversary of the Independence of the USA. One of my Wheaton classmates, Dr. Bobby Sherwin, was now a medical doctor in Philadelphia, so she gave Naomi her physical. Naomi was OK. At that same time, the hijacking of Air France with 100 Jewish hostages to Entebbe, Uganda, was ongoing. As we drove north to New York on July 4, we heard on the radio of the daring and successful rescue of these hostages! We were so thankful! Prayers were answered. Terrorism against Israel was beginning to rear its ugly head, and soon it would be against the rest of the world.

Back in March 1968, after we had spent 17 days in Israel, we stopped in Germany to see former students of mine at Bryan College who were now missionaries there. Don and Joyann Walker took us to the Dachau Concentration Camp. They did not want to take our sons, as they thought it would be too traumatic for them. It was very disturbing; but seeing the ovens of the crematoria and other remains of the camp was important for us.

Our interest in Israel and commitment to the Jewish people everywhere continued to grow deeper. The only way we could possibly understand the terrible persecution against Israel, done for no apparent reason whatsoever, was that they were the Chosen People of God and, therefore, the primary target of the enemy, Satan. True, the Jews for the most part were not living according to God's teaching, or Torah, and therefore were under God's discipline until they repented. But the accusation of the Catholic Church, that the Jews were "Christ killers" and therefore rejected by God in favor of "The Church," and eternally damned, is totally from the mouth of Satan. We will take our stand with Israel and Jewish people anywhere, anytime! Genesis 12:3, "I will bless those who bless Israel..." has remained in our minds and hearts since early days.

Our summer travels took us to New York and Niagara Falls, to Toronto, Canada, to visit friends, to Wisconsin with friends, and back to Wheaton in time to register for all the schools. In between school activities, the boys and I had some odd jobs so they could earn spending money. Naomi and I traveled extensively for mission conferences around the country. We had bought, and shipped home, many woodcarvings done by Ifugao carvers that we knew. One interested Wheaton friend, Dr Ken Geiser, arranged an interview for us with the local newspaper. They took pictures of us with our pair of life size carvings of a native man and woman, representing Wigan and Bugan, the first two Ifugaos that had escaped The Flood. He also had us speak to the local Lion's Club.

Ray singing bass, joined the Men's Glee Club at Wheaton College. He enjoyed the camaraderie of this select group very much for his three years at Wheaton. He started majoring in Physics. But he was disappointed that his dorm roommates would not help him, for fear that he might get better grades than they. In his later years at Faith, everyone helped each other in the dorm. The competition at Wheaton was "too much," and did not reflect the Christ-like attitude that we expected. Randy at Wheaton High joined the band and the wrestling team. Ron as a freshman joined the soccer, basketball, and track teams. Randy graduated from my old high school 30 years after I did.

With schools finished for the summer, all five of us packed up and left for California and saw a few things on the way. We said good-bye to Ray and Randy there. Ron flew back to the Philippines with us. Ray and Randy drove back to Wheaton to get busy with their summer jobs. Both would be in Wheaton College in the fall and both had partial scholarships, but there were many other expenses. They were pretty much on their own now. We helped out the best we could. Randy lived with the Fitzwilliam's for the rest of the summer and worked in maintenance at Judson College, where Jack was the business manager. Ray worked at a summer camp in Wisconsin with Steve Fitzwilliam. They were with friends and kept busy, which made the time pass. This was a comfort to us.

# CHAPTER 15

## Fifth Term
## BIBAK Tyrannus Center
## at 19 Gen. V. Lim St.
## 1977-80

We arrived in Manila to find that the German couple had left two days earlier. They claimed that they had already organized BIBAK Bible Fellowship and that documents were ready for it to be incorporated as a church. They told people that there was no more need for the Walkwitzes. They had finished the job. They had said nothing to us during the year, so we were all quite surprised, wondering what kind of missionaries they were. They obviously were ashamed or afraid to face us and left just before we arrived. How then could they face the Lord?

When we got to Baguio, we found the Center rather dirty and messy. They had spent all the money I had earned at Brent, but there was not much to show for it. So with Elisa and a few volunteers, we cleaned up the place and reclaimed our furniture from storage. The "documents" that he had were the same ones we had before. These were part of a previous preliminary attempt by some in the lowlands. But these were only half completed. If they had been submitted, the Securities and Exchange Commission or SEC would have rejected them.

We learned later that the man would secretly come to the Philippines. He had made mail contact with some of our marginal students who were now living elsewhere in the country, and he had paid them to be his missionaries. He could then report to churches in Germany that these were his disciples and he was supporting them to pastor his churches. He tried to undercut everything that we had done. This kind of fraud in missionary work is not the norm, but it is certainly not unique! We know of other cases as well!

We got the Center organized with a classroom and chalkboard, and a library. Regular Bible classes were scheduled in the evenings. There was also a small bedroom and bathroom downstairs that we used for the frequent guests that came to visit us. Several came from Wheaton. I also had my office downstairs. We lived upstairs in a two-bedroom apartment. The large garage had three rooms upstairs for servants' quarters. We made that the ladies dorm, with a bathroom downstairs. Part of the garage was partitioned off to make a small one-room men's dorm and a bathroom was built to go with it.

We took Ron down for the opening of Faith Academy for his sophomore year. He was a natural athlete and was put on the varsity basketball team. It was a championship year, so he enjoyed traveling to Japan for the Far East Tournament.

## Fifth Term. BIBAK Tyrannus Center

On Sunday's, the church still met at the Baguio Health Club in the middle of town. As we considered our growth, we decided to "multiply by dividing." Right next to Baguio City was the town of La Trinidad, the capital of Benguet Province. Quite a few mountaineers were coming to the Baguio Health Club from there, a one jeepney ride away. A jeepney is an opensided jitney that goes on regular routes and carries about a dozen passengers. Originally, they were made from US Army surplus jeeps after the war. That's how it got the name. If we moved the church to meet at the Center on the other side of Baguio, that would mean a long walk after the ride.

Three American young men were coming to Baguio as summer workers on a two-month exposure to missions, in June 1978. It would be best if they could help pioneer the expansion into La Trinidad. But to do that, we needed a place for them to live and a place for the new congregation to meet. The La Trinidad folks were looking but had come up with nothing. The three men were arriving in a week. I got on my little motorcycle and went up and down the main road in La Trinidad looking for a place. On one side was the campus of Benguet State University or BSU. We wanted to have a place very near this campus that could serve as a Student Center and Bible teaching center, a church meeting place, and living quarters for the three men — another "BIBAK Center." That was a tall order.

Right along the road I noticed a building with a glass window front that looked like it had been an automobile showroom, but was currently empty and being vandalized. This looked like a good possibility. In Old Testament style, I walked around the property twice, claiming it from the

Lord. He knew we needed it, so I asked Him for it. I found someone around who told me that it was the building of the Cummins Diesel Company. Business had gone down so they had moved out, at least temporarily. The actual owners lived next door and had stored a lot of their construction equipment in the back.

I telephoned the Cummins Diesel office in south Manila and talked to the vice-president, telling him that we wanted to rent the building. He said, no, because the company was planning to re-open sometime. I said, OK, but asked to talk to the president just the same. We made an appointment for the morning before I would meet and pick up the summer workers on the north side of Manila.

I arrived a bit early just to be sure I would not miss the appointment, as traffic was not predictable. The VP was a Filipino. Soon the president was available and we went into his office. He was an American. The vice-president told him what I wanted. The president said just what the vice-president had told me on the phone, that they were planning to re-open sometime in the future. I said that that was fine, but "in the meantime, the building is being vandalized. If we could rent it on a temporary basis, we would clean it up, repair what was needed, and we could have a good Student Center, Bible teaching center, and space for church. Then whenever you decide to re-open, just give us a short notice and we will be out."

The president agreed with me immediately, but said, "we'll give you a month's notice and we will have to charge you $1.00 a year to make it legal." He then told the vice-president to have the secretary type up the lease contract for him to sign. While the secretary was typing the contract, the VP and I sat down for a cool drink.

He asked me, "How long have you known Bruce?" Bruce Martin was the president. I replied, "Oh, I just met him." He could hardly believe that Bruce would let me have the building so easily, since I was a total stranger to him until that moment. But just like in the Bible, God controls the minds of people to accomplish His purposes. I was absolutely sure that God had let me see that building in the first place, that He would honor my faith when I walked around the building twice and asked Him for it, then phoned the company and gone there. I was sure that He would give it to me. We needed it. We had found no other option. I had no alternate plan in mind. If Bruce had refused, what then? I do not doubt God when I am sure of His plans. With the Contract in hand, I drove across town to the mission office where I would meet the three summer workers. We all rejoiced in the Lord, packed up and headed north for Baguio.

The next day, I notified the key La Trinidad persons that we had the building, and that we needed a lot of help to clean it up. The double front glass door was missing, so we made a wooden one. One office could be made into a room for the three men. They would have to rough it a bit. They decided not to prepare meals, but rather eat in a restaurant nearby. By rotation, one would come to Baguio each day to stay in our guest room overnight, have a good hot shower and wash some clothes, and have a couple of home-cooked meals. By the weekend, we were ready for our first gathering of what now would be the La Trinidad Bible Church.

After the service, we talked about the next step. We decided on a Grand Opening in two weeks, on a Saturday afternoon and evening. Pepsi Cola made us a large banner to put in front of the building, and we stocked about 15 cases of their products. We anticipated a full house, possibly around 200 people. Adequate refreshments would be expected. The different tribal groups were asked to come in their native attire and be prepared to participate in the various tribal dances, which we knew they all enjoyed very much. There were the war dances, the courtship dances, the festival dances, and so forth. They all were beautifully done, and they looked wonderful in their g-strings and skirts, all of hand woven multi-colored material.

During breaks, some of our people gave testimonies; I gave a short Bible lesson and invited them all to come by for fun and fellowship, as well as for Bible studies and church services. This gave the summer workers a grand opening to make friends and influence people for the Lord, at the Center and on the BSU campus across the street. After the three summer workers left, some of the single men students from the congregation moved in to take over. This was the beginning of a dorm for La Trinidad.

And guess what? We used that building for more than three years! Eventually a couple of executives came up to Baguio to inform us that they were going to re-open their Cummins Diesel business there. We said, "Thank you very much!" As we prepared to move out at the end of the month, the congregation found a house that was way too small and way out of the way. I was very disappointed, but this was their decision and their provision. They needed to have more vision and trust in the Lord's provision, more inspired leadership. But it just was not there yet.

As soon as this transition was made, we vacated the Baguio Health Club and began Sunday morning activities at the Baguio Tyrannus Center. The mission had a large tent that they had used for "tent campaign evangelistic meetings" in various areas south of Manila. It was no longer in use, so we brought it up to Baguio and set it up in the concrete area in front of our building during the dry season.

We had nightly meetings under the tent for about a week, using a visiting Gospel Team from Australia. The speaker was also a chalk artist, who taught some of our men how to do it. The mountain people are very intelligent and innovative when given the chance, so they learned quickly. Our own musicians and singers participated and gave testimonies. Many students made decisions for Jesus Christ and were discipled by congregation members.

Meanwhile, back in Wheaton, Ray's former roommate at Faith who had bonded with him, Paul Varberg, persuaded Ray to sell books for Southwestern Company with him during the summer of 1977. Ray was still a bit on the shy side, so selling books door-to-door all summer long would be quite a challenge. Southwestern had dozens of college students doing this every summer, as a chance to earn lots of money if they did well, and to train and develop students in confidence and hardwork.

Ray was already a diligent hard-working person. During that summer, his self-confidence developed greatly. He earned a lot of money and earned many awards. Ray and Paul then decided to sell books the next summer. In 1979, both being a bit tired of college, they agreed to sell for a long summer and then leave in October to travel around the world until they arrived in the Philippines and each went to see his parents. That trip could have been a chapter in itself, but Ray is no longer on earth to tell it. He arrived in Baguio about a month before Ron graduated from Faith Academy at the end of April 1980.

# According to Roger

Randy had quite a surprise when he moved in to the Wheaton College freshman dorm. His roommate was a black from Ohio. After a short while adjusting to each other's culture, they became good friends, together with another black student on campus. The next summer, Randy lived and worked in Ohio with the second one. The black family was somewhat wealthy and enjoyed Randy's company very much. Halfway through his second year, Randy dropped out and came to the Philippines to be with us.

College was meaningless to him at that time. He did not know what he wanted to do, so he was just spending money and wasting time. After about six months, he returned and enrolled in George Williams College, a YMCA college near Wheaton, that specialized in physical education, sports, camping, and pre-med. Randy thought of going into sports medicine, so he took up pre-med. He also got a job managing the DuPage Racket Club. The job was more fun than college, and he was earning money, so that was the end of his college career. A few years later, George Williams College closed for good — bankrupt. When Randy dropped out, that must have been the last straw?

In August 1979, tragedy struck. My Mom had been run over by a car and was in the hospital on life support. Mom was living at the Retirement Center in Hendersonville, North Carolina that she and Dad had bought into before he died of leukemia. Mom walked every day around the campus, looking for birds, which were her hobby. Those who had cars at the Center parked them in a long row of covered spaces. Mom was walking along behind them when a lady suddenly backed up without even looking behind her and ran right over Mom. Her chest had been crushed.

## Fifth Term. BIBAK Tyrannus Center

My sister came down immediately while Mom was still awake, but bleeding internally.

The doctors wanted to sedate her and put her on life support to give her lungs time to heal and stop bleeding. Mom did not like that, but they insisted that that was the only way they might save her life. After about 10 days, they tried to bring her out of sedation and back to breathing on her own. She never came back. She had already died.

As with my Dad, I did not go home for the funeral. My brother and sister took care of it all. Some months later, we each got a check for $4,000, the sum total of the accident insurance of the driver. That was also the sum total of inheritance I received from my parents. While they were living, they had given away much to many people in need, and spent the rest of the money. Mom's social security paid her maintenance at the Retirement Center. Mom and Dad had given me a good upbringing in life. That was enough. I was not looking for money. I was a bond slave of the Lord Jesus, so it was up to Him to care for me.

In Baguio, the impetus of having the Tent Evangelistic Meetings motivated the BIBAK members, both of Baguio and LaTrinidad, to train themselves to do things like that. They had a lot of natural talent which, when given over to the Lord to serve Him, would be blessed and enhanced. The men formed their singing Gospel Team, with Naomi as their director or coach. Mountain people enjoyed the southern gospel type music, which Naomi also specialized in.

The men called themselves "The CIA Guys." CIA could have been misunderstood as something else, and maybe was a few times, but the meaning was Christians In Action.

They had special meetings in various places around the area. Philippine schools go from June to March, so when Ray arrived, he joined them with his rich bass voice and Men's Glee Club experience. They spent a couple weeks having special outreach meetings in the mountain interior, including in a hospital with chicken pox patients. The staff assured the team that the patients were no longer contagious, but Ray at his age still came down with a severe case, something he had not had as a child.

By 1979, we were convinced that 19 Gen. V. Lim St. could be our Center location for some time to come, if we could get a long-term lease and build on the property. With graduate engineers in the congregation, we envisioned a lean-to chapel building attached to the present building, completely covering the paved area in front of it, reaching to the wall on two sides. This would measure 30 feet wide and 60 feet long, large enough to accommodate at least 250 people. Using folding or stacking chairs, the area would be very adequate for celebrations that included native dances and weddings.

The owners lived next door at No. 17. We were on very good terms. The husband was a retired building contractor and the wife was into real estate and other things. They were one of the prominent families in Baguio. After prayer, with a design in hand, I went to talk to them of this possibility. I asked for 10 years; I should have asked for 15. They readily agreed to 10 years, and drew up a contract with an increasing rental charge for the whole 10 years to take inflation into account. The mission treasurer signed the contract, as all rents are paid from the Manila office. Renters appreciated this because rents could be paid regularly with no hassle, direct to the owner's bank account.

## Fifth Term. BIBAK Tyrannus Center

We began building immediately, making our own concrete hollow blocks with volunteer student help. A block layer was hired to work and to coordinate everything, and our engineers, Joe Eming and Dave Angiwan supervised it all. It was a family team effort. Dave was the architect as well. Usually, building plans are finished and then submitted to the proper city department before a building permit is issued.

We did it the other way. As Joe, Dave and the others were putting up the building from plans in their heads, Dave was drawing up the plans accordingly. When the basic structure was almost complete, the plans were finished and submitted the early part of May. However, there was a lot of interior work to be done. Another missionary couple, Bill and Pat Arvan, agreed to come to Baguio to take our place for the year, to supervise the final construction and to continue our teaching ministry. Elisa stayed on to help them, as well as help in the children's ministry.

The CIA guys did a final recording session with Ray and then treated him to a cookout. We went down to Manila for Ron's graduation from Faith on April 30. Ray met his friend Paul there. They continued with their around-the-world trip. We returned to Baguio to wrap things up. The mission's Annual Conference was in Baguio that year. I finished my duties on the Field Council for another term.

In the Banaue culture, a crazy person was termed '7/11.' The people have no idea where the expression came from. So, were we 7/11 or what? Our building permit was issued on Wednesday May 7, and we had our first service in the completed shell on Sunday, May 11! That surely looks like a 7/11 to me! For sure we were blessed for being "crazy

135

enough" to trust the Lord completely. Now, here again was evidence of His blessing. The congregation had a farewell party for us in the evening. Then we traveled back to Manila. Naomi and Ron flew to Chicago to settle in at 114 Kellogg Ave, Wheaton, Illinois, another Furlough Missionary Home that we qualified for.

I had to return to Baguio to finish some business for a few weeks, and then fly to Anchorage, Alaska. The mission had a work in Alaska inherited from another mission. Every summer a bunch of summer workers come to Alaska to help in various activities such as building, discipling, children's work, and whatever was needed. Since it was June, it was daylight practically all the time. I had to put blankets over the windows so I could get a little darkness so I could sleep. I even took telephoto pictures of snow-capped mountains at 10:30 PM with Kodachrome film speed at only 25. It was an amazing place!

My assignment was to orient these young people about the challenges of career mission work in the Philippines. I gave them a brief survey of the various possibilities and ministries in progress, and then taught them about Acts 19:8-10, the story of BIBAK and its School of Tyrannus. I hoped to challenge them to low-key Bible teaching as a biblical way to disciple people into understanding the Gospel and responding accordingly. My very gracious hosts for part of the time in Alaska were Wayne and Doris Eames, who oriented me to the variety of ministries in Alaska, which I appreciated, as there are always new things to learn. I then flew home to join the family in Wheaton.

# CHAPTER 16

## In Wheaton for furlough 1980-81
## Ordination, Ray engaged

With family headquarters again in Wheaton, this time at 114 Kellogg Place, each son had a home to come to when needed. Ray was off again selling books with Southwestern in Texas, at least part of the time. He needed to finish selling in time to start classes again at Wheaton College, especially to join again with Men's Glee Club after a year off traveling around the world. Randy was happy with his Health Club job and had no intention to get a college degree. He did not need it. As soon as Naomi and Ron got to Wheaton in June, a former missionary friend, Dick Thompson, offered Ron a job running big IBM computers on the night shift. He continued this job for the next nine months and also started Wheaton College in the fall.

So when I arrived from Alaska, everyone was busy. I could relax at our new home with Naomi and figure out just how we were going to handle the year. Naturally, we were going to travel, as we needed to report to all our supporters around the country, at least as many as we could practically reach. A family in Detroit that had known us for a long time lent us one of their cars, which was in good shape. He worked for GM. We were thankful. We spoke at several Bible Conferences, churches and camps during the summer.

When a ministry with the Lord becomes successful, more critics appear for many reasons. For many years, outsiders had criticized me and BIBAK, saying, "Your missionary is not even ordained. How can you listen to him?" These comments came from those who thought of Christian ministry as just another type of job, being a professional religion person, like a lawyer, or doctor, or licensed contractor and so on. Most of Christianity thinks in these terms: one is either a clergyman or a layman. Even though I was a foreign missionary, I was not a clergyman. I had been commissioned, but I was not ordained. I was not a "reverend."

This criticism did not bother me or any of the people in BIBAK, because I had taught them that the clergy – laity division in Christianity was not biblical. Jesus taught against it, saying, do not be called Rabbi, Teacher, Father because you are all brethren. He warned against any division in His Body. The only true meaning of *Nicolaitanism* in the book of Revelation was the meaning of the word: *nikao* = to conquer or dominate and laos = the people of God. God said He hates it. In the Ephesus church, they would not allow it, and God praised them. In the Pergamos church, it had become established practice, like in the Roman Catholic Church, for controlling salvation. God hated it.

To avoid any semblance of a division between brethren,

BIBAK was established as a non-professional, no clergy. No one was paid for ministry. The only exception would be if a member went to another country as a missionary and was not allowed to work to earn in that country. Only then could that member receive support. Through all the years of our ministry, I have never allowed anyone to address me with a title. I am "Roger" to everyone who wants to use that. Some might say "Sir Roger" or just "Sir" as Filipinos are very respectful. Some would call me "Mr. Walkwitz." We are family in BIBAK.

Any respect is earned by the life one lives, not by the academic training one has had, or by ordination by some group. Letters after one's name are noted, but the teaching and life of the person had better back them up. I have known some Believers who had never gone beyond elementary school who yet have a spiritual insight beyond that of some seminary grads. Church leadership is based on spiritual maturity, not academic success or political power. Most importantly, it is not for someone who wants a paid job.

However, I thought it might be a good idea to silence the critics. During the fall, I asked the Elders of College Church if they would like to ordain me. I told them that I considered ordination as recognition of a proven ministry, not the result of an academic achievement. I had academic achievement, but I did not want ordination for that. I wanted them to evaluate my ministry for the last 30 years, in the church and later on the field, as a basis for ordination. If they approved, then it was OK. If not, it was still OK.

They said yes to the proposal. But one ThD professor Elder wanted me to read through Chafer's *Systematic Theology* and report on it. OK I said, no problem. I got one volume at a time, read it and made a few notes, then got the next one. There must have been about 10 volumes, I can't remember. This took a few months to complete since we were travelling around. My notes did not fill even one page. It was all Dispensational Theology, which I had been raised on. It was not a problem then, until I learned more later on.

As our furlough was coming to a close, Saturday, May 16, 1981, was scheduled for me to be questioned by the Elder Board. It was very enjoyable, as I like theological debate and Bible questions. They knew me, and I knew most of them for years. Dr. Earle Cairns, a history professor, asked me what person in church history I admired the most. I thought for a while, and decided on Martin Luther because of his boldness to attack the system, which in a sense I was also doing.

However, I learned later of Martin Luther's strong anti-Semitism in his later years. His ideas were later used by the Nazis to justify their actions before the Nuremberg trials. Luther expected the Jews to respond to his new approach to the Bible and to religion. When they did not, he turned on them. His writings are terrible! If he had only spoken about his ideas and not writen pamphlets, they would have been forgotten. I had to remember that fact as I wrote this book. I want people to remember what I write here, and learn much from it.

I cannot remember any more specific questions. I was fully approved. The following day was Sunday. During the evening service, the Elder Board laid their hands on me with prayer, and I was given an Ordination Certificate, signed by some of the "important ones" of Evangelical Christianity. College Church has plenty of them.

After the service, an older retired missionary from Africa, Paul Stough, whom I had known for years, told me, "Never allow yourself to be called Reverend. Look up Psalm 111:9." I never intended to do that either, but I did look it up. The KJV says about God, "*holy and reverend is His name*!" Wow, this was confirmation of His stand and mine as well. Thank you Lord! Spurgeon deals with this issue at length in his commentary on Psalm 111. He questions why this title is allowed to be used, saying it should be discarded. Who are we to be revered? I have noticed that in modern translations, the word has been changed to something else. The clergy translators have tried to cover it up.

In the spring of 1981, I went on a furlough missions trip without Naomi. There were times when it was not necessary for her to go with me. At these times she preferred to stay home to take care of her three sons, who were all busy with school and work. In fact, her life was pretty much wrapped up in her sons, to give them the home that she did not have in her youth. They are still very much attached to her, and she to them.

When I came home, there was a girl sitting in the living room. That was quite unusual for our family! While I was gone, Carolyn Moore and our Ray had met and were dating! They had met at a college-age Bible study at the home of my other best friend, Harold Cook. Ray came in late and the only empty chair was next to Carolyn. Afterwards he tried to recruit her to sell books the following summer with Southwestern. Recruitment was part of the job off-season. He would get a team together for the next summer. Ray was not thinking of romance at all. He talked with everyone about selling with Southwestern. The experience had done a lot for him, and he knew it would do a lot for others.

Carolyn was thinking otherwise. She had stayed out of Wheaton for a year in order to break off a relationship that she did not like. This was now her senior year and she was still unattached. She and a girl friend asked Ray to go with them to something in Chicago on the weekend. Ray was totally not experienced with girls, but the attention pleased him. The only dates he had ever had were as required escorts to banquet functions or the like.

So here was Carolyn sitting in our living room, waiting to meet Ray's Dad, who was due home any minute. Carolyn was a somewhat charming young lady, a music major playing the violin, who had grown up in Ecuador, of missionary parents with HCJB radio station. Her Dad was an electronics engineer. He spent two terms with HCJB and then resigned to work with Texaco in Ecuador as their communications engineer. Texaco has oil fields in Ecuador.

In about a month Ray and Carolyn were engaged. Ray needed a ring. My Mom had died over a year ago when we were in the Philippines. My sister had her ring. She sold it to Ray for a good price, since it would stay in the family. The diamond was large but had a small defect. Carolyn preferred to have it ground down to remove the defect even though it would be smaller. It was set with a new band and design. It was now ready to be given to her at the reception after her graduation violin recital. Carolyn's parents, Bob and Dolores Moore, came up from Quito to be there and to meet us. Carolyn did a great job with her violin performance.

Carolyn graduated in good style. She and Ray were getting ready to sell books for the summer, together with the team that Ray had recruited. We got acquainted with the Moores who were a nice couple. Randy would continue with his Health Club business. Ron had now transferred to work with AT&T Bell Labs in Research & Development, learning all about computers from the ground up. He now had a good job and was earning money. It was a daytime job, so that was the end of his college days. Randy and Ron got an apartment to share.

The 30<sup>th</sup> Class Reunion of my college class of '51 was during graduation week. I stayed for half of the main meeting, and then said "Good-bye" as we were off to O'Hare Airport for our return to the Philippines, this time without the boys. Ray & Carolyn had tentatively set their wedding for December, so we knew we would be coming back for that. Ray would continue at the college in the fall after the summer selling, while Carolyn would work in the Wheaton area at various jobs.

# CHAPTER 17

## Wedding, Ecuador, Tabernacle, Israelis, CBC, LaTrinidad Center 1981-85

We were at the BIBAK Tyrannus Center and back to our enjoyable ministry. The building was completely finished now, except for the stage up front. We needed this for the plays and dramas that the people loved to do, and for the weddings. I designed and built the stage about 2 feet high, with entrances onto the stage from both sides. For the curtain, I made it opera house style, looped and coming down from above. It was quite elegant. I also built in a PA system to eliminate any cords to stumble over.

Weekly classes began again. We had Missionary I for every new person. This included memorizing 100 Bible verses, plus a classroom study of Abraham, Moses, and Paul. These servants of the Lord who lived in different time periods had similarities and differences. Missionary II and III were for the more advanced students. Genesis was basic for everyone to have a good foundation. The

Book of Acts was also a semester course for everyone. We wanted to provide all the academic study the students needed for ministry. At the same time, we gave them on-the-job experience in using their learning, all while living in their regular environment.

We discouraged anyone from going to Bible school or seminary because we had seen the poor results. The graduates became proud, wanted to be addressed as "Pastor," and wanted to be separate and above the people. Yet they were financially supported by the people. They also did not want to get their hands dirty doing manual work, because they had been trained to be leaders! OK, now it would be interesting to see if they would have any followers. The culture had something to do with this situation. Missionaries in Manila said that neighbors were displeased when they were seen working on their cars. In the mountains, people respected us for being able to work on our car.

One new course we started was the study of the book of Exodus, on the establishing of the nation of Israel. It was fascinating to understand the redemption of Israel from slavery in Egypt, the ten plagues, the Passover and the crossing of the Red Sea, and their parallels to our Redemption through Jesus Christ, Yeshua the Messiah.

Then there was also the way of life that was given to Israel as God's Chosen People, the marriage proposal of God to Israel and their acceptance with the Ten Commandments, the supply of water and Manna, and especially learning how to worship God, His Way, in The Tabernacle. To do the course well, the students in the class built a scale model of the Tabernacle, using 1 inch = 1 cubit, to make it easier and more fun. This course eventually took one year to complete, but the model was beautiful.

We had the Tabernacle on display in the large Center that we had built. Visitors who came would see it and ask, "What is it?" Even some missionaries did not know what it was! Why? Because as is true today, the Old Testament was not taught much, and structures like the Tabernacle were relegated to ancient history with no relevance for today. How wrong that is! Just look at what *The Interpreter's Bible* of the Methodist Church says about The Tabernacle in Exodus in Volume 1, page 1027:

> "5. *The Tabernacle (26:1-37). The tabernacle here presented never actually existed. It is a product of the priestly imagination, an ideal structure. Two historical objects helped to give shape to the imaginary structure which was to illustrate a new theological conviction.*"

Wow! This is heresy! Blasphemy! The Tabernacle never existed? The Tabernacle is the only building designed by God and commanded to be built by God to be His dwelling place with His people, His family! No other nation on earth ever had this privilege and distinction! It is God's Picture Book of Redemption. We all need to learn it well! How can church leaders say it never existed? Maybe they don't think God exists either. Churches are infiltrated by pagan clergy!

During our first year back, an Israeli couple came to Baguio to develop a strawberry plantation of 32 acres just outside Baguio, for a Philippine corporation. Other missionaries had met Shmuel and Hanana Even and soon introduced them to us. Immediately Shmuel asked me, "What is the difference between you and the Roman Catholics?" After a quick prayer, I answered, "We teach the whole Bible. We are not persecutors of Israel. We love Israel and have been there."

According to Roger

Every Jew knows of the terrible persecution that the Roman Catholic Church has done to them. They consider Christianity a worse enemy than Islam. I already knew some of this, but needed to learn more. Once Shmuel realized we were friends of Jews, we had a good conversation. Shmuel had walked out of Romania after WWII to come to Israel as a 14-year-old refugee. Hanana was a third generation Israeli Sabra. A Sabra is a native-born Israeli, named after the native cactus which is prickly and tough on the outside but very sweet inside! We have found Israelis to be really sweet, once they get to know that one is a genuine friend.

As we talked, an idea came into my mind. This was surely from the Lord. "Shmuel and Hanana, would you be willing to co-teach a new course with me at our Center once a week in the evening? The title will be, Modern Israel and Fulfilled Prophecy. You teach one hour on Modern Israel. I will teach the second hour on Fulfilled Prophecy. Our courses are two hours, once a week." They readily agreed. "We will start in two weeks to give you time to get organized."

They contacted the Embassy of Israel in Manila and brought up literature and films. They did an excellent job, teaching all about life and institutions in The Land. And then of course, they stayed for my hour on Fulfilled Prophecy, about which they had no idea until then. This continued for a year. When strawberry season was in full swing, they brought the most delicious, large strawberries for all the class to enjoy. At that time, they were harvesting 3,000 pounds a day! Most were shipped to Manila and abroad. They also introduced us to the Ambassador of Israel and the Embassy staff. This made it easier for us to get films and materials later on.

We became good friends and have kept in touch ever since. When their 2-year contract was up, they were replaced by Ami and Bluma Solomon, both Holocaust survivors. While all four of them were there, they made us promise to come by Israel to visit them the next time we left the country. We said, OK! And we did visit some time later.

Ray and Carolyn had set their wedding date for the afternoon of Saturday, December 12, 1981, at the College Church. We flew home a week ahead to get over jet lag and prepare for this wedding. We stayed with Randy and Ron. Ray and Carolyn were going down after the wedding to Quito, Ecuador, where her family lived, for a reception with all of their friends there. They asked us to follow about a week later, so we could see where Carolyn grew up and learn something about Ecuador.

We did follow and had an enjoyable time seeing not only Quito but also Shell, where Nate Saint lived. We also flew into some of the places related to the five martyrs. Nate Saint happened to be a classmate of mine at Wheaton, and Jim Elliot and Ed McCully were friends in the athletic teams. Ed ran on the track team as I did. We were studying at CBC when the news came. In Ecuador, Spanish seemed to be the only language spoken, so we had to depend on Carolyn for all communication, except when we visited HCJB facilities and the Alliance School for Missionary Kids.

With our connection now established with the Embassy of Israel, we invited the Ambassador to speak at BIBAK any time he might be in Baguio City for vacation or whatever purpose. On a hunch one morning, I phoned the Embassy in Manila to inquire about the Ambassador. The secretary said he was on his way to Baguio right then! Knowing that he and his security would be staying at the Baguio Country Club, I drove over there to wait for his arrival. Of course he was surprised to see me, and probably wondered how this lapse of security could happen. I asked him if he would be willing to speak at BIBAK the following evening, and he agreed. I needed to come and get him, or at least, lead the police security caravan to our place.

We phoned community members to invite them for his talk. A good number showed up. I started by asking Ambassador Dr. Uri Gordon to tell us about himself, his life in Israel while growing up and so on, his career, plus Israeli politics. His security man was Asher Goffer. I also asked him to tell us about himself. We all had been learning about Israel from the Evens and Solomons, and we wanted to know their stories also. Asher was very alert. Across the street, someone lit a firecracker. He jumped to his feet to investigate and had the Baguio police check it out. Our people were very impressed with Asher's alertness as well as with both of their talks.

Chemistry majors do not study Greek, unless they go into medicine, since so many terms come from Greek. Over the years, I got tired of hearing teachers saying, "The Greek says so and so." How could I know if this was so? I felt vulnerable as a Bible teacher when I could not verify if what was said was true or not. I decided I needed to learn Greek. Naomi had had a year of Greek at Bryan, but she had forgotten it all. We discussed this with our students and they agreed to study with us.

I contacted our friend Dave Salstrom, who taught Greek at the seminary in Manila. He sang at our wedding years ago. I asked if he would be willing to come to Baguio for a couple of weeks during summer vacation to teach us a crash course on Greek. He did. So we studied Greek from 8 AM to 8 PM, every day except Sunday for two weeks. That covered the first semester. The next summer, we did the second semester, covering the whole grammar book. A dozen of us took the course. After the first summer, one pre-med student came to live in our dorm. He was a new believer. Andy was brilliant, apparently with a photographic memory. He wanted to join the second semester of Greek, so I gave him the grammar book to study on his own the first semester material. He accomplished it, as well as the second summer lessons, with ease. Later, Andy would become a well-known kidney specialist doctor.

One Sunday, a lady from a prominent lowland family living in Baguio came to BIBAK. She lived and worked in Manila, had come to faith in Jesus there, and was in Baguio for a visit. She had heard in Manila about the type and quality of our ministry, so she came to ask if someone would try to reach her parents and siblings with the Gospel. We agreed to have a Bible study with them to explain the basics, if she would make an appointment with them and let us know.

Her father, a medical doctor, was a nominal Protestant who knew next to nothing of the Bible. Her mother was a devoted Roman Catholic and knew even less. Their home compound was very near the Baguio Cathedral. Mrs. Abellera had recently had a stroke and was crippled, and was in a wheel chair all the time. The appointment was made for the coming Saturday afternoon. Mrs. Abellera was there with three other ladies. One was Nene Bowman, the executive vice-president of the Baguio Colleges

Foundation or BCF. We had an enjoyable visit and study. They invited us to teach them every Saturday afternoon if we could. Since they were all ladies, I decided to turn the class over to Naomi. I thought they would probably be more open with questions.

Nene Bowman did not show up the next Saturday nor the next one. During the week, I went to BCF to see Nene to find out why she had not come, when she had seemed very interested. She confirmed she was very interested, but she could not come on Saturdays. She was the editor of the Gold Ore, one of two weekly newspapers in Baguio, a city of about 200,000 at the time. The paper came out Sunday mornings. That was no problem for me, so I offered to come to the college during the week and teach Bible to her and her family and others, if they were interested. She was very happy about this. She had actually wanted something like this, but had been hesitant to ask.

Nene had come to faith in Jesus about a year earlier through an itinerant evangelist. She had been baptized, along with two other ladies, who were her friends from childhood. However, there had been no follow up and no discipling, which is so typical of evangelism, whether private or public. One of her lady friends was a daughter of the Abelleras, who had married an American GI and was then living in the US. That was why Mrs. Abellera had invited Nene to that first Saturday meeting. She had also heard about us. I found it amazing when she told me that over the last year, she had asked several missionaries to come and teach her, but they had all been too busy. Discipling takes time, and missionaries want quick results. Some hired Filipinos to do the regular work while they played golf. Nene hated golf.

So every week I went to BCF to teach. Nene had her mother and some sisters, and some of the key workers there to learn. Some came to faith in Jesus. Soon Nene asked me if I would teach a weekly luncheon Bible study at the Baguio Country Club. The president of the Southern Baptist Seminary taught one for men on Friday noons. I had not heard about it because these are not mountain people. Nene said, "Why couldn't we have one for ladies on Wednesdays?" Why not? I also thought. So, we started the next Wednesday.

The Club provided a private dining room for us with a set menu at a set price. Everyone paid for his own meal, including me. That was my practice. We would eat from 12 noon until 1 PM. Then I taught from 1 PM to around 2:30 PM. As a result, several came to faith in Jesus. After a while, some husbands started coming, and some of them came to faith in Jesus as well.

When Passover came, we did a shortened Passover demonstration right at the club. The Seder is usually in the evening and takes at least three hours. We could not take that long, then. Even then, some of the ones attending began to see the mistake the church had made by substituting Communion or The Lord's Supper for Passover. The Lord had called us to the mountaineers, but the "upper crust" of lowland society needed the Gospel too! This class became regular for all the rest of our time in Baguio. Nene also developed into a good teacher herself. The Spirit has given her good insight into the Word, and others respected her testimony.

For the 40th Anniversary Convocation of BCF, she arranged for me to be the speaker rather than the usual Catholic priest. I did not do a very good job for that; I did not have enough jokes. I had not yet learned to be a somewhat secular public speaker. I knew a lot of things like chemistry and current events, but I wanted to speak on only one thing, the Bible. I was even invited to be the speaker at the Rotary Club of Baguio. For the first time in fifty years, they had a Bible lesson! The inviter said to speak on anything I wanted to, and I did. They did thank me for it, however. No one was offended.

Naomi continued with her Saturday afternoon class at Mrs. Abellera's house for many months. Soon Mrs. Abellera understood and responded by faith to Jesus and was quite outspoken about it. She phoned Naomi, "Is it all right if I accept Jesus now and call myself a Christian?" A few weeks later, she and her husband invited us to go to their beach house, about an hour's drive down the mountain to the ocean, and to bring swimming suits. After we arrived and had changed into swimming suits, she told me that she wanted to be baptized, right then! Being a cripple, she needed several inner tubes to stabilize her. I said, "Wait a minute," and took some time to explain more about what baptism meant, as we had not studied that at all. She agreed to everything, so down and under she went.

She had spent much money buying idols. Now she wanted to get rid of them. However, she hesitated to burn them because they cost so much, and so she gave them back to the priest who sold them to her. Later on she wished she had burned them to powder. She became a regular at the Wednesday luncheon Bible study at the Baguio Country Club. On the other hand, her doctor husband continued to avoid a confrontation with Gospel Truth. He had supposedly made a profession of faith in Manila, but we saw no evidence of it. He had a stroke that hospitalized him. He knew he was dying and said he was afraid to die. We hope he made a decision that the Lord accepted, but we will never know. The family asked me to conduct his funeral. It was hard to figure out what to say and still be honest.

In the fall of 1982, we learned that CBC was now having a Student Body Project each year to benefit an alumnus missionary on the foreign field. Any alumnus on the field was welcome to submit his proposal for consideration by the student body committee. This was just in time for us, since we had lost the Cummins Diesel Company building in LaTrinidad. The house then occupied by the congregation was way too small and too far from the campus of BSU to be of any use to attract students. They had been over a year then in this house.

So without telling anyone except Naomi, I drew up a proposal for a building near the campus to serve like before as student center, Bible teaching center, and church, specifically for the mountaineers that come to BSU for their college. I also described the various tribal groups that make up BIBAK, and the School of Tyrannus method from Acts 19:8-10 that the Lord had led us to implement. The CBC Project would supply us with $10,000 and a summer team selected by our criteria from the student body. Again, I knew inside that we had a "winner"!

Our BIBAK project was submitted. The CBC student body committee would be sorting through the proposals to make their selections to submit to the student body soon after the opening of school in August 1983. The vote would be taken fairly soon and the winner announced, so that fund raising among the student body and faculty could begin and the team selected. We had heard that the selection would be from Asia in the coming year. This was great for us!

# According to Roger

The first Sunday of every September is the anniversary of the founding of BIBAK. We usually have something special on that day. September 4, 1983, was a beautiful day in Baguio. For that day, we had several Bible study classes in different tribal languages before the usual service in English. I was downstairs in a language class. The English class was upstairs in our apartment with Naomi. The leader asked for any prayer requests. The current mission director happened to be there on vacation. Naomi spoke up and asked for prayer for the proposal that we had submitted to CBC, that we would be chosen. A few knew about it by then and were praying for it.

The director responded to the effect that there was no use praying for that, as BIBAK was an unknown ministry in the US. Surely the CBC committee would pick the high-profile ministries that advertise their needs widely. Naomi just kept quiet, prayed silently, and told me about it afterwards. Toward the end of September, the director phoned me from Manila to inform me that the student body had voted for BIBAK! The final vote came down to a choice between a church in Japan or us. To me, that was no contest. What student body would pick a local church in Japan over a vibrant ministry to mountain tribesmen? I uttered a simple "Thank you, Lord."

Now we had to get busy. First, we had to find a building to lease or buy. Buying would not be possible for the size we needed. One of our long time members in Baguio knew of a family in LaTrinidad that was putting up a building that would meet our needs. But they had run out of money and stopped building. We could make a deal to lease for 10 years by paying a good sum up front to have the building finished in time for the arrival of the Summer Team from CBC. We looked over the unfinished

156

three-storey building and made a deal. We made a contract in January 1984 to have a 10-year lease, pay $3,000 upon signing, $2,000 more in one month, and $2,000 more in two more months. This would pay for three years rent, then we would start paying monthly.

The bottom floor would be configured into four rooms on the right side for a men's dorm and open on the left side for church services. At the end of the long building was a kitchen on the left and showers and toilets on the right. The second floor would have four rooms on the right and two rooms on the left for a ladies' dorm, with the space for two rooms open on the left for a classroom. There would be a kitchen at the end, as well as showers and toilets.

The third floor would have two regular rooms on the right and a double room with a kitchen at the end, and more showers and toilets. The third floor would be for a missionary family who would stay to oversee the campus ministry and teach weekly Bible classes, just like in Baguio. The church would continue to function on its own, since it was organized with its own leadership. The church would pay a nominal rent for its space, and each dorm student would pay some amount for utilities in addition to rent. The building was barely done when the team arrived.

The next big task was to come up with our suggestions for the team that would come. Since we had a lot of college students and some young married families in the church, in addition to the outreach we wanted to do, we requested for some grad couples and singles from the undergrad program. We ended up with three young grad couples, one single girl and one single man. The three couples stayed on the top floor. The girl had one room in the ladies' dorm and the man had one room in the men's dorm.

Besides that, one faculty man came along for a few weeks to be sure the team would be OK.

Besides giving the team experience in ministry on campus, I wanted them to be involved in the teaching of the School of Tyrannus, in Baguio and also LaTrinidad. They would not have time to create courses, so I decided to use the other $3,000 of the $10,000 grant to buy some of the CBC extension courses that they might already have taken. These were on cassette tapes with extensive syllabi. They could choose what they wanted to teach and design the course as they wished. I gave them a lot of freedom to jump in and let the Lord lead them in pioneering a ministry. They chose their own team leader as well. The two months went by quickly. Some of them experienced real freedom in ministry while others could not quite get over their fears. Only one couple eventually got on the foreign field and stayed for several terms. They have returned home to stay and are now pastoring a US church.

All eight of the team were back in school in the fall to give their reports. We finished our term a bit early to be able to get home in March 1985 in order to get on CBC campus to have a reunion with the team for one more time before graduation. While there, I was asked to give a message in the chapel service to further motivate students and faculty to consider the School of Tyrannus method in their ministry and teaching.

This time our furlough would not be in Wheaton. None of our sons were in college there anymore. Randy and Ron were living together and working in the Wheaton area, so we would visit them and other friends from time to time, but we had a house in Florida now! We needed to see it, and Ray and Carolyn, who were living in it. How did that happen?

## Wedding, Ecuador, Tabernacle, Israelis, CBC, LaTrinidad Center

At the end of December 1981, after Ray & Carolyn's wedding, we were scheduled to fly to Ecuador. Our flight began in Miami. Randy and Ron decided to drive us to Miami from Wheaton after the wedding, just for fun and fellowship. Time with family did not come very often. Ron had bought a big Olds 98 Regency, which had plenty of room. We stopped by Morriston, Florida, for a few hours to see Ralph Mount, Naomi's pastor from her childhood in Ohio. He had retired and bought some acreage to subdivide with the idea of starting a friendly Christian community.

He and a block layer from his Bible class on Sunday afternoon had started building a house for a pastor friend in New York. Halfway through, the pastor's wife decided she did not want to move to Florida after all, so the construction stopped. While the boys were busy watching football on TV, Ralph took me over to see the house. It was only a shell, with a few dividers up. He thought he could give me a good deal on it, since he had a lot of money tied up in it. His concern for us was that we had no place on earth now to call home. I was convinced that it would be wise to cash in some of my time deposits and buy this place.

When we got to Quito, I talked it over with Ray and Carolyn. They had no idea about exactly where they were going from there — back to the US, of course, maybe Wheaton and work. Ray had not finished college yet. They decided to come to Florida, get jobs, help finish off the house and live in it. So we bought the house, as is. This would eventually be our home base and a "shelter in the time of storm" for the family no matter what happened. Ray and Carolyn finished off the inside, got the occupancy permit and moved in. While visiting them, we put two screened-in porches on the house and a two-car carport in between. It was only a two-bedroom house, but it was adequate, on one acre, with our own well and septic tank. We are 5 miles from the nearest convenience store and gas station, and 11 miles from the nearest supermarket.

Passover came while we were there. The Bible study group that met at the Mount's place each Sunday afternoon made all the preparations. We were simply guests. Carolyn played her violin. Everyone enjoyed doing the Last Supper Passover just like Yeshua and His disciples had done. We had learned that it is totally wrong to take two items out of the context of the Passover and make a Eucharist, Communion, or Lord's Supper out of them. This happened about 200 years after Yeshua when anti-Semitism came in and Gentile Believers started breaking off from the Messianic communities. The Gentiles started developing their own religion, separate from the Old Testament, which became Christianity. This satanic hatred of Jews has caused untold suffering and great confusion in biblical understanding and practices.

Ray and Carolyn lived in guest quarters at the Mount's while working on the house. After moving in, Ray started selling Encyclopedia Britannica. He also had most of his Wheaton credits transferred to the University of Florida and ended up graduating with a major in history. During long breaks between classes, Ray would go out to the Gainesville airport, just to watch the planes. As a boy in Banaue, he got interested in flying because of the MAF (Mission Aviation Fellowship) and JAARS (Jungle Aviation And Radio Service of SIL) airplanes that came in to our marginal airstrip on top of a mountain. He built several model airplanes from school paper and sticks to give to his brothers. One day at the Gainesville airport, an old WWII pilot asked Ray if he wanted to learn to fly. Of course Ray said, "Yes, but I don't have much money." This man taught Ray to fly and said he was a natural as a pilot. Ray enjoyed taking us for some rides in his Mooney, a small sports plane.

With all three sons in the US, we started taking short furloughs and shorter terms. After a few months, we gladly kept our promise to stop by Israel to be the guests of Shmuel and Hanana and Ami and Bluma on our way back to Baguio. The cheapest flight was on Singapore Airlines. But it stopped in Cairo, not in Israel. We would take that, take a 3-day tour of Egypt, and then take the bus to Tel Aviv. Israel and Egypt had then established diplomatic relations, so this land trip was now possible.

In Egypt, we toured the Egyptian Museum, which was very interesting, and the great pyramids. We actually went way down inside one of them, to the burial chamber of the pharaoh. The passageway was narrow and low, but we made it. It was rather smelly down there. There was much more in Egypt that we would have liked to see, but we did not feel very comfortable there, especially when we got to the border crossing by bus.

The place was dirty. The Egyptian officials tried to get our money and harassed us. I only showed them my credit card. They did not even know what it was. The Israeli side was clean and had green shrubbery. The officials were polite and asked only one question. "Where are you going?" "To Rehovot to visit our Israeli friends there." He said, "Ok", and stamped a 90-day visa on our passports. It might have helped that I had a nice four-inch long beard and looked quite Jewish, but without a kippa on my head or tassels on my shirt.

161

According to Roger

Bluma was waiting for us at the Tel Aviv bus station. She and Ami had finished their work in the Philippines and were now doing agricultural development in Panama. Ami had to stay to work, but Bluma came back to Israel specifically to host us! We were amazed at that, but it confirmed that Israelis are wonderful friends once they know you love them. Is that not true for anyone? Probably. But I am not too sure about some others, who seem to have a totally different attitude about life and other people who do not share their faith.

Bluma took us to Bethlehem in Galilee. Moshe and Adina lived there. We did not know there was such a place, but it is mentioned in Joshua 19:15. This is why the Gospels say Bethlehem in Judea. Moshe had driven trucks up the "Burma Road," the alternate road to Jerusalem during the War of Independence. Their life stories are fascinating, yet the events are tragic. Ray and Carolyn named their second son after him: Benjamin Moshe Walkwitz. Bluma hosted us for five days, then the Evens for five more days. Shmuel and Hanana showed us many places and even brought us to a large family gathering. In the yard of the host, I saw a pomegranate on a tree for the first time. Jewish sages suggest that the fruit on the tree in the Garden of Eden was a pomegranate, not an apple. The juice is purple and very delicious; it has hundreds of seeds, more seeds than the 613 commandments or *mitzvot* in the Torah.

The bus route from Tel Aviv back to Egypt went through Gaza, which was a somewhat sandy desert area. The bus was going to pass along a road by the Cairo airport, which was a long way from Cairo. So we asked the driver to let us off by the roadside. We dragged our luggage across the highway into the airport. It would be more interesting to wait for our flight at the airport, and we would not have to pay for a taxi from Cairo. After a while, we heard a wedding celebration or reception with lots of music going on in the restaurant upstairs.

Singapore Airlines, of course, goes to Singapore before flying on to Manila, so we had arranged to stay a few days there. In Baguio, we had met a missionary from Singapore who had brought a group there for a retreat. He arranged for a couple of his disciples to show us around. Singapore is a beautiful, clean place. We would come back some years later to do some significant teaching. From Singapore, it was on to Manila and Baguio!

We were always ready to teach the Bible and do what was necessary to help the growing congregations in Baguio and LaTrinidad, including the many others now out in the mountains. There are interesting stories that will be told someday about how these many churches got started as a result of teaching the Bible in Baguio and LaTrinidad using the School of Tyrannus method. It was about time that we evaluated the ministry to see if we were about to reach our original objective - that of having fruitful disciples who could carry on without us.

# CHAPTER 18

## Passover in BIBAK
## and Randy's Wedding
## 1985-90

BIBAK Bible Fellowship has now expanded into many congregations, the result of doing ministry following Paul's new method that God led him to start in Ephesus. In his first two journeys, he traveled widely. In Ephesus he stayed and taught, and others did the traveling. The results were quite amazing. However, we do not want to imply that this method is the only answer. This is doing God's work, God's way, for each particular place and time. God has many ways to do His work to bring glory to Himself and accomplish His purposes. That is our objective, His Glory! Our situation in Baguio City paralleled Paul's in Ephesus. We believe it is a basic plan that should be used as much as possible. Actually, the "School of Tyrannus Method" is an implementation of what Paul told Timothy to do in 2 Timothy 2:2:

*"The things that you have heard from me among many witnesses, the same commit to faithful men* (anthropos = people), *who shall be able to teach others also."*

This spans four generations: Paul – Timothy – faithful persons – others also. If we as disciplers see our disciples carrying on to the fourth spiritual generation, we can then be confident that we did it God's way with those whom He has chosen. Trying to disciple someone who is not truly born from above, not chosen by God, still dead in sin, will not work.

The many churches that have been spawned through BIBAK have decided to band together a bit more closely. They did not want a denomination, but a closer alliance. They formed themselves into the Fellowship of BIBAK Bible Churches or FBBC. I helped them write a constitution and by-laws that limited FBBC to certain activities, leaving each church autonomous in its functions. Again, because politics is so prominent in Philippine life, we tried to make all documents and procedures that would avoid this situation that is hated by the Lord. So far, so good. We hope things continue that way.

The churches in the provinces can find or build facilities rather cheaply. In the city, land is very expensive. Eventually, BIBAK Baguio and LaTrinidad would need to buy land and build. But for now, the Lord had provided more-than-adequate facilities for them to grow and to multiply we hope, without any stress regarding a place, at least for a few more years. Each large Center that we had leased was for 10 years, which is enough time for them to get established.

We continue teaching, especially newer things we were learning from Jewish and historical sources that we did not know about before. It seems the subtle anti-Jewishness in the churches prevents many teachers from even considering Jewish sources and practices that are biblical. With such emphasis on the Newer Testament, the foundational Older Testament, or Tanach, has been neglected. *Tanach* or *Tanakh* is an acronym from the *Torah, Neviim, and Ketuvim*, or **TNK** with vowels put in between. These are the three parts of the Hebrew Scriptures: Torah or Pentateuch, Neviim or Prophets, and Ketuvim or Writings. Psalms is the first book in the scroll of the Writings. As Yeshua said:

> *"And he said unto them, These are the words which I spoke unto you, while I was yet with you, that all things must be fulfilled, which were written in the Law of Moses, and in the prophets, and in the psalms, concerning me. Then <u>he opened their understanding</u>, that they might understand the scriptures."* Luke 24:44-45.

Please note that the disciples were able to understand Scripture only after Yeshua opened their understanding to do so. Human wisdom is not enough. Intense secular scholarship and research is not enough. This Truth is indicated many times in the Bible. It is a Truth that many people choose to ignore, including those who claim that they know the Truth. Peter's insight in Matthew 16 was credited as *"flesh and blood has not revealed this unto you, but my Father who is in heaven."* We dare not be presumptuous.

With our love for Israel and being honest with many Bible passages, and with historical backgrounds that we were now learning for the first time, we began to see many things in a new light. We wondered why seminaries do not teach what we have found to be most important. Could it be that they have mistakenly concluded that "the church" started in Acts 2, rather than in the breaking off from the Messianic communities 200 years later?

Acts 7:38 informs us of the *ekklesia* in the wilderness with Moses, which was the continuing Messianic community from the beginning. Speaking of Moses, it says:

> *"This is he that was in the church (ekklesia) in the wilderness, with the angel who spoke to him in Mount Sinai, and with our fathers, who received the living oracles to give unto us."*

The Messianic community in Acts 2 is just a continuation of this *Ekklesia* from the time of Moses! Acts 2 is actually the implementation or launching of the Great Commission! Three thousand <u>disciples</u> were made, they were <u>baptized,</u> and they were <u>taught</u> everything that Yeshua had taught, for many weeks, maybe months. This was the exact procedure specified by Yeshua in the Great Commission in Matthew 28:18-20:

> *"And Jesus came and spoke unto them, saying, All authority is given unto me, in heaven and in earth. Therefore, wherever you go, <u>make disciples</u> of all nations, <u>baptizing them</u> in the Name of the Father, and of the Son, and of the Holy Spirit, <u>Teaching them</u> to observe all things whatsoever I have commanded you; and lo, I am with you always, even unto the end of the age. Amen."*

When we discovered Luther's pamphlet against the Jews, it was quite a shocker. Why had he written against the Jews? They had done nothing to warrant such hatred. I had a course in seminary on the Reformation, but this fact was never brought out about Luther. Constantine's letter to the churches after the Council of Nicea in 325 C.E. was also shocking! This was not brought out in seminary either. His hatred of the Jews was such that he declared that anyone who celebrated Passover from then on would be charged as a criminal! He and the bishops would build Christianity on a foundation different from the Old Testament.

To Constantine, the Jews were miserable wretches, the scum of the earth. Why? Jews had done nothing against him or the Roman Empire. The Empire long ago had excused the Jews from worshiping the emperor, so that was no reason to hate them. None of this was brought out in seminary either. Then there was the terrible persecution of the Jews by the church with its Inquisition. It was too much! We must go way back to discover what is called "the early church" of Jesus and His Apostles and start over on a correct foundation.

Passover came again in April 1986. We decided to teach on it and to experience it. If "Constantine and his successors" wanted to criminalize us, that would be just fine. Luke 22:14-20 records the significant items that Jesus called attention to during that Last Supper Passover. There are four parts of the fifteen part *Seder* that He asks all Disciples to do in Remembrance of Him.

*"And when the hour was come, he sat down, and the twelve apostles with him. And he said unto them, With desire I have desired to eat this Passover with you before I suffer; for I say, I will not any more eat of it, until it be fulfilled in the kingdom of God. And he took the **cup** (#1), and gave thanks, and said, Take this, and divide it among yourselves; for I say unto you, I will not drink of the fruit of the vine, until the kingdom of God shall come. And he took **bread** (#4), and gave thanks, and broke it, and gave unto them, saying, This is my body which is given for you; do this in*

*remembrance of me. Likewise also <u>the cup after **supper**</u> (**#11**), saying, **This cup** (#13) is the new testament in my blood, which is shed for you."*

The *Seder* means the orderly arrangement of all the 15 parts of the celebration, with #1 being the first cup of wine called *kiddush* or sanctification of the evening; #4, the broken unleavened bread (*matza*); #11, the festive supper; and #13, the cup of wine after supper. Jesus had not explained #4 and #13 in previous years, but now was the time to do so. In its anti-Jewishness, the church has taken #4 and #13 <u>out of its context</u> and made them into the pagan Eucharist of the Roman Catholics, bringing back into their worship what they practiced before becoming "Christians." Protestants and Evangelicals are still blind to what happened in 325 AD and at the Reformation, and have not come clean with Truth. They continue in what they call the "Lord's Supper" or "Communion" instead of going back to Yeshua and the Passover. Tradition is so comfortable. We prefer being correct.

We had a full house for our Last Supper Passover Seder! Everyone enjoyed it, and many have continued to do the Seder each year since, having been convinced that this is what Jesus said and meant. Inevitably, "Constantine and his successors" eventually condemned BIBAK and us for going back to the Foundation of Yeshua and the Apostles, celebrating the biblical festivals instead of the whitewashed pagan festivals that the church brought in from Constantine's time and continue to celebrate.

Back home in Wheaton, Illinois, Randy had found a girlfriend. He and Janie planned to get married October 4, 1986. They asked if we could come home for the wedding, and if I would   officiate the ceremony. Well, why not! I replied. Actually, we would not have missed that for anything! College Church was quite strict as to who did weddings there, but since they had ordained me, and Randy and Janie had gone through their pre-marital counseling program, it was OK for me to do it. Some of the pastors who were there said I did a great job. My voice quavered a bit only when I announced them as "Mr. and Mrs. Randall Edward Walkwitz."

The reception was at a very nice restaurant with a great meal. Janie is the youngest and an only girl, with three older brothers. None of the rest of the family were at that time believers. Her mother died of cancer when Janie was only 14 years. The family is nominal Roman Catholic, but they all came to College Church for the ceremony. Her father, AJ Sabella, was a builder who remodeled a trashed house for them. This was a huge help to them financially. He also died of cancer several years ago.

Considering everything in BIBAK, we decided to set a goal of phasing out slowly, take short furloughs, and set June 1990 to terminate our fulltime ministry in the Philippines. We had been very busy involved with the lowlanders living in Baguio as well as the mountaineers, and had enjoyed it all very much. But being foreigners, and out of our own conviction for an indigenous ministry, we believe there is a time to leave. It is sometimes hard to tell when that time is. We had such a variety of ministries, but we felt somewhat comfortable with June 1990. It was a bit too early for the lowlander ministry, but just about right for BIBAK.

What should we do then? Retirement from the mission was required at age 65. I still had a few more years to go. OK, we will go to Israel to study for a year! I was due for  a 'sabbatical' anyway, and this would be a good transition. We were hungry for more background information on the Scriptures.

The Institute of Holy Land Studies in Jerusalem had some courses to help us. Ray had visited there with Paul on their round the world trip and recommended it. Also, a year in The Land would allow us to observe how Israelis celebrated or observed all of the LORD's Appointed Times summarized in Leviticus 23. These are usually called Festivals in our Bibles, but the Hebrew word *Moedim* means 'a gathering by appointment.' We would take a short furlough to go to Israel and check them out.

In the spring of 1988, we went home to Florida to see Ray and Carolyn and to plan our trip. We would fly to Miami on Eastern Airlines, pick up El Al Israel Airlines going to Montreal, Canada, and from there, fly direct on El Al to Tel Aviv. Ray had already been to Israel with Paul in 1979 and with us in 1968. He insisted that Carolyn also have a chance to go. Now, traveling with us was the best opportunity.

Joshua Nathaniel Walkwitz, Ray and Carolyn's first child and our first grandchild, was already two years old. He was born on March 2, 1986. Ray could already handle him while Carolyn joined us in Israel. She could not be gone too long, so she just came a few weeks after we had left. Ray was developing his Flight School then, and Joshua would ride in the back of the airplane when Ray would take a student up for instruction.

We were waiting in Orlando for our flight to Miami. Bad weather was delaying its arrival from Tallahassee. We did not have much time between flights in Miami. I phoned

El Al in Miami to advise them of our problem. Eventually we got there and ran through the terminal with our carry-on baggage to the El Al counter. It was all good. The plane had not left.

We had checked our baggage through to Tel Aviv. When they did not arrive at the El Al counter, staff called Eastern to see where the baggage was. Since our Eastern flight from Orlando was very late, Eastern assumed that the El Al flight had left, so they put our baggage, unaccompanied, on an Eastern flight to New York to connect with an El Al flight there! How presumptuous that was!

El Al is very strict on security. Unaccompanied luggage is generally not allowed. Soon our El Al flight left for Montreal. We all then transferred to a big El Al 747 and found our seats. The plane was almost full when we got there, because our group from Miami was a bit late. The other feeder flights had already come from other US and Canadian cities to consolidate on a single flight to Israel.

We waited on the 747 for a long time. We were served some drinks and snacks. Finally it was announced that a mechanical problem that would take some hours to fix had been found, so we would be put up overnight in the luxurious (to us anyway) airport hotel and leave in the morning. That was fine with us! We were tired anyway, so a good night's sleep would be wonderful. Shmuel and Hanana would find out about the delay and meet us later.

When we arrived the next day, they were there to meet us at the airport, all excited. We had been delayed because a call came that a bomb had been placed on the plane. It was all over Israel TV! Of course we were not informed about that. The plane was searched all night, but nothing was found. It was another harassing hoax, but it was better to be safe than sorry. El Al is the safest airline in the world.

Our checked baggage? They were not there on our arrival in Israel. We reported it to the baggage office. The people there said they would deliver them to the Even's house in Rehovot as soon as they arrive. We had no extra clothes in our carry-on baggage — this was a big mistake. We had planned to rent a car and be on our way after a day visiting; but now, we could not proceed. No baggage, no clothes, no going! We were a bit embarrassed because Passover was in a few more days.

The Evens invited us to go with them. We bought some underwear locally and we borrowed some clothes from them so we would look presentable. The *Seder* was to be in a fancy hotel along the Sea of Galilee up the hill toward the Golan Heights. There were about a hundred attending. The leader was a popular Israeli entertainer so he could dramatize the story better. We each had a Haggadah, the narration booklet. Ours was in English and Hebrew, although all the talking was in Hebrew. We enjoyed it very much.

Since it finished late at night, and Rehovot was about three or four hours drive away, we stayed overnight with the Evens daughter and son-in-law up on the Golan Heights. They and a few others were pioneering a new Moshav. Ilan and Ruhama had come to Baguio to visit us a few years earlier on their year-long trip after army days. After the stress of three years in the army, (two years for girls), many Israelis travel the world to exotic places for many months or even a year. Usually couples are not married when they travel. If things work out, they get married later. Some go to college. Once married, they have to buckle down to work to establish their family. There would be no time to travel then. That is the usual way. Ilan and Ruhama wrote us from somewhere in South East Asia at their eleventh month of travel. They had one more month to go, but were running out of money. What could they do? Go home and get married!

Now they were living in a caravan, a temporary dwelling, while working to establish this *Moshav*. When we woke in the morning, they asked if we had been disturbed during the night. We had not. An intruder from Syria had tried to break through the security fence to attack their village. They all had been called out to defend the place. We had not heard a thing. I wished I could have gone with them. After all, I was an army man!

Our baggage finally arrived after one week! The bags had been forced open to be inspected for bombs. Unaccompanied baggage is a no-no. Our stuff was all there, although with some damage. Carolyn arrived after a few days. We met her at the airport, brought her to Evens to meet them, and stayed there overnight before we went on our way. We checked out the Institute for Holy Land Studies and decided that we would study there for the school year 1990-91.

We showed Carolyn the country from top to bottom in about two weeks. She met many of our friends, including Adina and Moshe. Adina had been a concert pianist and Carolyn was a top violinist, so they bonded well. She enjoyed being with Bluma and Ami also. We videoed their life story in Europe during the Holocaust. We then flew back to Florida together.

Back in Florida, Ray had flown with Joshua somewhere in the Midwest to buy a twin-engine plane to add to his fleet. He wanted to offer multi-engine training while at the same time building up his hours of flying time. He was too tall (6 ft 5 in) and too old to get in the Air Force, and commercial flying at that time paid only a pittance for entry level. So his own aviation business was the best way to go. He was too busy to be selling books for Southwestern or for Encyclopedia Britannica anymore. He was a family man now.

Back in Baguio, we began to wind down our activities. The local leadership was doing just fine. We continued with the Baguio Country Club Wednesday lunchtime Bible study. With all our contacts now, we were invited to several big celebrations, like a debut for an eighteen-year-old daughter, Christmas parties, birthday parties, all with the upper crust lowlanders. We had learned to be comfortable with them, but were right at home with the mountaineers too, as they were more like family.

By January 1990, we began selling off what we did not need and packing in steel drums the things we wanted to take home. We gave Elisa a generous severance pay for her faithful 25 years serving us and the Lord, and hoped that she would find a good job after we left. In some ways, it was hard to leave, as this had been our home and second family for many years. But it was best for them. They were maturing in the Lord and He would care for them.

# CHAPTER 19

## ISRAEL. Institute of Holy Land Studies, Jerusalem 1990-91

We were very excited about the opportunity to study in Israel for almost a year! At our age, there are so many things we wanted to learn. In contrast, the young usually do not know what there is to learn. But before we departed for Israel, a great tragedy hit Baguio, seven weeks after we had left. An 8.0 earthquake devastated the city, demolishing hotels and dwellings, killing many people. There were many aftershocks, so people were sleeping outdoors, even in the parks.

An Elder of BIBAK, Rufino, had his travel agency office off the lobby of the Hyatt Terraces Hotel. As soon as he felt the quake, he shot out the door just in time, as the lobby ceiling collapsed right behind him, killing another believer. Our BIBAK Centers in Baguio and LaTrinidad both survived with minimal damage. There was no use going back to help, as everyone was in dire straits, with no water, no electricity, and food shortages. We would have only been a burden. We got through by phone to inquire about the damage to the BIBAK community, and then we had to proceed to Jerusalem.

Naturally, we were the oldest of the students. Many of them were still in college, but that made it more fun. At 61 and 59, we were still in good shape. We did well in all of our classes, except Modern Hebrew. It was a reading course, not on conversation, which we had wanted. All the students had had some Hebrew before they came. We had not had any, so we were trying to catch up the whole semester. One semester was enough, but it did give us a few expressions, enough to make conversation with Israelis we met, and some ability to read the Hebrew Bible. Bible script is very different, so we learned both on our own.

The class we enjoyed the most was on Physical Settings of Israel. In class, we studied the land in sections, one area at a time. Then we toured that area and had a quiz on the details. By the end of the semester, we had a fairly good grasp of this wonderful land. Other classes included Jewish Thought and Practice taught by a rabbi; Islamic Thought and Practice taught by a practicing Islamic PhD; Rabbinics; Second Temple Period; the Greek Orthodox Churches; and more.

The Festival of *Sukkot* (Tabernacles) came in October. Friday is the Muslim weekly holiday. On the Friday during Sukkot, after prayers at the Al Aksa Mosque on the Temple Mount, hundreds of Muslims came swarming out with big rocks in hand to throw over the wall at the Jewish worshipers below at the Western Wall. The rocks had been stockpiled for some time. An alert guard shouted to the Jews below to back up, so that no one was hurt badly.

We saw the pile of rocks which was about three feet deep! The Muslims then began attacking the police, who fired back with rubber bullets to protect themselves. Then later, they apparently had to use live ammunition and killed 19 of the attackers. The incident caused a big international blast against Israel, as usual. This was the Islamic objective all the time! You can be sure that any news in the media about Israel will be twisted against them. It infuriates us when we know the truth about Arabs instigating incidents just to make trouble against Israel. Israel is totally the victim. For centuries, the Jews have been the scapegoat, and will be again and again until Yeshua returns to straighten out this evil world system. As God's Chosen People, Israel, the Jews, are the primary target for the hatred of Satan and his people, who are in the majority.

This would never have happened except for the stupidity of Gen. Moshe Dayan, the Chief of Staff of the IDF, the Israel Defense Forces. The leaders of Israel do not understand Islam and do not understand even themselves!

When Israel conquered Jerusalem in the Six-Day War in June 1967, the Muslim leaders in charge of the Temple Mount, the *Waqf* as they call it, gave the keys to their buildings to Gen. Motti Gur, the conquering general of the IDF. He gave them to Gen. Dayan, who soon gave them back to the Islamic leaders, saying that Israel was not interested in conquering religious sites. What a stupid, naïve act, that has caused untold deaths and problems for Israel ever since. Give Islam an inch of consideration and they take a mile, because they consider any bit of consideration or kindness as weakness. This only motivates them to go for the kill more and more.

There is one extra day added to biblical *Sukkot* called *Simchat Torah*, the Joy of the Torah! The big celebration was at the

Western Wall plaza in the evening, a few days after the rock attack. IHLS is only a 10-minute walk from the plaza, so we went right after supper. What we saw and felt that evening was the most impressive of our whole time there.

A platform at the north end of the plaza held a small klezmer band which plays a certain joyful type of Jewish music. The plaza was full of people, mostly men, some with their two or three-year-old kids on their shoulders, and a few women. Whenever the band played, they would line up to dance, men with men, and women with women. The lead person held a Torah scroll. Everyone was smiling and enjoying the evening. When the music stopped, someone gave a talk from the platform. We had no idea of the content of the talks. But the joy that was expressed told us this, "We Jews are the possessors of the actual words that God gave to Moses. We are the guardians of God's words!"

What a privilege this is, given to no other people on the face of this earth. We are so used to referring to our English Bibles as the Word of God. No, His words are in Hebrew, and Greek for the Newer Testament. My Bible is only a translation, fairly accurate I hope, but nothing like the Hebrew text for those who know Hebrew well, so I am told. These Israelis speak Hebrew as their native language!

Then there was the Gulf War of 1991. Pressured by their parents, many of the students left for their home countries. Our Israeli friends appreciated the fact that we stayed on. The school continued as well. Saddam fired 39 Scud missiles at Israel during that time, mostly at night when we were sound asleep, or on Friday suppertime when every Israeli family is celebrating the beginning of *Shabbat* (the Sabbath).

I kept track on my calendar of every one of them. Since no one knew if the Scud carried an explosive or a chemical warhead, we had to gather in a sealed room instead of the usual bomb shelter. Bomb shelters are below ground, and gas would seep into them. We wore gas masks just in case it was a gas attack. From the sound of the alarm until the Scud hit, we had 2 minutes to get some clothes on and scamper to the one common sealed room.

Naomi had a difficult time putting on her gas mask, partly from being afraid of not being able to breath. But one of the ladies helped her. I did not notice her predicament, as I was busy listening to my battery-powered radio. Only the Israel Defence Forces Radio was allowed to go on air during an emergency. We had to listen to know when it would be safe to leave the sealed room, and to know if it was a chemical attack or explosive. Many buildings around Tel Aviv were damaged, but only one person was actually killed by a direct hit. There were several accounts of miraculous escapes. God is always watching over Israel, but very few see it yet.

Passover arrived. The school was going to celebrate in the dining hall, since the Last Supper Passover includes the evening meal. When we entered to find our seats, an elderly man looked at me and said, "I know you, young man. You are a missionary in the Philippines!" Wow! How did he know me? Do I still look like a young man?

Hillel Munce was a retired schoolteacher from Michigan. He still remembered me from my talk at either a Gideon Meeting or Christian Business Men's Committee meeting in the Detroit area many years ago, long before I understood and accepted the Messianic teachings. When I got back home, I looked it up in my appointment book and found that it was in 1963! It was now 1991. We had not seen each other in those 28 years, and we did not even get to know each other at that time. It was just a meeting, but God had His plans also. He and his wife, Miriam, lived in Caesarea, and had come to IHLS to spend the week of Unleavened Bread with their friend who was the secretary at the school.

The next day Hillel asked me if we would be willing to live in and take care of their house while they went to the USA for the summer. Miriam had retired from teaching school in Illinois. It was their second marriage since both their spouses had died, and they had families there to visit. Of course we said, "Yes!"

When the school year ended, IHLS awarded me a Graduate Certificate in Middle Eastern Studies. Hillel came to pick us up and brought us to their house. The next day, I drove them to the airport for their trip to the USA. I would be picking them up when they returned. We had the responsibility to keep the yard in good order and take care of their dog. Using their car, we were able to travel on weekends to visit various Messianic synagogues. There is no public transportation on Shabbat.

This opportunity was a wonderful provision of the Lord since we wanted to get a good exposure to the total Gospel ministry in Israel, Christian and Messianic Jewish. In Jerusalem, during the school year, and now throughout the rest of the land, we found that Messianic congregations were made up of Jews and Arabs, and some had other nationalities too. No pictures were allowed, since some orthodox Jews were strongly opposed to any Jew becoming a follower of Jesus. If he were found out, the believer might lose his job, as his employer would be pressured to fire him. Arab believers could be killed.

We were not able to develop any kind of friendships with any in these congregations. Our friends were the secular ones that we met here and there over the years, and a very few Messianics, like Hillel and Miriam. With the use of their car, we got to visit our friends during the weekdays and many other sites that we wanted a second or third look at. It was very interesting to shop in the outdoor produce markets which had fresh fruits and vegetables produced locally, and at the supermarkets and other kinds of stores. We were not tourists now. We "belonged" here in Israel! At least, we thought so.

In the afternoon on one Shabbat in May 1991, we were returning to Caesarea from visiting a Messianic group near Tiberias. We had the car radio on to the one station that gave news in English. Suddenly a flash bulletin came in. "The IDF has just completed Operation Solomon!" Almost 15,000 Ethiopian Jews had been rescued from Ethiopia in a shuttle airlift in 24 hours. Many Russian Jews were also coming to Israel at this time.

Why was it called Operation Solomon? (I am so glad you asked!) This is one of several interesting, and important, Jewish historical backgrounds that we have studied. The last Emperor of Ethiopia before the Communists took over in 1975 and slaughtered his family was Haile Selassie. He called himself The Lion of the Tribe of Judah and claimed direct descent from King Solomon and the Queen of Sheba, as did all the emperors before him! Their son was Menelik, who was raised in Jerusalem by Solomon. When Menelik was trained and ready to return home to Ethiopia, he took with him a replica of the Ark of the Covenant in order to set up Jewish worship. This history is based on 1 Kings 10:2 and 13:

# According to Roger

*"When the Queen of Sheba heard of the fame of King Solomon concerning the name of the LORD…and when she was come to Solomon, she talked with him of <u>all that was in her heart</u>….And King Solomon gave unto the queen of Sheba <u>all her desire</u>, whatever she asked…"*

We have no reason to doubt the above history, nor its interpretation and understanding. We also have no reason to doubt any part of Scripture. Numbers 12:1 is a problem for some and is used by critics to point out a "glaring mistake in the Bible." Everyone knows that the wife of Moses was Zipporah, the daughter of Jethro (or Reuel), the priest of Midian, in Exodus 2:21. So who were Miriam and Aaron complaining about?

*"And Miriam and Aaron spoke against Moses because of the Ethiopian woman whom he had married; for he had married an Ethiopian woman."*

Now, did Moses marry an Ethiopian woman or not? The Bible says, Yes! Doubters say No, because Midianites are very light colored, not black like Ethiopians, and there is no other mention of this in the Bible. Some Bibles say a woman of Cush, because Cush is the Hebrew word for Ethiopian or black person. Cush was a son of Ham. So what is the solution?

Again we turn to history, this time the book of *Josephus* in his *Antiquities of the Jews*, Book II, Chapter X, page 58. In a fascinating love story, we read of Moses being appointed general of the Egyptian army when the Egyptians were being pushed back by an invasion by Ethiopia, in the south of Egypt. God gave Moses wisdom to change tactics and drove the Ethiopian army back into their territory until he came to the castle of the king, which was surrounded by rivers and high walls.

184

Tharbis was the daughter of the king of Ethiopia. From on the walls above, she saw Moses and "fell deeply in love with him," and sent her faithful servant to Moses to "discourse with him about their marriage." Moses "accepted the offer on condition she would procure the delivering up of the city," which she did. Moses then "gave thanks to God and consummated his marriage" to Tharbis, his Ethiopian wife of Numbers 12:1. There are no mistakes in the original Hebrew and Greek manuscripts. Apparent mistakes are due to faulty translations or lack of understanding of the historical backgrounds. We should study until we find solutions to all apparent mistakes, or wait until more information is available. But we should never condemn what God has written.

In the mid-1980s, Israel's IDF made its first secret airlift of Ethiopian Jews to Israel. Can you guess what it was called? It was called Operation Moses! Jews know their history. Why don't Christians know this, since Christians claim to know the Bible?

My answer: because of Replacement Theology! That "since the church replaced Israel in the plan of God, there is no point learning any history before the Gospel accounts. The Hebrew Scriptures are old and of little value to Christianity." According to Constantine, Christianity is built on a different foundation from the Tanakh. That being so, Constantine and his bishops built Christianity on paganism! This is what we have been discovering, and are very disturbed about it. To think that for many years, we had been guilty of propagating what Constantine & Co had developed. Still, we are thankful that the Reformers of the Reformation turned back, at least partially, to the original Foundation.

By the way, was the Ethiopian Eunuch in Acts Chapter 8 a Jew or a Gentile? Nearly always, whenever I ask that question, the answer I get is "Gentile." No, he was a born Jew, descended from either Moses or Solomon, not even a proselyte like many commentaries like to say. If he were a Gentile, then God would not have sent Philip to witness to him, because Peter had not yet brought the Gospel to the Gentiles, in the person and family of Cornelius in Caesarea. Peter had the Keys; Philip did not.

So what has been <u>your</u> idea about the Keys of the Kingdom of Heaven? The Catholic Church claims that they have the Keys. Sorry, they do not! The Catholic Church is full of lies and perversions of Scripture. This is why we are pulling out of anything and everything that they have changed over time. Back to The Foundation of Yeshua and His Apostles is our objective!

The Keys of the Kingdom of Heaven were given to Peter, and to him alone. He could not and did not pass the Keys on to anyone else. Here is the only biblical evidence of how the Spirit of God guided Peter in using the Keys, as he probably did not know what it was all about. He was the leader of the twelve, but that is not why he was given the Keys. He was given the Keys because of his statement that Yeshua is the Messiah, the Son of the living God. Peter was now the one to "open the door" to the Kingdom of Heaven on the basis of the now completed Gospel to each ethnic group, especially to those who had been <u>looking forward to the Coming of the Promised Messiah since the time of Adam & Eve</u>. Peter's message was that the Promise has been fulfilled in the death, burial, resurrection and ascension of Yeshua, the Messiah, the Son of the living God.

That is why Peter was the spokesman on the Day of

Pentecost to all the Diaspora Jews who had come to Jerusalem for Shavuot, (Pentecost), in obedience to the Torah requirement. Peter "opened the door," using the Keys to the Kingdom of Heaven to all the Jews present there at the Temple courtyard. As a result, 3,000 more responded and entered the Kingdom.

That is why Philip's ministry in Samaria was limited until Peter came from Jerusalem, recognized the problem, and put his hands on the Samaritan Believers. They were then born from above and showed the joy of a changed life by the indwelling Spirit. By the way, there is no "tongues speaking" mentioned here! What was the problem? There had been centuries of hatred between Jews and Samaritans. This had to be solved <u>before</u> God would bring Samaritans into His Kingdom. Harmony must prevail. By putting his hands on the Samaritans, Peter demonstrated acceptance, the elimination of this hatred in the Body of Messiah. Only Peter could do this, because only Peter had the Keys.

That is also why God told Cornelius in a vision to send for Peter, in Joppa at the time, to tell him what else he needed to know. Philip was living in Caesarea at the time. Philip knew the completed Gospel just as well as Peter did. It would have been simple for God to tell Cornelius to just go down the street and talk to Philip. But no, Philip did not have the Keys. Peter had to come all the way from Joppa to Caesarea to "open the door" to the Kingdom of Heaven directly to Gentiles, represented by Cornelius. This act of God through Peter was "earth shaking" to Peter and the Apostles. It was necessary to <u>break the hold</u> of wrong rabbinic teaching that Gentiles were unclean and could not have a place in the world to come unless they first converted to Judaism!

**Matthew 16:13-20** is so badly translated, and therefore so badly interpreted and falsely applied, that we need to deal with it now. If I repeat some of this again later, that would be good, because it bears repeating many times until the Truth is firmly fixed in our minds. I will correct the translation and explain or paraphrase as I go along:

> *"When Yeshua came into the district of Caesarea Philippi, he asked his disciples, saying, 'Who do men say that I, the Son of man, am?' And they said, 'Some say John the baptizer, some Elijah, and others Jeremiah or one of the prophets.' He said to them, 'But who do you say that I am?' Simon Peter replied, 'You are the Messiah, the Son of the living God' Yeshua answered, 'Blessed are you, son of John! For flesh and blood has not revealed this to you but my Father, who is in heaven.'* (Insight into Spiritual Truth is <u>revealed</u> by God, not discovered by scholarship alone!) *'And I say also to you, that you are Peter* (a small stone) *and on this rock* (a huge boulder, referring back to what Peter had just said, the <u>rock-solid-Truth</u> that Yeshua is The Messiah, The Son of living God) *I will (continue) to <u>build up</u> my Ekklesia* (Congregation of the LORD, Messianic Community since the time of Moses, NOT start something new called the church!) *and the powers of death shall not prevail against it. And I will give <u>unto you the Keys</u> of the Kingdom of the Heavens, and whatever you might bind on the earth shall be having <u>already been bound and still bound</u> in the heavens, and whatever you might loose on the earth shall be having <u>already been loosed and still loosed</u> in the heavens.'* (This sentence is <u>past</u> tense, not future as it is in all translations! Being past tense, Yeshua is telling Peter and the rest that any and all decisions regarding life practices must be based on <u>what has already been decided</u> in heaven and

brought down for man, meaning the Torah, the only way to live God's way on earth. By using the future, translations open the door to all kinds of abuses, primarily that the Catholic church has the "right" to make changes in the Bible because "the Pope has the Keys of Peter." This is a total lie and blasphemy!) *Then he warned the disciples that they should tell no one that he is the Messiah."*

I hope you now see how important it is to have the correct translation of this passage in your Bible! It is not only about the twisting by the Roman Catholics. All other Christian churches, to some extent, have followed the changes that the Catholics have made. Mainline liberal Protestants are sometimes worse than the Catholics in that they approve of homosexual behavior, even for their clergy!

Back to Caesarea, Israel. Our visas would run out one month before the Munce's returned. I had gone to the Immigration Office to get an extension. There were many people waiting. I sat next to a Jew from Chicago. He was wearing black, so he was Orthodox, but friendly. As I told him my situation, he said, "Never mind. They won't care if you are over by a month as the paper work and waiting is not worth it." I took his advice. It is always wise to listen to the natives!

On our way out in August, the Immigration clerk noticed that we were a month overdue. I told her that we had been here for school in Jerusalem for the year and that the Gulf War had come along so that we had not been able to finish on time. OK, she said, and she thanked us for staying throughout the war. Israelis are sensitive to this issue and evaluate who their friends are based on this fact.

Do you cut and run when it is time to fight, or do you hold your ground and stand by what is right? We will stand by Israel every time Israel becomes an issue. This is because we have a good background of first hand information, as well as of God's Promises in the Bible, relating to attitudes toward the Jews, His Chosen People forever.

# CHAPTER 20

## Transition to Menorah Ministries
## 1991-94

We certainly enjoyed our year in Israel and we learned so much! Somehow, we are happy wherever we are, so we were happy to be home in the USA again, excited about our next step following our Lord and Savior, Jesus the Messiah or *Yeshua HaMashiach,* as we now call Him in Hebrew. Home base would always be Morriston, Florida. Ray and Carolyn were living in our house with Joshua, now five years old, and Benjamin Moshe, now two years old.

While we were still in the Philippines, the owner of the house on the next acre offered to sell it to us, as I had asked him for first chance if ever he wanted to sell. Our two-bedroom house was too small to keep guests. He was the builder who also helped Ralph Mount build ours. Both had the same floor plan, small but efficient. Together with Ray, we bought the house. We stayed in this second house when we were not traveling around the USA for meetings in supporting churches and Conferences.

We knew the Lord had a new ministry for us, while we still helped those in the Philippines. I have patterned my ministry after that of Paul, who traveled but always kept in touch with those groups that he pioneered, by letters, visits, and especially prayer. This is in contrast to clergy teaching, which says that when you leave a church for another better employment, you have to cut your ties to the first church so that the new clergyman can mold his new church the way he wants it, without any personal loyalties to deal with. The pastor is not to build close ties with anyone, as these will cause problems for his successor. Missions are sometimes guilty in this regard as well.

This is the business model, which I totally reject! Ministry in the Bible is not business! That is the corruption that came in when the Body of Messiah was divided into clergy and laity, instead of the equal brotherhood that Yeshua taught. It may also be a reason why personal discipling is not done much, especially by the pastors, so as to not develop personal loyalties. In contrast to clergy practice, we major on discipleship because that is the one specific command in the Great Commission of Matthew 28! The Navigators have a book called "The Lost Art of Making Disciples." Church leadership should read this good book!

The Walkwitz Flight School was growing. Ray needed to put up an office at the Ocala Airport, rather than in his VW Van! It would make life easier if they also moved into Ocala to be near the airport, as our place was 25 miles out in the country. So during the fall of 1991, they did both. By January 1992, it was time for me to go back to Baguio, alone this time, to see what help we could be.

## Transition to Menorah Ministries

BIBAK would be OK, but the Baguio Country Club Luncheon Bible Study Group of prominent lowlanders was rather new in the faith and needed lots of help. In addition, besides the 8.0 earthquake, another terrible tragedy had happened in June of 1991. Pinatubo Volcano erupted with terrible violence and results. Even though it was about 50 miles south, ash still came down on Baguio. It was described as when day turned into night, because of the clouds of ash that darkened the sky for days. Airplanes could not come into Manila for a few days because the engines would suck in the ash, and destroy them, and cause crashes.

I was in Baguio for about three weeks, mostly teaching the non-BIBAK people. Even meal times each day had to be used for teaching as they had so many questions. Their Bible knowledge was minimal, because they had not been given a good foundation in their churches. This is so typical. The earthquake and volcano explosion caused one family to move back to Manila. Dan was a pilot for the Ayala Corporation. I came down for a few days to help do some teaching before leaving for home. Dan and Emy Reventar had gathered 25 friends for a potluck supper and teaching. A field trip was suggested for the next day, to the Embassy of Israel and the Synagogue.

Ambassador Yoav Behiri invited us to the Embassy, since he had the whole morning free. He welcomed me with a big bear hug, as we knew each other quite well. He taught us about Israel until noon. We had lunch and then visited the Synagogue. We had a good tour and talk from the rabbi. We met again in the evening at the Reventars, with questions going past midnight. They were saying, "We never hear any of this in our churches!" Just plain good Bible study is absent from most churches. They were very hungry to learn and thanked me profusely. I had to cut it off, as I had an early morning flight to Honolulu.

Naomi met me in Honolulu for the month long Missions and Prophecy Conference at Kalihi Union Church. I did most of the teaching the first week, all day Sundays and the nightly meetings during the week, through two weekends. On Saturday morning, we went with a Jewish friend from KUC to a Messianic congregation meeting at the Community Center in Waikiki. A Messianic Jewish teacher spent February in Hawaii and taught there each Shabbat. He was an interesting scholar. We learned some more about the place of Jews and Israel in God's plan, and our place as Gentiles in the Good Olive Tree.

Then we flew back to Chicago to stay at my brother Don's place and prepare to go to Detroit for another Missionary Conference at Ward Presbyterian Church in Livonia, the church that we helped pioneer as Interns. Moishe Rosen of Jews for Jesus was the main Bible teacher. We had a display featuring our Philippine ministry and a flag of Israel for our new ministry.

I taught on Israel and the Bible to an adult Bible study class Sunday morning. A Lebanese woman came in late, sat in the back, after a while, stood up to loudly object and then walked out. She poisoned the atmosphere. She apparently hated Israel. With Moishe Rosen teaching in the main sessions, my display of a flag of Israel, and my teaching on Israel and the Bible, she must have figured I was the easier target for her anger. She obviously did not know, or did not believe Genesis 12:3 and the following verses that those who <u>bless Israel will be blessed,</u> and those who despise Israel will be cursed.

Apparently, she succeeded. The church dropped our support a few months later. The missions pastor was pro-Arab as well. God says He loves Israel "with an everlasting love," so how can those who claim to trust Him have such hate for Israel? Also, since Gentile Believers are grafted into the Good Olive Tree together with Jewish Believers, how can brethren have such hate? It was shocking for us to find such things in evangelical churches! Does the Holy Spirit really live in them? Are they really born from above? If so, do they listen to the Holy Spirit? It is an enigma to us.

Another Independent Evangelical church, Elmbrook Church in Wisconsin, also dropped our support when they learned that we were interested in Israel. We explained our position from the Bible, but they were not interested. If we went into Muslim work or back to tribal work, they would keep us on, but not for Jewish ministry. So in a short time, we lost almost half of our financial support from friends and churches that had "loved us to death," until we took our stand with Israel.

Because "Replacement Theology", (that the church had replaced Israel in the plan of God since "the Jews killed Jesus.") so persuaded the churches, they had no interest in the Jews or in Israel. In their eyes, God was finished with Israel. So why try to reach out to them? They conveniently forget that God's Promises to Israel do not fail! God is not a liar. He does not change His mind; otherwise, John 3:16 is not valid either. God promises to bless those who bless Israel, and curse those who do not.

Although before this time, we had not known the term "Replacement Theology" and what it meant, our early teaching reflected it. How? Just like everyone learns in churches today, any and every passage was "interpreted" to refer to us — the church. We are the salt of the earth, we are the light of the world, and the return of Jesus is for us, for the church. These are all partly true as an application for true Disciples of Yeshua, but the interpretation is for Israel, for those in God's Good Olive Tree, Jew and Gentile together.

We had not realized how deeply ingrained and subtle an anti-Jewish, or anti-Semitic attitude prevailed in nearly all churches. Some claimed to love Israel but did not like Jewish people! Their "love Israel" stance seemed to be based on their pre-Tribulation Rapture theology; Israel needed to be in place so that the Lord could return and take the church out first, and then let "all hell break loose on the Jews" who would be left behind for the Great Tribulation. If you have read the "Left Behind" series of books, forget what you have read, because they are deceptive.

"**The** Tribulation (*thlipsis* in Gk) the great one" in Revelation 7:14 began with the stoning of Stephen in Acts 7 and will continue until the Arrival of Yeshua HaMashiach as He comes down to earth, bringing all Believers with Him. John is watching **The** Tribulation in progress, which is why "no one can number them." John also says in Revelation 1:9: *"I, John, who also am your brother and companion in The Tribulation..."*

John testifies that he is in **The** Tribulation at the time he wrote Revelation. It was not to start in the future. Check your Greek NT or your Interlinear New Testament to find and verify every time *thlipsis* occurs in the singular with an article in front of it, meaning **The** Tribulation, a specific one.  Do not be fooled by translators who use synonyms like trouble or persecution.  *Thlipsis* should always be translated Tribulation.

The Apostle Paul adds his testimony to John's, making the two required witnesses.  See Romans 5:3-4:

*"And not only so, but we glory in tribulations also, knowing that **The Tribulation** works patience; and patience, experience; and experience, hope;"*

Paul knows that he is in **The** Tribulation as he writes, but gives further information about its ebb and flow over time in 2 Corinthians 4:17, in a literal translation:

*"For the present lightness of **The Tribulation** is working for us exceedingly upon exceedingly  an eternal weight of glory..."*

In other words, **The** Tribulation will not always be severe, and not always in every place.  History bears out that "the present lightness" of the tribulation (or persecution) against Messianic disciples was not severe all the time, although it was always there, somewhere.  They needed to be on their guard all the time,  while being bold in their witness and teaching.

Back in Florida, Passover was approaching again.  The Bible study group of Ralph Mount had so many extra people coming to celebrate Passover with them that there was no more space in his school building.  Therefore, Ray and Carolyn decided to have Walkwitz Flight School sponsor another Passover celebration in Ocala at the Radisson Inn, on Friday evening April 17, 1992.  That evening was the beginning of the 15th of Nisan, right on schedule with the Bible. This would relieve congestion at Mount's and give opportunity for more who lived in Ocala to join. Mount's place (and ours) in Morriston was 25 miles from Ocala.

The dining room was packed. The chef had worked for Jews in New York, so he knew just how to fix the kosher meal. The next morning being Shabbat, I decided that we should go to visit the Reformed Synagogue in Ocala to see what the rabbi had to say. It was our first visit, so we sat in the back. The rabbi went on to tell of the items in the Seder that they had celebrated the night before. But he admitted that for many of the items, he did not know the reason for what they did or what these meant! If only he had given me the chance to tell him and the congregation! The Gospel of Yeshua is in the Passover celebration!

Our year of furlough for reporting back to our friends and supporters was more than half over. A decision needed to be made regarding our next ministry. We asked for a Jewish-oriented ministry. The mission replied that they had no administrative category for Jewish ministry and that they were already too busy expanding into Europe. Actually I think they were typically church-thinking — "why bother with the Jews?"

Since at this point we had served for 35 years in various capacities, they had to offer something that we would enjoy doing. To get themselves "off the hook," they asked us to go on-loan to a Jewish mission for administrative purposes. Our present mission would still handle our finances, as donations were coming to them. That meant I would receive a salary until I turned 65 years of age IF contributions met the requirement, and an expense account beyond that from whatever funds were given. We had already lost half of our support, so we received only a partial salary and began to use our savings. Finally, I decided to take my Social Security two years early to supplement our income.

We accepted all that, because Yeshua was in charge and He had better plans. We now began to search for that Jewish mission. To hasten matters, I went to Moody Bible Institute in Chicago to see Dr. Louis Goldberg, head of the Jewish studies program there. I explained everything to him and he understood very well. He told me to go see his friend, John Fischer, in Florida. John is the academic dean of St. Petersburg Theological Seminary, the Head of Netzer David Yeshiva, and the Rabbi of Ohr Chadash Messianic Synagogue, with a PhD and ThD. He was born in Europe of Holocaust Survivor parents right after WWII.

We made contact, and on Friday May 22, 1992, we went to Clearwater, Florida, to talk it over. After we explained the history of our ministry, John understood very well and readily agreed to put us under the umbrella of his **Menorah Ministries**. "Financial involvement? None. Job description? None. You have been in ministry longer than I have. You know what you are doing; just do it." The mission and John did some paper work to satisfy everyone.

I was now free to follow the Lord's leading! I called my new ministry THE OLIVE TREE MESSAGE! Romans 11 is so clear that Jew and Gentile Believers are together in God's Good Olive Tree! It is wrong to separate them into Israel and the church. There is only one Family of God, Israel, with believing Gentiles grafted in! My Olive Tree Message begins with Genesis 1, to be sure we know what God we are talking about, and then encompasses all the Bible.

About that same time, a flight student from Israel was

learning his basics in southern Florida. He inquired around at different places as to where he could get the best advanced flight training. The answer was always, Ray Walkwitz in Ocala, Florida. Ray was a perfectionist in many things, so his flight instruction was the best. He would show his students a picture of our marginal airstrip on top of the mountain outside of Banaue in the Philippines and tell them he wanted to train them to be able to fly in and out of a strip like that. It was not straight, but had a "dog leg" in the middle, at 4,400 feet altitude, with a cross wind most of the time. Marginal? Definitely, Yes!

Dr. Avi Bar-Lev made arrangements to come to Walkwitz Flight School in Ocala. Carolyn picked him up at the Orlando airport. He had supper with all of us. Many years later, while visiting him and his wife in Israel in 2006, Avi told us that he was touched that a Gentile would treat him like family and care for his every need while training with Ray. Our friendship continues. Avi is a medical doctor as well, and does all the annual physicals for private pilots in Israel, in addition to a regular medical practice. He is a very busy, humble man. There has been no spiritual response yet, however.

The Messianic Jewish movement came out of hibernation as a result of the Six-Day War. We needed to get exposure to its varieties, as we were just getting involved. In the summer we attended the annual conference of the MJAA, the Messianic Jewish Alliance of America, at Messiah College in Pennsylvania. This is the largest organization, for individuals, and it is growing, with thousands attending. In August, we attended the annual conference of the UMJC, the Union of Messianic Jewish Congregations. This is also large, but for congregations or synagogues.

## Transition to Menorah Ministries

We also drove around Florida to visit the many Messianic congregations here. We offered our help to teach but no one responded, except for a Jewish couple in Ormond Beach. Even then, the leader of their synagogue made trouble for them for doing something outside of his jurisdiction, symptomatic of the old domineering clergy principle. We taught Friday evenings for an interested group at their place for several years.

People are the largest export of the Philippines. These Overseas Workers are also the largest US dollar earners for the Philippine economy, as they send a lot of money back home. When some from BIBAK do go overseas, we try to keep in touch with them for encouragement and continuing discipleship. Two young ladies who went to Canada asked me to stand in for their fathers, to walk down the aisle on my arm at their marriages to Canadian young men.

We drove to Ottawa, Ontario, to be at Mary Gumihid's wedding to Danny Parkes on October 10, 1992. There were many Filipinas there. It seems it is the young ladies that go abroad, while the young men marry and stay home. So it gave us another opportunity to disciple these who had been gone for some years. Everyone needs a spiritual push at times and a touch of God's love through someone.

Back in Florida, with our Israel experience, I persuaded a church in Gainesville to let me give a series of teachings in January on the Arab-Israel Conflict. With flyers printed, I went to the University of Florida Jewish Studies office to leave one, with a personal invitation. The director said that an expert from Israel was already teaching on that. The semester was just beginning, and I would be welcome to sit in! I did, and so a long friendship began with Yaacov and Ronit Bar-Siman-Tov from Hebrew

201

University, Jerusalem. They have a lovely home in a new suburb of Jerusalem, Mevasseret Zion, where we also have several friends, including the people from Home For Bible Translators.

Through that friendship, we met several more Israelis, who were either involved at UF or working temporarily in the US at their professions, which were mostly in the medical field. They have all returned to Israel now, so we visit them there! Israelis appreciate Gentiles for our pro-Israel position, because they have very few friends in the world. But when it comes to the Bible, they mostly do not want to talk about it.

The terrible persecution of the Jews by the Catholic Church and other Christians for centuries, and the horrors of the Holocaust are such huge stumbling blocks for them. It is only by the Spirit that the blindness will be removed. We can only do our part, to show them the love of the Messiah, and wait for Him to open the conversation into His Word.

We celebrated Passover in '93 with the Bible Study group in Ormond Beach. Then we flew with Ray and Carolyn to the Bahamas to do some teaching for a missionary there and to do a Passover demonstration. Passover seems to be the entry point to understand Yeshua and His Apostles in their context, without the changes the church made centuries ago.

By this time, Ray had moved his flight school to Arthur Dunn Airpark in Titusville, Florida. The administrators there really pushed him to move, as the terminal building was in bad shape without any aviation program going on. It now became Walkwitz Aviation, Inc. It was an expensive move and it separated us. We kept our grandsons for longer periods of time, as Naomi helped with their home schooling, when the pressure of business was such that Carolyn did not have the time to teach them. Even when they lived in Ocala, Naomi helped out many days and the boys stayed with us. In the end, we were thankful for this time with them, as they were snatched away from us too soon in the fiery plane crash in the Bahamas on March 22, 1998.

At Bryan College, I was the track coach. One of the team members was now a pastor of a rural Baptist Church in Michigan. Dave Marsteller phoned me one day to ask me to come to participate in a missionary conference. We went and enjoyed it very much. The congregation apparently liked me, so I was invited the next year to do a Bible conference. We agreed that I would teach on the Tabernacle from the book of Exodus for one week.

Months ahead, I started building my scale model of the Tabernacle that could fit in my van, or maybe the trunk of a large car. The scale this time was 1 centimeter = 1 cubit, a bit smaller than the one we made in Baguio (centimeter is less than half an inch). Since this was all from Exodus, we did a Passover demonstration complete with a kosher meal! It was not the 14th of Nisan, so we just called it a teaching demonstration. We have done this for several churches that are open to some teaching from the Hebrew Scriptures, and all have enjoyed it and learned a lot.

Another trip to Israel in '94 was helpful. We visited many of our Israeli friends and got their understanding of the situation in Israel. Each one tried to be optimistic, but felt "what else can we do but to give in to the demands of the world powers?" In this regard, the USA is not the real friend of Israel as it claims. Our relationship with

Israel is motivated more by self-interest, rather than the genuine needs of Israel and the position that God gives to Israel in His Word.

Also, the lies of the enemy against Israel that are promoted by a prejudiced media are believed by many, and foreign policies usually are strongly influenced by these lies. It is always a double standard against Israel. They can't win, no matter how much they give in to please the world. The leaders of Israel are just groping for solutions. They are not good solutions because these leaders do not have the spiritual strength that God gave to His leaders in the Bible. Spiritual blindness is still on our friends. But God promised that someday He would remove it, and for the nation as a whole. What a day that will be!

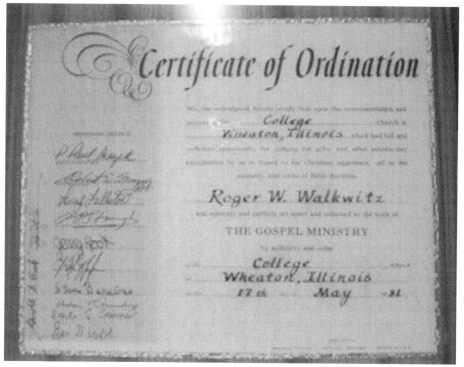

Ordination Certificate for Roger Walkwitz May 1981

Walkwitz sons 1981

Baguio BIBAK Center 1982

Naomi with her Bible Class Baguio City 1983

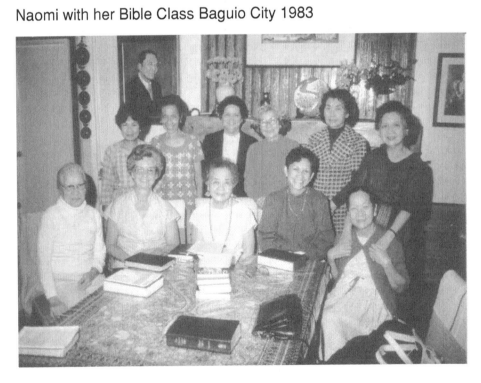

Roger & Naomi at Western Wall, Jerusalem 1990

Roger at Golden Dome in Jerusalem 1988

Roger and Naomi at Garden Tomb, Jerusalem 1990

Roger during Gulf War 1991

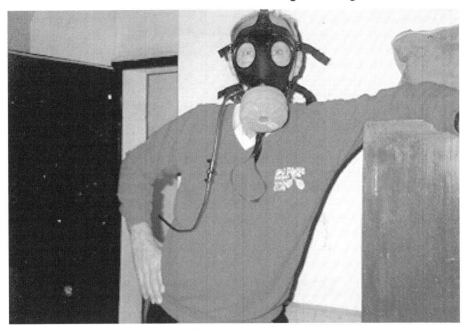

Roger with Jack and Alice Fitzwilliam 1998

Roger speaking at Messianic Synagogue in
Calgary, Alberta, Canada

BIBAK Team in Rehovot, Israel with Shmuel & Hananah 1999

BIBAKers in Israel

# CHAPTER 21

## The Olive Tree Message
## 1995–97

On September 1, 1994, I was enrolled in Medicare. On September 14, 1994, I reached my 65th birthday. That meant we would officially retire from our mission after 37 years of service and our salary would be stopped. Our IRA would be invested somewhere with the income meant to supplement our Social Security. While talking over details, the US director asked what we preferred for our award for our 35 years of service - rings with the mission logo on it or watches? We chose watches. These "milestones" are awarded in 5-year increments at each Annual Conference in the US.

The next Annual Conference was in July 1995. It was special as it was the 50th anniversary of the beginning of the mission by GIs at the end of WWII. All the messages and activities were enjoyable. Then came the last evening event when the general director gives out the "milestone" awards with pertinent comments. Starting with 5 years, the counting got up to 25 years - and stopped. I should have shouted, "Wait a minute! Where is our 35 year award?" But I did not. I just swallowed hard and asked afterward, "what happened?"

Somehow, the office just "forgot" about us, again. That hurt. The conference was over, except for breakfast and a short prayer meeting, during which, we were told, the error was announced. But most of the people and we had already left. That was the last time we had anything to do with this mission. It had failed to meet us upon our first arrival in the Philippines, put obstacles in our way as we tried to obey the Lord's Calling upon us, and did not give us credit for all the accomplishments and service of 37 years.

But the Lord knows all about it, and He knows that we were not working for honors or awards, but that we were serving Him and enjoying all that we were doing. Maybe someday He will say, "Well done, good and faithful servant." However, everyone likes and needs to be appreciated in some way. The LORD does that very well. He uses His written Word and the love and appreciation expressed by many of our disciples.

We were now part of Menorah Ministries with **The Olive Tree Message!** What is The Olive Tree Message? It is taken from Romans 11. God through Paul is speaking to believing Gentiles with a clear message not to be proud against Jewish people, thinking that they, the Gentiles, have replaced Israel in God's good olive tree. On the Jewish calendars that I buy each year, this summary of Romans 11 is printed at the bottom:

*"I am speaking to you Gentiles…if some of the (Jewish) branches were broken off (because of unbelief), and you, being a wild olive, were grafted in among them (Jewish Believers), and became a partaker of the root and fatness of the(ir) olive tree (since you also Trust in Yeshua), boast not against the branches. But if you do boast, remember it is not you that supports the*

*root, but the root supports you."*

There is much to learn from this illustration that God gives. The good olive tree represents the <u>one family</u> of God, composed of both Jewish Believers and Gentile Believers. Gentiles have come from their wild olive tree, which is not part of the family of God. When a Gentile is saved, God takes him out of the wild olive tree and grafts him, contrary to nature, into His good olive tree. The Gentile does not replace anyone, but joins with Jewish Believers in Yeshua. Harmony is expected to prevail. The lifestyle is the Torah lifestyle, which the Jew has grown up with.

The newly saved Gentile is expected to adjust and adopt the Torah lifestyle, which is the only lifestyle ever given by God. The life-giving nourishment from the root that causes growth is distributed equally to natural and engrafted branches. Branches that do not grow and produce fruit are broken off, by pruning, whether originally Jewish or Gentile engrafted branches. God reserves the right to engraft back Jewish branches that originally were broken off, when the Jewish person becomes a Believer.

These facts were quite an eye-opener to me when I realized that the mainline churches, maybe all churches, had the idea that they had replaced Israel, or that somehow there were two olive trees, Israel and the church. And for centuries, the church has tried to make Jewish people into gentilized Christians, forcing them to leave their Torah lifestyle, as if the church is the wild olive tree! And maybe it is!

To illustrate, Ray and Carolyn were attending the large evangelical Presbyterian Church in Ocala. Joshua was in the pre-school program there. Israel was never mentioned in the Sunday messages, so they asked to meet with the large pastoral staff. The conclusion came out that, yes, they believe in Replacement Theology. The church has replaced Israel in the plan of God and the church now inherits all the blessings promised to Israel. Of course all the curses were still upon Israel. If Ray and Carolyn could not accept this, they were asked not to come to the church anymore.

Ray and Carolyn looked in the Yellow Pages and decided to attend the Grace Brethren church. After some time, when Passover was approaching, a young couple in the church, the husband a Gentile Believer and the wife a Jewish Believer, were invited by the parents of the wife to join them for Passover. The husband had never done that and wondered if he should attend. So he asked the pastor. The pastor told them, especially the wife, that they were Christians now and could forget all that Jewish stuff! What heresy!

Both churches are way off the biblical Foundation, but are typical of all the rest. Our job became more clear and urgent - to wake people up to Bible Truth! However, we found that very, very few people that we met in the USA were interested in Bible study. They were happy in their comfort zone of church tradition. Their attitude seemed to be, "Don't confuse me with the facts!"

Another big eye-opener for us was the symbol used for Christianity. Every church that I have seen displays a cross very prominently. Is the cross really God's designated symbol for His people? The message of the cross in the Bible is basic to the message of salvation. Without the cross and what Yeshua accomplished on it, the message of salvation would be incomplete. Yeshua's sacrificial death and burial are essential factors, but the resurrection is THE essential factor! Anyone can die, but only God can rise like He did.

The Roman Catholics display the cross very prominently. But they leave Jesus still hanging there on the cross. The resurrection is not stressed in their teachings. The Catholics have used the cross as a weapon to conquer many people around the world, especially in South America and the Philippines. The cross came in with Constantine. When he was fighting to become the next emperor of the Roman Empire, he supposedly had a vision of a cross, where he was told, "In this sign you will conquer!" So he put the cross on the shields of his army. He also issued the Edict of Milan in 311, making Christianity the legal religion in his area of the Empire. Therefore, many Christians joined his army. He was able to defeat his challengers and become the sole Emperor. As far as we have found in our studies, this is the time when the cross began to be used as a symbol for Christianity. Before that, it was the fish.

We cannot find the cross being used anywhere in the Bible as a symbol for God's people. So is there a symbol that God has designated in the Bible for His people? Yes, there is. Look at Revelation 1:20:

*"The mystery of the seven stars which you saw in my right hand, and the seven golden lampstands; the seven stars are the messengers of the seven ekklesiai and the seven lampstands which you saw are the seven ekklesiai or Messianic Communities."*

Lampstand = *Menorah* in Hebrew. The *Menorah* is here clearly designated as THE Symbol of His people! The *Menorah* is used today as the symbol of the State of Israel.

A large *Menorah,* donated by Great Britain, stands on the grounds of the Knesset, Israel's Parliament building in Jerusalem, the Capital. The *Menorah* is also the symbol used by Messianic Communities. No cross is ever used by a Messianic Community, as it is a symbol of death. On the other hand, the *Menorah* is a symbol of life and light; it is God's symbol.

This history and the use of the *Menorah* is a basic part of The Olive Tree Message! In our Logo, notice that the *Menorah* is central with the Hebrew letters for Yeshua above the *Menorah* where the flames would be. Yeshua is The Light of the world while we, His Disciples, are the "light holders," the *Menorah.*

We carried on with a few teaching opportunities around the USA and then were off to Baguio City again for the 25$^{th}$ Anniversary of BIBAK. These are occasions when some who have drifted away from the Lord come back, admit their failures and renew their commitment to Him. They realize the blessings of "the good old days" of being in fellowship with God and His people as they participated with BIBAK. It also seems that when "sir and ma'am" arrive, everyone perks up, eager for anything we have to teach them, especially on Israel. What a blessing this is for us!

When we left the Philippines this time, we went to Japan to teach for five days, in Tokyo and Sendai, for the Japan Messianic Fellowship! This was in November 1996, a first for us. Many months before, I had received in the mail a general letter informing people about the activities of this new venture, the Japan Messianic Fellowship led by Takashi Yokoyama. Since we could stop over in Japan on our way from the Philippines, I wrote to Takashi and offered my teaching if I could be of any help to him.

He was very happy about that, so we made plans to meet at the Tokyo airport and then follow whatever schedule he had arranged. He had me teaching on the Arab-Israel Conflict, the Olive Tree Message, the Tabernacle, and anti-Semitism, from 9:30 AM to 8:00 PM. These were subjects that I was prepared for at any time. Of course, he had a translator for me at each place! I enjoyed the Japanese food, but Naomi was just OK about it. Chopsticks are not for her. Thankfully, I had learned how to use them when I was in high school.

Back home in Florida, Naomi went north to be with Randy and Janie for the birth of their first child, Jake Ronald Walkwitz on June 5, 1997, the same date that our first son Ray was born in 1958! She said that Jake was "just perfect, so sweet!" Aren't all babies like that?

With an invitation for a Reception at the Ambassador's residence, I headed back to the Philippines for Israel's 49th Independence Day celebration. In the Philippines we could participate, while in Israel we were just bystanders! Ambassador Amos Shetibel stayed for 5 years, so I got to know him quite well. At the reception, I also met the rabbi for the congregation, the first one that I can remember being there. He is from Israel and speaks several languages, so I was told, but was only learning English now. This is essential for the Philippines. Before that, I had been in Baguio for several weeks, teaching to the various groups, especially the Luncheon Bible Study at the Baguio Country Club.

While I was back home in Florida again, Takashi informed me that he was coming with a small group to stay with us in our Guest House for several days to study the Tabernacle. He learned that we had made the model, which would help their learning. The second house near us that we bought was specifically for this purpose as a Bible Study Center. Using both bedrooms and the living room hide-a-beds, we can sleep eight people. Besides Japanese, we have had Indonesians, Filipinos, and Americans stay with us, some for study, some for a respite from the cold north. Although the house is fully equipped, Naomi fixed all the meals for the Japanese at our house, American-style meals for the most part.

There is a Hillel Jewish Student Center right near the University of Florida campus, 35 miles north of us. The rabbi at this time, Jerry Friedman, had classes in the middle of the day for community members. I joined the classes whenever I was home and able, as this Rabbi was a good teacher and welcomed Gentiles like me. Coming from Brooklyn, his first language was Hebrew, so he knew it well; his second was Yiddish and his third was English. His English was very good.

When we are in the US or in Israel, we participate in the celebration of the Appointed Times of the Lord, sometimes with the Jewish people. Shortly before *Shavuot* (Pentecost), the Rabbi invited me to join their all-night Torah study, which is the way they celebrate Shavuot.

Jews have calculated that the tribes of Israel reached Mt. Sinai about the time of *Shavuot*, or Feast of Weeks, and received the Ten Commandments at that time. Therefore, to celebrate it, they study Torah all night, with some snacks and coffee! I joined them and found it interesting. We as a family have joined their other celebrations as well, for the purpose of learning and being a blessing and witness to the Jewish people.

A few years back, a New Tribes missionary whom we had known in the Philippines learned that we were retired but still active this time, now in Jewish type ministry. Angie Brunemeier put us in touch with their missionary in Bolivia who had a tremendous ministry to Israeli backpackers as they travelled the world after their army service. How it developed through friendliness is an interesting story by itself.

Bob and Joyce Wilhelmson were not thinking of starting such a ministry. The Lord just dumped it onto their laps. Traveling Israelis learned about them from logbooks kept at Embassies and sporting goods stores. They phoned the Wilhelmsons when they got to Cochabamba, Bolivia, and came to their home at the agreed upon time. There they looked at picture books of all the ones who came before them to see if any of their friends had been there.

Then they watched a slide show of the NTM Gospel work among the primitive tribes people. After that, they were served an Israeli type supper, which they enjoyed very much, like a touch from home! After supper they had a 2-hour Bible study on the prophecies and fulfillments about the first coming of Jesus The Messiah. The teaching is in English but the readings are all in the Hebrew Bibles that they have available.

The Wilhelmsons were getting older, with some ailments, and were looking for a replacement. Since we had been corresponding, they asked us if we might be interested. Of course I was, but had my doubts if it would work out. However, they invited me to come down to observe anyway. In November 1997, I spent two weeks with them and enjoyed it very much. It would be a very fulfilling ministry. They were averaging about 1,000 Israeli visitors per year! There needed to be some way to follow up on these contacts. We did not know any Spanish either, so living there would be difficult.

It did not work out for us, but the Lord provided another NT missionary couple to take over, a younger couple. Blessings on them! We are sure that some Israelis eventually came to trust in Yeshua, because the questions they asked indicated they were beginning to see the Light. The Bible passages in Hebrew were truths that they were seeing for the very first time only.

However, we learned in 2008 that this couple also had some health issues and had to quit. No replacement could be found, so the ministry stopped. That is sad! It would be wonderful if we could move to Israel, find a location in Israel for a Center like we had in the Philippines, to continue this Bible teaching ministry to these open young people and any others that came along, using the School of Tyrannus pattern. We know of a lot of ministries in Israel and most of them are doing something worthwhile, but are only partly on the Foundation of Yeshua and the Apostles. Most are still "church on Saturday" in the clergy–laity format, so that discipling and the whole Body working together are still not there.

# CHAPTER 22

## Tragedy Strikes
## March 22, 1998

We drove up to Plymouth, Michigan, to participate in another weeklong Missionary Conference. Thankfully, my part was mostly on the first day, Sunday, March 22. We were invited for a lunch and Bible study with a businessman the next day. The church had put us in a motel for the weekend, since the ladies were winding up their Retreat on Saturday and would not be prepared for guests until Monday. Monday morning, the lady that was to host us had come to the motel to give us directions and a key to her house.

While we visited, the motel clerk came to tell me that two men wanted to talk to me, so I went with them to a seminar room. They asked who I was and if Ray and Carolyn Walkwitz were related to me. I said, yes. Then they handed me a dispatch from the US Embassy in Nassau, Bahamas. It said, "Raymond, Carolyn, Joshua, and Benjamin Walkwitz had perished in a flaming plane crash Sunday evening at 5:10 PM on Eleuthera Island, Bahamas.

Two others were with them in the plane. There were no survivors."

Whew! I just bowed my head in my arms on the table and talked with my Lord, not crying or making any sound, and thanking the Lord for taking them Home to be with Him. It had to be His will. I was just too shocked. Soon Naomi came in, as the hostess had left and the clerk said the men wanted to talk to both of us. Naomi looked at me. She later said that I was as white as a sheet. She asked, "What's wrong?" I told her, and she quietly left the room and went to our own room.

The men were plainclothes detectives from the local police department. They offered any help that they could give, but I said, thanks, we will just depart right away and drive back to Florida to take over Walkwitz Aviation, Inc. and do what is needed for the bodies. The motel offered the use of their telephone toll free to take care of notifications. Our would-be hostess was called back and the church sent some people to comfort us and help as needed.

The Lord gave us strength and calmness, so that I think we comforted them more than they did us. I notified our family and Carolyn's family, who really took the news very hard. Everyone thought that we ought to fly back as they thought we could not possibly drive back with this news to handle. No way! How would we get our van back home? We were perfectly OK in the hands of Yeshua, our Lord and friend.

It took two days to drive back home first, then over to Titusville and the business on Wednesday. All the employees wanted to continue working for us. Ray had asked in his Will that I would continue his aviation business. Ron was not working at the time, so I made him the General Manager. He had been working with Ray for a while and he knew something about the business. I took over as President and Treasurer, got the bank accounts changed over and began paying bills and payroll.

A contact with the largest church in town resulted in their offer to host the Memorial Service Friday evening free of charge and to video the service. The tragic news had been on Orlando TV for two nights and in the newspapers. They gave out the news of the Memorial Service, so we knew we would have a big crowd. In addition, Ray was well known all around as a very honest businessman, an excellent pilot and flight instructor.

The cause of the crash is still an unsolved mystery. Our other two sons, together with Dave Hotham, a friend of Ray's who flew over from the UK when he heard the news, chartered a plane and flew over to Eleuthera Island to view the crash site and identify the charred bodies. The other two in the crash were pilot friends of Ray from Europe. They came every year for update training. Ray made many flights to the Bahamas, one of the specialties he offered. This time, Ray borrowed a Beechcraft Baron, a six-seater, since all of his fleet of planes had been booked by his other customers. He had flown this plane for the owner before and knew that the maintenance had not been the best.

A typical clergy-led memorial service would not do. As Ray's father, I knew I had to be the one to do it. People would want to know what motivated Ray & Carolyn to be so hospitable, to be so honest in business, to be joyful, as their testimony by life was quite widespread. Several friends gave eulogies; Ron, Randy, and Naomi gave testimonies; and I gave the message.

I wanted to explain that we were born into God's Family by the New Birth and that there was a Way to live as His children, to Love God first of all by obedience to Him, and then to love our neighbor. I said that we believe the Bible exactly, including Creation, and we seek to live by it. God is real and that there is no happening outside His control, including this plane crash, terrible and tragic as it was. As promised in the Bible, Ray, Carolyn, Josh and Ben are "present with their Lord." We will join them eventually. The crash was terrible, but not a tragedy as the world counts tragedy. "The Lord gave and the Lord has taken away. Blessed be the Name of the LORD."

From the Program for the **Memorial Service:** This text was written one year before the accident and printed in the Faith Academy Newsletter. The editor had asked Ray about himself and his business, so part of what he wrote is quoted in this Newsletter.

\* \* \* \* \* \* \* \* \* \* \* \*

Like many kids, Ray Walkwitz loved airplanes when he was growing up but thought he could never fly because he wore glasses and the training was too expensive! His parents were missionaries with SEND Intl. in the Philippines. Ray attended Faith Academy along with his brothers, Randy and Ron.

Ray attended Wheaton College, where he met his wife, Carolyn. Her parents were missionaries in Ecuador where Ray and Carolyn honeymooned. On the way back, they traveled through Florida, and liked it so well that they decided to settle there.

# Tragedy Strikes

Ray transferred to the University of Florida as a history major and got into flying.

Ray and Carolyn now own Walkwitz Aviation, Inc. in Titusville, Florida. "We have been in business for 9 ½ years and have about 16 employees and 10 airplanes that we use for flight instruction and rental. We are a full service Fixed Base Operation, offering fuel, maintenance, pilot supplies, aircraft tie down, and pilot training, which is our main service. We even offer fully furnished apartments to our students.

"We specialize in advanced and especially multi-engine training. We look forward to the occasional missionary pilot in training from various mission organizations around the world.

"My purpose in business is to operate according to Biblical principles, as I learn and understand them, and to be a blessing and witness to those that work here and those students/renters who come here from literally all over the world (half come from overseas). It is my prayer that this business will be pleasing to God and bring honor and glory to Him. I feel that the Bible is our total handbook for operation of our lives, not only personal, but also as work in business. Christianity is a walk that should permeate our total lives. We also are called to be witnesses and to make disciples. I grew up wanting to be a missionary bush pilot; however, since the world is coming to us, I haven't had to go anywhere to do this.

"Trying to operate Biblically has been very difficult, mainly because the employees that we've had over the years have not been interested in spiritual things. Several have been very antagonistic because of our Biblical stand and have literally tried to destroy the business. I have been really blessed in the last few months with the most wonderful staff that I have ever had! Over half are believers now, and several eagerly look forward to a prayer/bible study meeting held almost every day. I must say that I am the one who has really benefited from the whole experience and grown in so many ways.

"My wife, Carolyn, has helped in the business for many years. She is currently home-schooling, full time, our two boys, Joshua and Ben who are 11 and 8 years old."

Ray Walkwitz for Faith News
Winter 1997

* * * * * * * * * * * *

## Memorial Service

Raymond D. Walkwitz
June 5, 1958 - March 22, 1998
Carolyn F.(Moore) Walkwitz
February 24, 1958 - March 22, 1998
Joshua Nathaniel Walkwitz
March 2, 1986 - March 22, 1998
Benjamin Moshe Walkwitz
May 11, 1989 - March 22, 1998

"Absent from the body;          Temple Baptist Church
Present with the LORD!"              Titusville, FL
2 Corinthians 5:8                    March 27, 1998

Ray Carolyn Josh and Ben Walkwitz 1994

Ben Walkwitz looking ahead 1996

Ray with favorite airplane at Titusville FBO 1997

Remains of plane that Ray & Family perished in March 22, 1998

Florida Today March 24, 1998

1998 Gravestone Front

Naomi and I flew over on American Airlines to authorize the cremation of the four bodies, burned beyond recognition except by those who knew them well. We stayed with friends of Randy in Nassau and then brought the ashes back with us. Burial was in a small do-it-yourself cemetery in Morriston. An appropriate headstone was made as a testimony to their lives, with a brief biography carved on the backside.

Walkwitz Aviation, Inc. was practically bankrupt when we took over because the bookkeeper had stolen over $40,000 from Ray. It was discovered shortly before Ray's death and she was fired, but she got away with it in court because Ray was not there to testify against her. Nevertheless, the Lord was watching over us as we built the business up with a frugal operation and took no salary myself.

As the months went on, we came to the conclusion that running the business was just work. We could not replace Ray. He was the core of the business. We had other more important things to do, like our teaching ministry in the Asia Pacific region. So we decided to sell now that we were making a small profit. When we did, we thought about what we would do with our half of the profit after all bills were paid. Carolyn's parents got the other half.

We each got $36,000. The business represented Ray's life work. We should spend it for something in line with what he would like. We could not keep it for ourselves. Ray and Carolyn both loved Bible education and Israel. We decided to take a group of faithful Bible teachers from BIBAK to Israel for three weeks, all expenses paid. Two weeks will be an organized Tour by the Institute of Holy Land Studies. The third week, we will rent two vans and a car to visit some of our friends and other places. We took fourteen from BIBAK. With Naomi, Ron, and myself, we were seventeen in all.

We termed these fourteen the <u>Living Memorial to Ray and Family</u>. One highlight of the third week was staying overnight in the homes of Israelis living on Moshav Kanaf on the Golan Heights, arranged by our friends, Ilan & Ruhama Matalon. We also had a *Shabbat* with an Orthodox rabbi who had come to faith in Yeshua while in Miami and brought his whole congregation to Israel.

They established a Kibbutz in the southern desert, which was flourishing until some radical ultra-orthodox Jews forced the government to cut off their water supply. Soon all the orchards died and the people were forced to go elsewhere to find work. The corrupt government in Israel tolerates this kind of harassment and persecution. Only Rabbi Simcha Pearlmutter and his wife were left. For Shabbat, others would come from around the area to celebrate with him. His eldest son was in the IDF. A homicide bomber sat next to him on a bus in the Hadera station and blew himself up, killing many people. So Simcha empathized with us in the death of Ray, our eldest son. Simcha himself died two years later with pancreatic cancer.

"What are you doing to decorate your heavenly home?" This was part of a newsletter from the Pacific Garden Mission in Chicago, as we opened a pile of mail, our usual task upon our return from travels. We may have thought about that, sometime. What made it more interesting was that my Dad, Clarence Walkwitz, spent many Saturdays at PGM mission talking to people about Jesus. Although a Protestant churchgoer all his life, he had not come to faith in

Jesus until he was forty eight years old. So he had a zeal to help others who also had not understood what they might have heard in churches, if the Gospel had been explained or if they had gone to church at all.

We knew also that Dad and Mom, and now Ray and family had decorated their heavenly homes and were enjoying them with Yeshua and all the rest of The Family up there. We also were very happy that Naomi's sister, Kennetha, had finally come to faith in Jesus and was now working for PGM. She was writing scripts for their radio program called "Unshackled!" which is about people being delivered from the shackles of sin by the Lord Jesus the Messiah.

During this time, we heard about the First Fruits of Zion, a Messianic Jewish organization that was developing teaching materials and holding seminars about the Hebraic or Jewish Roots of Christianity. These Roots showed a distinct difference from what the church has been teaching for many centuries. They were not the only group doing this, but we read about their seminar in Denver called "The Letter Writer," about Paul the Apostle.

Since Naomi's sister Kennetha and family lived nearby in Colorado Springs, we decided to make the trip and visit them as well as attend the seminar. We learned a lot and met some of the FFOZ personnel, particularly Tim Hegg, who was a good communicator with good content. We also learned of their 14-lesson study called *HaYesod, The Foundation*, excellent lessons on the foundational truths that the Messianic Communities were built upon in the first century. Dave Angiwan, a BIBAK Elder in Baguio, asked me to teach this the next time I came to the Philippines. I decided to check it out by teaching it first here in Florida for a few interested people. We found it to be very good and have adjusted our teaching and practice accordingly, and added some of our own learning.

# Tragedy Strikes

The Elders of BIBAK asked us to come back to help them celebrate their 30th Anniversary in September 2001, and do some more teaching. These are always a blessing, to see disciples maturing and making more disciples. This time my teaching would be the *HaYesod* program. This became an eye opener to some. Others resisted the implications, thinking, "Have we been wrong all these years on certain things by following church Tradition? Where and when did these Traditions come from? Some teachings and practices seem to be clearly in violation of Scripture."

No one had heard the truth about why and when *Shabbat* was changed to Sunday, something we ourselves learned only in recent years. The evidence is available, but clergy are comfortable in their positions, and saw no need to bring up such things? Those clergy that know the Truth willingly keep their congregations in the dark. What deceit, what hypocrisy! It reveals the total abdication of responsibility to learn the Truth by everyone claiming to be a Believer, by learning only what the clergy teaches them without doing any research themselves. We had determined early on to teach everyone all the Truth that we knew, and keep it up. We never pretend we know everything, and we correct errors when discovered.

To complicate matters, a few years earlier, the mission had assigned a couple under questionable reasons to work with BIBAK in Baguio. BIBAK welcomed the help at first, but things turned out differently. This couple tried to undo much of what we had done, and the Elders resisted. Thankfully, we had given BIBAK a constitution that limited non-mountaineers to associate membership with no vote and no office. Even then, the man joined with the Elders all the time, trying to influence them against us and our principles.

Mountaineers are very gracious. So although they did not rebuke him, they did not follow his ideas either. His wife was good with the music program, so the couple was tolerable for that reason. At the end of their 4-year term, the mission asked for the usual evaluation. The BIBAK congregation gave a negative report. That should have ended their career in the mountains as well as in the Philippines.

However, a year later the mission re-assigned them to Baguio to start another church for mountaineers! This couple was claiming that "there was no church in the area that met the needs of the mountaineers." What a lie! BIBAK already had four churches for mountaineers in the area! Preposterous! They were not able to destroy BIBAK from the inside, so now they would start another church to try to destroy BIBAK from the outside! As deceitful politicians, they lied to the BIBAK people about their new assignment while they were preparing the groundwork for this new church. They did their best to hire away some of the BIBAK-trained men for leadership and entice BIBAK members to come with them. A few did, for selfish reasons, mainly money. So what is their point?

Such a display of perverted "Christian" Ethics should never happen, and never will happen from us. The mission has lost its credibility. At first, BIBAK was blamed for being mostly students, then it was honored as a model for church planting, and now it is being criticized for sticking to its original no-clergy stance. This couple even tried to entice BIBAK to hire a lowland pastor, who wanted a nice house, a car, and a big salary. BIBAK flatly said, "No Way!" They don't have these things themselves. Events like this only confirm my opposition to the clergy system. It is basically wrong, even though there are some good people in it who just do not know that it is wrong! They have been deceived by Tradition.

# Tragedy Strikes

After the anniversary celebration, we went to Banaue to do some teaching. There is a nice hotel there now, and this is where we usually stay. There was none when we used to live there. One of our early disciples, Butch Sarol, is the controller of the hotel. As I walked out of the dining room one evening about 8 PM, a foreigner walked in the door carrying a gallon jug of water, something we all take with us when we travel. I said "Hi" and asked where he was from. He said, "Israel!" I responded with a few Hebrew expressions to welcome him to Banaue! We joined his family in the lobby, as they had just arrived. Soon we had a firm invitation to visit them in Taipei, where Meir Lavi managed a branch of an Israeli hi-tech firm.

Since they arrived after dark, they asked if we could show them around the next morning. My teaching was scheduled for the evening, so we agreed. We took them up to the View Point where the whole valley of rice fields can be seen. It is an amazing sight, the largest terraced rice paddy in the world.

Mary Namulngo, George's widow, was living there in a makeshift hut since her previous hut had burned down. I took the Lavi family to visit her. They were amazed to see on a bare plywood wall twelve pictures of Israel, from the calendar I had given her the previous year. They found that at this "end of the world" place, many people knew about and prayed for Israel, the result of teaching the Bible and bringing in current events about Israel.

"Every Believer should be ready at a moment's notice to preach, pray, or pass away." This is one of the sayings I have when I teach people. This hit home to our Filipino friends again, when one of the participants in our BIBAK Trip to Israel died of injuries suffered in a vehicular accident. He was a well-liked, honest elementary school principal.

Someone had sponsored a trip for a dozen such principals during summer vacation. On the highway, a truck plowed into their bus and killed four of them.

We happened to be in Baguio at the time of the first anniversary of his death, so I was invited to speak to the teachers and pupils in an assembly at his school, about the new life in Jesus that Eugene had lived before them. I explained that they could have that kind of life now by believing what the Bible says about Jesus and accepting Him as their Lord and Savior. Then they would have the assurance of eternal life, which Eugene is enjoying right now.

A regular practice of mine is to go to the Embassy of Israel when in Manila to keep up our friendship with the Embassy Staff and the current Ambassador. We want them to know that here are some Gentile Believers in Yeshua the Messiah who love Israel and Jews everywhere. We tell them we are your friends and ask if there is anything we can do for them. Sometimes there are things they can do for us that benefit them as well. The Ambassador this time was a lady, Irit Ben-Abba. I phoned and made an appointment to meet her.

When I arrived, after going through security, she brought me into her office, said "Hi," and asked me, "How do you know Asher Goffer? He has been calling and wants to see you." I told her that he was the security for Ambassador Dr. Uri Gordon when the two of them came to Baguio some years ago and spoke at BIBAK. I had lost track of Asher. She said he is now in business in Manila and heard through the Embassy security personnel that I was here in town and coming to the Embassy. "Just a minute, I will get him on the phone for you."

# Tragedy Strikes

Wow, what an introduction! Asher had been impressed with us in Baguio, had thought of us often, and now wanted to see us again. We made an appointment for supper that evening. Then I sat down to get acquainted with Irit Ben-Abba. She was still a fairly young divorcee, with a 10-year-old son, and probably an atheist. I assured her that we were very pro-Israel and all of our congregations in Baguio and the mountains were the same. I asked, as I usually do, if we could have our picture together with the flag of Israel. The security had kept my camera, so she told them to bring it in. I was not a terrorist! We had our picture. I would see her again several times, and keep in touch by email.

On our way back home to the US, Naomi went on ahead while I stopped by Japan to do some more Seminars for the Japan Messianic Fellowship. This time it was 10 short Seminars in 10 different towns in 10 days! This was my third time to have this privilege. Usually my Seminars in Japan have been for congregation leaders, but this time everyone was able to come. Their interest was intense and their questions, very good. They asked me to come again. I promised I would as Yeshua opens the doors. Then I proceeded to Wheaton to enjoy the 50th Class Reunion of my Wheaton College class of '51. As usual, they were getting older all the time, and a lot of them were now missing. I wondered how many more reunions would I be attending?

# CHAPTER 23

## Asia Pacific Messianic Fellowship
## 2002 Onward

Takashi Yokoyama had been contacted by email by a person in the southern Philippines who wanted him to come to teach them, since he was the head of the Japan Messianic Fellowship. This person had been searching the Internet for a Messianic teacher in the region, and Takashi was the only one he could find at the time. Takashi was very busy at that time; and so he passed the request on to me, knowing I go to the Philippines anyway.

I went and found that the family and a few others had been kicked out of their church for celebrating Passover! Their Seventh Day Church of God meets on Saturdays but would not do the other Appointed Times of the LORD from Leviticus 23. The family found this inconsistent. So they did Passover on their own. Now they felt like orphans, like they are the only ones like this.

I assured them that they were not alone. Ever since the Six-Day War, the Messianic movement of going back to the basics of Yeshua and the Apostles was growing worldwide among Jews and Gentiles. After spending a few days to encourage and teach them some basics, I went to Baguio. Naomi had gone ahead. I taught for a week, and then went to Banaue to teach for a week. After that, I went down to Manila and later , went on to Singapore.

In 1985, we had passed by Singapore for a few days. Our host at that time had since gone to Chad as a missionary, but was home for a while and asked us to come to Singapore for a visit again. I told Evelyn that if I could do some teaching, especially on Jewish Roots, in addition to visiting the country, I would be happy to come. She asked her former pastor, who was now a college professor, regarding this. Paul Tan had left the pastorate as he began to see defects in the clergy and church system and was now searching for the original Jewish Roots of the Apostles. He was very happy to have us come to teach *HaYesod*.

Before leaving Manila, I asked Ambassador Irit Ben-Abba to arrange a meeting for us with the Ambassador of Israel in Singapore, for Paul's team and us. She did and we had a lovely meeting at the Embassy. Ambassador Itzhak Shoham was happy to know of these Gentile Christians in Singapore that he could depend on to back Israel if he needed any locally. The team was also welcome to avail of the Embassy if there was anything that they could help them with. We had a lovely picture of all of us, by the flag.

Paul Tan assembled 40 selected pastors who he knew were also searching. We studied all-day for the three days following Palm Sunday. Thursday was Passover, so we did a *Seder* for the group to learn. Friday we had a meal to welcome *Shabbat*. On Easter Sunday, I spoke in the evening service at a large Anglican Church. We felt creepy with all the religious stuff around. After I taught, the pastors got a happy-happy speaking tongues extravaganza going. We just sat tight. We did some shopping on Monday and flew back to Manila on Tuesday.

On Wednesday, we flew to Taipei to spend some days with the Lavi family whom we had met in Banaue. We had promised to come, so we came. We especially appreciated going to the Chinese Museum and seeing the ancient oracle writing, as it is called, on tortoise shells and inside of brass urns. In Singapore, we were given a book that explained this ancient China writing and information, as being close to ancient Hebrew writing and information, indicating a close connection of ancient Chinese to Israel. However, we did not realize the significance of this until we read the book later on.

The eldest son of the Lavi's was to turn thirteen the next week, just after we left Taipei. He would be having his *Bar Mitzvah* at the Synagogue. We had attended a couple of *Bar Mitzvahs* so we knew what he was expected to do. I asked him what *Torah* or *Haftarah* passage he would be reading. He told me and read it for me in Hebrew, as Hebrew is his first language, but not necessarily biblical Hebrew. He was supposed to explain it a bit, so we talked about it. Later on he told me privately that he did not believe a word of the Bible. He was doing this only for Tradition's sake and for the family. This is so sad, but quite typical of Israeli families.

A *Bar Mitzvah*, meaning "son of the commandment," is a ceremony when a boy turns thirteen and is then considered an adult, responsible for himself. A *Bat Mitzvah*, '"daughter of the commandment," is for girls when they turn twelve.

We have since spent time with the Lavis in Israel. They are back home now for their sons' schooling, with the eldest now in the army. They also keep in touch by email. There has been no spiritual opening yet, however.

Flying back to Manila on China Airlines, the pilot announced, "We thank you for frying with us. We hope you fry with us again." We might! We then headed up to Baguio for several weeks of teaching and for the wedding of Leah Angiwan to Honor Salayao on May 4, 2002. Leah is the first child of Dave and Mancy, our very close associates in the ministry. The previous year, we had promised to be there. It was a lovely wedding, with some native dancing after the ceremony in the large gymnasium that they had rented for the occasion.

With this flurry of travel around the Asia Pacific area, teaching groups of Believers wanting to return to the Roots of biblical faith and practice, and seeing how they thought they were alone in this endeavor, I began to get an idea from the Lord of a central Bible Conference to include them all. We would find a good Messianic Jewish Bible teacher. Participants would learn a lot from the Bible and have fellowship with others from far and wide and be encouraged. They would also learn what the Lord was doing in this regard in Israel, the USA, and other countries of the world, bringing Jews and Gentiles back to their Roots.

Thus began ASIA PACIFIC MESSIANIC FELLOWSHIP. We would not make it a denomination. It would not control any congregations. It would not be clergy-centered! It would be for teaching the Word and historical backgrounds. It would be a Fellowship of like-minded Believers in Yeshua the Messiah who wanted to live as He and His Apostles lived, in obedience to His commands.

First of all, we would sponsor a Bible Conference in Baguio City. Where? The best place was the Conference Center of the Asia Pacific Theological Seminary of the Assembly of God, located on a lovely campus just outside of Baguio. Out there, we could breathe clean air and drink clean water from the faucet, both not possible in Baguio! We reserved their available dates, June 3-9, 2003, and made a deposit.

Who would we get to be the Bible teacher? John Fischer was not available. Tim Hegg was not available. These were the only two good ones that we knew at the time. What about the writer of *HaYesod* and the books, *Torah Rediscovered* and *Take Hold*? Ariel Berkowitz writes well. Maybe he can also teach well. Where could I find him? I never want to invite any person without first having met him personally. We were told that he was not in the USA at that time. He and his family were in Israel. But even if I had his phone number, a call would not do. We had to meet to see if the Lord gives His approval. We decided we would go to Israel later to find him.

We left Manila for Los Angeles and rented a car. We first drove to Glendale, Arizona, and visited Randy and the family for a couple weeks. Then we spent two weeks driving up California, Oregon, and Washington to visit friends who were mostly from BIBAK and former missionaries. It was Memorial Day weekend, when we drove north from California to Oregon. Suddenly, I noticed that the yellow line on the highway was jagged. We went to the emergency room of a hospital to have my eyes checked. The right one was OK, but the left one had a blot to the left of the center vision. <u>Macular Degeneration, the wet kind, had occurred</u>!

They could do nothing at the hospital for me. By Tuesday after Memorial Day, I was able to see an ophthalmologist. He took pictures. It was too late to stop the bleeding of the macula. The spot had enlarged to cover the central vision. With only peripheral vision in the left eye, I could still drive with depth perception at a distance, but close work like threading a needle was now impossible. We continued on our journey, arriving back at Randy's and meeting more Messianic Believers there. Then I turned in the car and we flew home.

When we got home, we went to St. Luke's Cataract & Laser Institute in Tarpon Springs, Florida to see what could be done about my eye. They decided to do the low power laser to cauterize the bleeding on July 1. In the meantime, we flew up to New Hampshire for the wedding of the oldest child of Topsy Tischler from Manila, now Topsy Black. We had visited them in California some years before and knew the family. Being half-Jewish, Kelli Black decided to forget her Jewish roots and just be a 'normal' person.

It was a Christian wedding in a church, but there was nothing spiritual about it. The groom was probably a nominal Christian. There would be a spiritual crisis a few years after this, but details were not given. Some of the family wanted to come to Florida to be with us and deal with it, but they never came. Later, I found out that Kelli divorced after only a few years of marriage. This was probably the crisis. Marriage must be based on the Word of God, but they had rejected it.

September came. I had a checkup on my eye, and then went off to Israel to find Ariel Berkowitz, the main writer of *HaYesod* and other books. From Ben Gurion airport, we took the *Sherut* (shared taxi) to Jerusalem, to the Youth Hostel, Beit Shmuel, where we sometimes stayed. I had the phone number of a friend who might know where Ariel lives and might have his phone number. He had it and I called and told Ariel briefly that we enjoyed the *HaYesod* and his books and would like to meet him. I told him we were staying at the Youth Hostel. He said he was coming to Jerusalem the next day anyway, and would drop by at a certain time.

Ariel had been with First Fruits of Zion when he did the writing, but was now independent. He was living outside of Jerusalem and teaching in Israel College of the Bible and IBEX, the Israel Bible Experience Semester in Israel for Master's College in California. We told him about our ministry and the Bible Conference next June. I asked if he would be interested to come and teach. He said he would talk it over with his wife and let me know later. We were going to rent a car to travel around Israel to see friends, and when we got back, I would phone him.

We had a wonderful time with our Israeli friends, especially with the Carmelis who lived in Zikhron Yaacov. We had met them in Florida a few years ago and had kept in touch. Varda took us up to Rosh Pina, a town in the North pioneered in 1882 by Jews from Rumania. This was in the first wave of immigration from Europe. Rosh Pina in Hebrew is "head of the corner," from Psalm 118:22. Yeshua quotes it three times about Himself in the Gospels, and it is also quoted in the Book of Acts and First Peter.

I pointed this out to Varda, but I do not think she caught it. When we got to her mother's place in Shlomi, way up in the Northwest corner of Israel, she got her Hebrew Bible and verified what I told her from Psalm 118. But we both had no New Testament with us at the time. I had given her a Hebrew NT when we met in Florida, but I do not know if she knew where it was. If the Spirit is working in her, He will make sure she finds the passages sometime.

We returned to Jerusalem about two weeks later and phoned Ariel. Yes, they would be in town the next day to have lunch with us and talk it over. When we sat down to talk, they were very positive about coming. The dates fit in their schedule, because his teaching in Israel would be over for the summer and they would be coming to the States to see their daughter, before proceeding to Manila. Any teacher I invite has to volunteer his time. There would be no honorarium. If he can pay his own airfare, that was good. If not, I will pay for it myself.

His wife D'vorah and son Yo'el came with him for lunch. As we ate together at a quaint restaurant of their choosing, I asked Yo'el what he would be doing next summer. He was nineteen, but was delaying his army service to a later time. So I asked him if he could conduct a children's program for our elementary age kids morning and afternoon. The kids would stay with their parents for the evening meetings. He agreed. I ended up paying for Ariel's airfare, they paid for D'vorah's and Yoel's. We had another two weeks to go to do the visiting that we intended, so we rented another car and headed out. A car in Jerusalem is useless, as there is very little parking. We take buses or taxis in the city.

Back in the Philippines, the year-long captivity of Martin and Gracia Burnham was going on. The Islamic terrorists in the Philippines were collaborating with some of the Philippine Military to get and share ransom money. This is a very sad story. We have to conclude again that God had His plan for them, as sheep for the slaughter, to be used for His Glory.

Martin Burnham was Randy's roommate at Faith Academy one year, so we followed the news more carefully. From what we learned in our class at IHLS on Islamic Thought and Practice, and with all the various news sources that we have, we have concluded that Radical Islam is an evil political system using a contrived religion of lies to deceive its followers, like the Kamikaze pilots of Japan were deceived. We also conclude that Radical Islam is the final world power of the anti-Christ empire of Satan, mentioned in Revelation 17 and 13. In the light of what is going on, we do not want to waste any time. The Return of Yeshua must be very near. Our responsibility is clear: harvest the Asia Pacific region and make disciples of as many as possible, who will also make disciples. We must multiply!

Back home in Florida, we got busy working on the preparations for the big Conference. The APTS Conference Center has small, medium, and large dormitories for economy-minded singles, and hotel type rooms for couples that want to stay together. Prices need to be calculated before sending out a brochure. The dining hall is cafeteria-style. We needed to work with the cook on a kosher menu. The schedule includes a weekend, so we would need to have a special menu on *Erev Shabbat*, a Friday evening celebration. This will require a small glass of wine. The APTS administration gave us permission to bring in our own wine for this, since it is a required cultural practice.

On Saturday morning, we will have a *Shabbat* service, with *Torah* readings, *Haftarah* (prophets and writings) readings, and Newer Testament readings, by selected participants, and some teaching on the *Torah* portion. After lunch we will resume the lectures. The Conference concludes by noon on Sunday. After lunch, we will have a two-hour cultural show, with many different dances of the mountaineers. Since mountaineers are sponsoring this Conference, we want the visitors from other countries and areas to know and appreciate our culture.

Then as a special, I will invite Ambassador Irit Ben-Abba to come Sunday afternoon to give a talk on Israel. Not only for the Ambassador, but in view of 9/11, security on the campus will be tight. Therefore, nametags will be required for entrance at the gate, and would be worn all the time. For music, we will need to have a small combo to lead us in singing some of the new Messianic songs, many with Psalms put to music. Edward Sano and the La Trinidad group can do that just fine. Also, we will have a bookstore of significant books on Messianic themes, and Judaica items like flags of Israel, pins, and *Menorahs* (lamp stands). We brought a lot of this with us from Israel.

Am I leaving anything out? Ah, yes, the brochures. Once we had all the details worked out, Kym Hotham, our graphic artist and color print shop owner in the UK, would make the brochures for us. They turned out in beautiful color, with pictures and a new Logo that Rachel Angiwan had designed. Advance registrations would come to us via email or mail to our P.O. Box in Baguio City. Those who lived in the Baguio area could commute or stay-in. The rest of the visitors, of course, would be stay-in.

And one more thing, it would be great if we had the cultural presentation on videotape, including the talk of Ambassador Irit Ben-Abba. Angel Channel was an upstart Christian company that videos events to put on local TV programs. We hired them to do the job. The result was acceptable by Philippine standards.

And yes, Ambassador Irit Ben-Abba agreed to come barring unforeseen emergency that could happen to prevent it, and provided the weather was OK so she could fly to Baguio. She did not accept our offer of a hotel-type room for the night, choosing rather to stay at the Baguio Country Club, the usual place for VIPs. She had one other reason to come to Baguio, to meet with the Shalom Club members.

Israel offers a variety of study opportunities for specialized persons in underdeveloped countries that can benefit their home country by such training. Requirements are fairly strict, and transportation to Israel is usually the person's responsibility. Those who have gone and completed their course of study and returned home became members of the Shalom Club. BIBAK has had at least half a dozen members qualifying and completing their courses, and would be attending our Conference. Irit would want to meet with them. Of course, our contacts with the Embassy helped to get the qualifying information to our people. BIBAK people, and now APMF people are very much Israel-oriented.

We flew to the Philippines a couple of months before the Conference. We wanted not only to get things ready, but also to travel around the country to motivate people to come. This would be something new to them. Most of them had never been to a Bible Conference, especially one for Asia Pacific people. Takashi Yokoyama will be coming with a couple of men from his groups. I urged him to bring his daughter as well. Michiru had finished college. Life as a Messianic single was quite lonely. She would enjoy the fellowship with a lot of other singles. A few were coming from Indonesia.

Typhoon and rainy season begins in the latter part of May, so we would be facing some potential problems. The Berkowitz family arrived a week early to get some rest after a very busy year. Even then, we took Ariel on a survey trip to Banaue. Yo'el got sick, so he and D'vorah stayed in Baguio. A typhoon came to our area right before the Conference was to start! We asked the Lord to control the weather for us.

Naomi did one better. Without telling me, she asked the LORD to give us good weather for the whole Conference as a confirmation from Him that the direction we were going was from Him. It was raining in the morning, but by lunch time the sky began to clear. The Berkowitz family and we transferred to the Conference site in partial sunshine. That was Tuesday, June 3, 2003. Good weather prevailed until June 10, after the Conference was over, when another typhoon hit the area. HalleluYah! The Messianic message and way of life was the right way to go. Let the critics talk. We know we have the blessing of the Lord and we will press on!

Registrations totaled about 180 participants from all over the Philippines. We had planned for 200, so that was OK. Such a Bible Conference is a bit expensive for some, especially those coming from other countries. When I was teaching in Japan the other year those 10 Seminars in 10 places in 10 days, Takashi started each one with a song that was new to me, in Japanese of course. I liked the lively tune and the message that was translated back to me. *Days of Elijah* was a song from an American Messianic singer. When I got home, we found it and decided to make that the Theme Song of our Conference.

I had asked Takashi to bring his transparency with him and have his group sing the song for us in Japanese. Everyone loved it! So we decided to make that the Theme Song for all of our Conferences in the future. The words and my Bible study on it are included in the Appendix. I had appointed several persons to give their testimony, one of them being Michiru. She had never done such in English, but did a great job with a good response from the audience.

Yo'el Berkowitz did a great job teaching the children about the Jewish Roots of Bible faith and practice. The Berkowitz family was originally from the USA and were Christian home missionaries until the Lord woke them up to the fact that they were Jews and should be living as Yeshua and His Apostles lived. Yo'el was very young when they moved to Israel, so his Hebrew speaking is very native and very good. The children loved him and he loved them. His English was also OK.

We were learning a lot from Scripture in its original context. We were learning to Think Jewish, to think like they thought when the texts were written. We were learning how Yeshua, Peter, James, John, Paul and all the Apostles lived. They obeyed all Ten Commandments, not just nine. *Shabbat* was very important. Passover was important. All the Appointed Times of the LORD were important, historically, currently, and prophetically.

When will Yeshua Return? At the time of the Fall Appointed Times of *Rosh HaShanah*, *Yom Kippur*, and *Sukkot*. When was Yeshua born? At this same time of year. What about the springtime festivals? Their prophetic significance were fulfilled at Yeshua's First Coming. The fall festivals will be at His Second Coming. It is all so clear now, once you clear your mind of the changes brought in by the

Catholic Church in its anti-Semitism. This is not easy. Tradition has been so ingrained, and everyone feels comfortable in it, so why change? We change because of Truth!

The second day of the Conference, I asked the participants what they were going to do with all that they were learning? I asked them to sit together at lunchtime and talk it over. As a result, some new Messianic congregations were formed, notably the Baguio City Messianic Congregation, or BCMC.

There were lots of requests to have another Conference the following year, in fact to make it an annual event. I said, fine, but they have to do the work next time and take care of the subsidy. I would find the teacher and get him here, and will help in whatever way, but they have to carry the load of organizing and subsidizing as necessary. I only charged the registrants for the bare cost of their meals and lodging to make it possible for more to come. My subsidy was about $4,000 in addition to our own expenses from the US, but it was well worth it and a great blessing to us. Now to get ready for APMF Bible Conference No. 2.

# CHAPTER 24

## Thailand
## 2<sup>nd</sup> APMF Bible Conference 2004
## BIBAK Building

Remember Paul's "Macedonian Call?" Instead of a vision, we got an email, "Messianic Movement in Thailand." A large group of churches there want to join APMF. Why? The gist of the message was that Christianity is seen as the white man's religion, used to colonize the countries of Asia. This is true for the Catholic takeover of the Philippines. Thailand is the only country in Southeast Asia that has never been colonized, so that after 200 years of Christian missionary work without a colonizing government behind them, less than 1% are Christians. "That the Messianic movement is going back to the roots which is Jewish, it removes the hindrance that the Thais have always had to the gospel. I believe this is what Thailand needs for revival." We agree!

We needed to be in Manila for a Regional Seminar on the Jewish Roots the first week of January 2004. Ariel and Yo'el Berkowitz would be teaching, but I was needed for a lot of logistical work and coordination. So we decided to go early to Manila, do what was needed, and then take a trip over to Bangkok for a couple weeks to check things out there, and then return.

Over 200 from the Metro Manila area participated in the weekend Regional Seminar, which included a Monday, a workday. Attendance held up well. We were very pleased and the participants seemed to appreciate it. It takes time to shift gears from traditional thinking and ways of doing things to honestly look at the Bible in its original context and face the differences. Some understand very quickly, the first time they look at the evidence, and make the shift. Others understand, but are reluctant to leave their "comfort zone" in Tradition and face the criticism that will surely come, which all of us have experienced.

We had never met Tony, the one who sent the email. He met us at the airport and took us to the hotel that he had booked for us. Tony is the son of an American soldier and a Southeast Asian mother. He is an ardent Christian evangelist, mostly focusing on the thousands of Israeli backpackers who come to Thailand. When in Bangkok, the Israelis stay in their own hotel in a busy tourist area. There is also a Chabad Lubavitch Jewish Synagogue and Center in the same area to cater to them. We went with him to see all of this.

The purpose of the visit, however, was to make contact with this group of churches in Northeast Thailand that heard about and wanted to go Messianic with us. Tony put us on a bus going to that area. A person was to meet us there. When we arrived, two men met us. Then we all went by car to a neighboring town, where we talked and stayed overnight.

This group of churches was Seventh Day Adventists. The foreigners in charge were too heavy handed with the Thailand leaders, who were looking if they could get out from under them and go with us. The catch was, the SDA organization was paying a lot of the expenses of the Thailand operation. If these churches went with us, we would be expected to take on that subsidy expense. When they learned that we only provide teaching, not money, that we follow indigenous principles and are non-professional with no clergy, they were no longer interested. They apparently took us to this other town so that they would not be seen hosting and talking to some Americans.

Again, we have learned that "money talks" or that money seems to be the "bottom line" of the church clergy-laity system. "Ministry" for most is a job, only another way to earn, not a Calling from the Lord. So instead of the few days Bible Conference we had planned on to be sure they understood what the issues are in going back to the Foundation of Yeshua and the Apostles, we were now on our own to do some sightseeing.

We took a bus the following morning to Chiang Mai in Northwest Thailand, a tourist area where a lot of missions have their headquarters. We found lodging at the YMCA at a reasonable price. It was walking distance from the main part of town. We knew that Wycliffe Bible Translators had a Center there, for their workers travelling in and out of China. We found it and had a good visit with several from Wheaton. One BIBAKer was working with them, but was not in town at the moment, so we left something there for her. After a couple of days, we took the bus to Bangkok, went back to the same hotel, met Tony again, and then flew back to Manila.

255

We learned something from this experience, something that I felt in the beginning of our ministry in the Philippines.

Christianity is seen worldwide as the <u>white man's religion,</u> because the ones who brought it to most of the world were the missionaries from England first, with their colonizing government, and now mostly Americans without a colonizing government. This need not have been so, if the message of these white missionaries had been the true message of the Bible. <u>Jesus is a Jew, not a white man</u>! His real name is Yeshua. The culture is biblically Asian, not Western. Clergy control over the laity does not fit the biblical pattern, as it copies the colonizing government and ends up as a business at best and a dictatorship at worst, like the Catholic control over salvation.

The Bible pattern is the Body of the Messiah functioning together, with everyone actively doing his part. There are no spectators and no performers. Genuine Love for the true Creator God of Genesis and genuine Love for each other is naturally illustrated in the Messianic Community. Genuine Love as defined in the Scriptures is different from the popular concept today. Yeshua said it clearly, "If you love Me, keep My Commandments!" Obedience, commitment, is what God looks for, not emotional ecstasy, glib promises never kept or meeting only a few hours on one day per week.

Yeshua explained to His disciples that leadership in the Body of the Messiah, the Messianic Community, is not to be like the pagan gentile political system. Those in power lord it over their people. Rather, leadership is to be like His example, building up His Body by humbly serving it as He did.

A very interesting, and appropriate, article appeared

in the December 2003 issue of *Mission Frontiers* magazine, entitled "Living Like Jesus, a Torah-Observant Jew". The author, Joshua Massey, is an evangelical missionary among Asian Muslims. He is advocating going back to Torah living, living like Jesus did, which is just what we are doing! He says, "Without major life adjustments, even the most spiritually vibrant among us tend to appear to Muslims as unclean pagans."

My suspicion is that the American Indians, Buddhists, Hindus, and other ancient religions might think the same way about Christianity, since they take their own religions much more seriously. The Gospel has hardly penetrated any of those in these religious groups. Is the way our message presented mostly to blame? Or is our message itself partly off base, not precisely how the Bible presents it in context? Our message must fit the text! Twisting the text to fit theological positions is wrong! And our lives must back up our words.

To do all the traveling and ministry that we do, our bodies need to be good servants to us! We are very thankful for the Veterans' Administration Hospital in Gainesville, Florida, about 35 miles north of us. I am a US Army veteran, so I am entitled to primary medical care. Once a year, I have a good physical exam with complete urine and blood tests. If anything looks suspicious, more tests are given. I make a co-payment and Medicare pays some.

Medical care for Naomi is entirely on our own plus Medicare A&B. We are thankful that we have minimal medical issues, mostly arthritic aches and pains, for which we take no medication. Regular exercise is our goal, but with all of our traveling, we are not consistent. When at home and the weather is OK, I walk two miles a day at a good pace and

Naomi walks maybe a mile. We try to eat healthy as well, finding the biblical menu a good start. Our bodies are temples of the Spirit, so we must take good care of them.

Our original church, BIBAK Bible Church of Baguio City, was finally able to buy a lot in the center of town and start building. It is on a hillside, which is common for Baguio, but a bit steep for older people to walk down to. Several floors were envisioned, but money dictates what they can build at the moment.

They built two floors, with the second floor divided into a dorm for ladies and a dorm for men, anticipating the student response we had some years before. However, times have changed and many students are living with parents who had moved to Baguio for business or other reasons. The city is growing, getting crowded. But that is all the more reason for a vibrant Tyrannus Bible Training Center! However, members and leaders have become too busy, so this ministry has declined. Now they have added the third floor, which is a spacious area for services, weddings and many other activities.

We were home in Florida this year when Passover time came along. The Bible Study group that used to meet at Ralph Mount's place each Sunday afternoon asked me to lead it. It was held in the home of one of the members and was really crowded. That was not just because I was such a popular teacher! It was because people enjoy celebrating their Festival of Freedom, physically for the Jews and spiritually for both Jew and Gentile Believers, from the "Egypt" of this world's system and the bondage of sin, through the blood of Yeshua.

It is also enjoyable because <u>Passover is family-centered</u>.

The patriarch of the family group leads it, or a selected friend who can tell the story well. It is not led by any clergy, whether a rabbi or a pastor. They enjoyed my edited *Haggadah* and said it was one of the best Seders that they have ever had. The *Haggadah* is the narration booklet that is followed during the evening.

When we read the Bible book of Exodus, it seems that Moses is the hero of the whole episode. Guess what? Moses is not even mentioned in the *Haggadah*. God is the hero, from start to finish! The Gospel is there, even though the basic *Haggadah* was written hundreds of years ago by Jewish writers who were not Messianic, as far as we know. We celebrate it every year, no matter where we are.

The 2nd Annual APMF Bible Conference was May 20-24, 2004, in Baguio City. The local committee was too late to reserve the APTS Convention Center like last year, so they settled for what is called the Green Valley Country Club. It did not have any golf course, but did have a gym, bowling alley, and swimming pool. There were others using these facilities while we were having our meetings in the long, narrow hall nearby. It was very noisy. We will not use this facility again.

We did use the swimming pool once, to baptize Bong and Arnold Acebuche, two brothers from the southern tip of the Philippines. They had been caught up in various religious groups and cults, but finally got straightened out through more faithfully studying the Bible and getting help online from our teacher for this Conference, Tim Hegg from Tacoma, Washington. Many are finding a lot of help via the Internet, but there is a lot of deception and garbage out there also.

The attendance was not quite as good as last year, but there were a lot of new ones, so we were happy and encouraged. When I first invited Tim Hegg to come, since we had met some years before, he said he would consider it and let me know later. Maybe a month later, he emailed me that he would be very happy to come. The dates were OK and the Lord had confirmed his coming by providing his airfare.

Soon after I had invited him, a lady gave Tim an envelope of money, saying, "I know you will need this," and said that there would be more. A few weeks later she gave him some more. The total amount was what he needed for his airfare! This time I did not have to pay the invited teacher's airfare. This was another confirmation from the Lord. We have been so blessed by blessing Israel, being obedient to Torah, and trusting Him for everything!

# CHAPTER 25

## 80-Day Trip, ISRAEL,
## 3rd APMF Conference
## Naomi's 50th Class Reunion

"Around the world in 80 days!" is the title of a book, I think. We went "Around North America in 80 days!" Why? We had an invitation to teach on Israel as part of a Bible Conference way up in Northwest Canada, Tumbler Ridge, British Columbia, to be exact. It was not a place that could be reached by any airline. The organizer of the Conference was a student at Bryan College when I taught there and Naomi was a student.

Ken Campbell was a well-known evangelist all across Canada. His Gospel message included attacking the social ills of the country. This Conference was "Calling Canada Back to God." We accepted the invitation (paid our own way, of course, which we do all the time) and decided to fulfill a longtime desire, to drive all the way to Alaska. It also completed Naomi's journey of driving with me in all 50 states of the USA and nearly all the Provinces of Canada. We left home in Florida in July and drove 12,742 miles and back home again in exactly 80 days. We did not plan it that way. It just happened.

The scenery was beautiful in many places. The Alcan Highway was muddy and bad in some places, but we came to see people! How many? We visited at least 65 people that we had known for many years: Filipinos from BIBAK, missionary colleagues, college friends, Army friends, former neighbors and other friends. Like the Apostle Paul, we make it a point to keep in contact with people, Believers or not, so we had many addresses on file. We just had to put them in order and follow the map, and make arrangements ahead of time as much as possible, by email and telephone.

At the top of Alaska, we visited one of Ray's flight students, who became one of his flight instructors. When Ray moved Walkwitz Aviation, Inc. from Ocala to Titusville, Joe Sigmon got a job with an airline company in Fairbanks, Alaska, about as far north as he could go from his home in Ocala, Florida. He told us that when he was building his house in Fairbanks, he and a friend were nailing on the roof at midnight. A neighbor came over to ask them to please stop since his wife could not get to sleep because of the constant pounding! In the middle of summer, the sun never sets, and in the middle of winter, the sun never comes up. It is hard to imagine it without experiencing it. Joe died in 2007 in an airplane accident in Alaska, leaving his wife Isobel and son Trustin.

During the week of the Conference in Tumbler Ridge, we were guests of a couple, Ron and Loreen, who were very much interested in Israel. As we talked about our coming trip on up to Alaska, they suggested taking the ferryboat from Alaska to Seattle on our return, rather than driving all the way around, retracing our trip a lot of the way. They happened to have a brochure about the US Maritime Highway ships that connect from Haines, Alaska, all along the Southeast panhandle of Alaska and western edge of Canada. Juneau in this panhandle is the capital of Alaska. There are no roads to reach these towns. Transportation is only by air or by ship, so this ferryboat makes a lot of stops between Haines and Bellingham, Washington.

We phoned the 800 number and made our reservation by credit card. All of the two-person cabins were taken, so we had to take a four-person cabin on the outside with a window so we could watch as we went along, if we were not up on deck. Some young people just slept in the lounges at night, as having a cabin was not required. It was just a ferryboat but a big one. Our car was down below with about seventy more cars, trucks, and campers. Meals were in a cafeteria staffed by Filipinos! They were not far from retirement. When the time came, they would go back to the Philippines and live like kings! We had a great time even if we did not see any whales.

Soon after we arrived home, Hanana phoned us from Israel. "Where have you been? I have been calling to see if you are okay from the hurricane!" A hurricane had gone through our area while we were gone, but it was mild and had only torn off some of the awnings on our guest house. But what worried Hanana was the fact that she had not received a *Rosh HaShanah* – Happy New Year card from us. In Jewish culture, a *Rosh HaShanah* card is usually expected from good friends. We had been on our trip when *Rosh Hashanah* came along in September and so we did not send any cards in 2004. Hanana thought maybe something bad had happened to us. Love and concern like that is not unusual from Israelis who come to know you well.

After we had chatted a while, she asked the inevitable, "When are you coming to Israel?" We replied that after that long trip we did not feel like spending for another one. Maybe next year, we said. However, on a hunch I phoned Northwest Airlines to see what the price would be from Tampa or Orlando to Tel Aviv. For a two-week trip, there was a special, less than half of the usual price! "Yes sir, I will take two tickets!" We booked November 30 to December 14, and started making emails and phone calls. The Lavi family was so happy they said they would meet us anywhere in Israel at any time...just name it!

This time frame would include *Hanukkah*, the eight-day celebration of the victory of the Maccabees against the Syrians and the cleansing of the Temple. This victory and celebration were in 164 BCE and has continued through the centuries. BCE means Before the Common Era; CE means Common Era. Jews do not like to say Christ, so BC is not used, nor is AD. Yeshua also celebrated Hanukkah, which is called the Feast of Dedication.

> *"And it was at Jerusalem the feast of the dedication, and it was winter. And Jesus walked in the temple in Solomon's porch."* John 10:22-23.

Hanukkah in Hebrew means Dedication in English. It is also called the Feast of Lights, as eight lights are lit, one the first night, two the next night, and so on.

We lit light No. 1 with the Lavis in Ramat Gan, part of Greater Tel Aviv; No. 2 and No. 3 with Yehudah and Yonah Avni at their Dude Ranch, *Vered Hagalil*, the Rose of Galilee, near Korazim. We met Yehudah on our first trip to Israel in 1968. He was from Chicago, we were from Wheaton, near Chicago, so we remembered him well. Yehudah came to Israel in 1949 to help in the War of Independence, stayed on and married locally.

We lit light No. 4 with Asher Goffer and family in Kiryat Bialik, Northeast of Haifa (they have since moved to Netanya), on *Erev Shabbat*; No. 5 and No. 6 with Miriam Munce, our now widowed friend in Caesarea; and No. 7 at Beit Dagan with Ilan and Ronit Keidan, friends we met in Gainesville, Florida many years ago. When the candles burned down and out they gave us the beautiful pewter *Hanukiah*! A *Hanukiah* is a lampstand with nine lamps, one higher than the other eight, which is the servant lamp. The servant lamp is lit first each night and then used to light the others. We did not get to light the eighth lamp since we were flying over the Atlantic Ocean at the time it was to be lit. I did carry a candle in my carry on bag, but I was hesitant to light it in the airplane cabin!

Ilan took us to the airport for our flight back to Florida. Beit Dagan is near the airport, so we turn in our rental car there, he picks us up and brings us to his house (it is a hard to find place, so it is better that he comes to get us), we eat and fellowship, then later in the evening he takes us back to the airport, since most flights are near midnight. Ilan is a pediatric anesthesiologist with four children, three girls and one boy. The oldest is a girl, Lee, who is in the army as I am writing this.

We returned to the Philippines in February to assist the local committee with preparations for the 3rd APMF Annual Bible Conference, April 6-10, 2005, again at APTS Conference Center outside Baguio. Tim Hegg will again be our teacher. He communicates well with good content. This time we will hire Angel Channel to video all of his teaching sessions, to put on DVD so that others can learn. Contact me if you would like to borrow them.

Tim tells in his first session what triggered him to go back to the Jewish Roots of biblical faith and practice. While talking in bed one night, his wife asked him, "Tim, how come we keep only nine of the Ten Commandments?" Tim replied, "I don't know. I never thought about it. The question has never come up, even in seminary. I will have to do some research." Commandment No. 4 on Shabbat has been ignored.

Tim's father was a fundamental Baptist GARB (General Association of Regular Baptists) pastor for fifty years. His mother was Jewish, but never practiced her Jewishness. Tim went to a GARB-approved college and seminary. He was a top student, so upon graduation he was offered many pastorates. He said, No, he had to work in the work-a-day-world for a while first, and started a printing business.

For some years he pastored part time with a team, then went fulltime on the request of the members and sold his printing business. Then his wife comes up with this question about Shabbat. Soon he confirmed that he should be meeting on Saturday, not Sunday, and should be doing the Appointed Times of Leviticus 23, not the substitutes that the Catholic Church brought in because of their anti-Semitism. Being honest with the Truth, he started a Saturday congregation along with the Sunday one for a while, and then left the Sunday one for those who want to stay that way.

Putting our research together, we came to <u>three definite conclusions</u> for Jews and Gentiles alike, which are:

1) There is only <u>ONE WAY of salvation</u> from the beginning of time until the end of time, which is by God's Grace through our Faith response or acceptance. It is not by works of any kind, but is a Gift from God, provided by

the shed blood of Yeshua The Messiah to make <u>full payment</u> for our sin, which is called <u>Propitiation</u>, not atonement. Atonement is the word for the Covering of sin by the blood of an animal at the Tabernacle. His burial, Resurrection, and Ascension to Heaven confirmed that Propitiation had been made. This is summarized in Ephesians 2:8-9. Jews have never been saved by works, and neither has anyone else.

*"For by grace are you saved through faith; and that not of yourselves, it is the gift of God – not by works, lest any man should boast."*

2) There is only <u>ONE FAMILY of God</u>, which is Israel with Gentile Believers grafted in together with Jewish Believers. This is clear from Romans 11, The Olive Tree Message. There are not two families, Israel and the Church. There is no "church" in the Bible. The church began slowly as a breakaway from the Messianic Communities, a departure from truth 200 years after Yeshua. It is a deceptive distortion to translate *Ekklesia* – the Messianic Community – as "church," which comes from *kuriakon* – a pagan temple in NT times. I checked my Webster's Dictionary for "church" to find this gem of truth. In contrast, theological books claim, wrongly, that church comes from *Ekklesia.* <u>Clergy write these books</u> and they are determined to say it their way regardless of the facts. The Messianic Community in Tanach (OT) times was called the Congregation - *Kehilah or Kahal* - of the LORD, which translates to *Ekklesia* in the Greek Septuagint – LXX for short – being the Greek translation of the *Tanach* (OT). There is no *kuriakon* in the Bible; therefore, there is no "church." It is a tragedy when Bible translators translate by their pre-determined theology rather than by being honest with the texts in their historic context. It is also a

tragedy that there are some fine, true Believers in Jesus Christ in some of the churches, and in the clergy, who love the Lord, but do not realize that they are on a partially defective foundation. What joy and peace have we who have shifted over to the original solid Foundation, that of Yeshua and His Apostles.

3) There is only ONE WAY to LIVE in God's one family, the Torah way as amplified all through the Bible, from Genesis through Revelation. Torah means teachings, not laws. This is clearly stated in Ephesians 2:10 as God's Expectation upon entering His Family, a verse which is usually left out when quoting Ephesians 2:8-9.

*"For we are his workmanship, created in Messiah Yeshua unto good works, which God has before ordained that we should walk in them."*

If God has "before ordained" that we should "walk in them," the "good works," the only conclusion possible is the Torah way of living, that is, according to the law, the only way God has given to anyone. God has "created us" this way when He brings us into His one Family. It should be the natural way to live, IF a person is genuinely born-from-above.

In fact, Ephesians 2 shows clearly that there is ONE New Man in Messiah, Jew and Gentile together, on the Foundation of the Apostles and Prophets, not on any foundation of the so-called "church fathers," who were Greek philosophers, nor on the reformers of the Reformation either! Torah primarily refers to the Pentateuch, or Books of Moses, and contains some laws, but the primary meaning is teaching. Therefore, Torah can refer to the whole Bible, as the Bible is full of teachings. This also means that all Ten Commandments are still valid, since Yeshua and the Apostles kept Shabbat. No one has the right to change something God wrote in stone with His own finger! That also means that our celebrations are the Appointed Times of God, summarized in Leviticus 23, times when God says He will meet with His people when gathered together. We need to meet Him <u>on His schedule</u>. Thinking Jewish, thinking like they thought when the texts were written, will show clearly that there were no "church meetings" on Sunday daytime anywhere in Scripture. Saturday night meetings, yes.

The Conference was well attended again, with nearly 200 enthusiastic participants. We left the Philippines for Florida and home, in time to go to Bryan College for the 50th Class Reunion of Naomi's class of '55, May 6-7, 2005, in Dayton, Tennessee. Naomi and I started at Bryan together, she as a freshman and I as faculty, teaching chemistry, math, and coaching track and cross-country. After my two years in the US Army, we also finished together, Naomi graduating with a BA with a major in English. This Liberal Arts background and Bible classes served her well for home schooling our three sons. Many good friends were there at the Reunion. There were some new buildings as the college was growing. We consider Bryan College as one of the best, or the best, because of its firm stand for Literal Six-Day Creation, just as Genesis 1 states. Departing from this foundational Truth leads to error after error. We have always been thankful for this college and its stand on Creation, and hope it never departs from it.

# CHAPTER 26

## APMF, Inc, Banaue Dec 2005, 4<sup>th</sup> APMC Apr 2006, ISRAEL Summer!

Bible memorization has been part of my practice since early days. When I was in the US Army, I always carried my packet of memory verse cards to review during break times, when most of the others were off smoking their cigarettes. Therefore, at each Annual Bible Conference, we have had memory verses to learn.

It is essential to have a large amount of God's Word stored in one's memory. We will never know ahead of time when significant opportunities come to give a witness for our Lord. We need to give His Word, not ours. There will be times for some people when Bibles may be taken away, or denied to us. What we have memorized may be the only Bible we have.

As soon as we arrived home, an email came from the mission treasurer. He was no longer going to receipt donations for our expense account, to help pay our ministry expenses. This is in violation of mission policy that provides for an expense account for retirees who have a continuing ministry, funded by donations to our account. In our on-loan agreement with Menorah Ministries, the mission agreed to continue to receipt donations for our expense account. But now, we will not have an expense account anymore. There was no official letter from the mission; just a back door way of cutting us off. There was no word from the office until two years later, admitting the change in policy. Why?

We assume that they do not like our Messianic ministry, but they are afraid to come out and say so plainly. It would expose their anti-Jewishness, which is the norm in most of Christianity. This is again an example of clergy domination and pride. Actually not much was coming in so that we had been paying most of our expenses anyway. God knows their motives. We are with Menorah Ministries now and John Fischer likes our ministry very much, and so do the people that we teach in the Asia Pacific region!

Some folks think that missionaries over 70 ought to be in their rocking chairs at home, not traveling the world to teach. However, we had a few friends that we knew would like to continue helping us, and there might be others. For their sake, we needed to have a way by which we could issue an IRS-approved tax-deductible receipt. Menorah Ministries would be happy to do this for us, but that would be more work for their office. Instead, we will incorporate Asia Pacific Messianic Fellowship and do the work ourselves! We had full confidence that this is what the Lord wanted us to do and He would bless us.

The first thing to do was to find a lawyer to draw up the

incorporation. A Jewish Believer lawyer in Ocala, Florida drew up Ray's Walkwitz Aviation, Inc. papers, so he could do it. He was willing, for a modest fee, of course. We needed a mission organization, a not-for-profit, religious educational corporation, and we needed to be able to qualify for an IRS 501 (c) (3) category to be tax-exempt and to issue tax-deductible receipts. The lawyer was happy to do the Florida State Incorporation papers and submit them. However, the IRS thing was too expensive and time consuming. He would not do that.

We asked a few other lawyers and CPAs, and they all said the same thing. "You don't have the money to pursue this." Of course we don't, so we will do it ourselves. I got all the papers, filled them out and mailed them in with the required dollar amount by check. In just three weeks, almost by return mail, we received our full Approval from the IRS! No questions asked. APMF Inc. is now a 501.c.3 Tax-exempt Corporation "qualified to receive tax deductible bequests, devises, transfers of gifts...as a public charity." We are equal to all the "Big Boys." Thank You, Lord!

That did not mean that we had any money! The Lord had just provided a channel by which interested donors could help us and still get the same credit as from any other mission organization or charity. The key to our immediate approval was trusting the Lord to have us write down exactly what we are. APMF has no employees and pays no salaries or compensation to its officers or Board of Directors. Everyone involved is a Volunteer. Monies received are spent only for reimbursement of expenses when on assignment for APMF Inc. activities. Being aware of a lot of fraud in charities, I knew the IRS would like us, and they did.

# According to Roger!

Our thanksgiving 2005 Newsletter introduced ASIA PACIFIC MESSIANIC FELLOWSHIP, Inc. and advised each one of this new channel for giving to us. Some new ones began to help and older ones continued, switching from the mission to APMF. Still not much comes in, but we are thankful for every gift, large and small. God is the one to "multiply the loaves and fishes" into enough to pay all the expenses necessary.

The rest of our expense money comes from our own pockets, mainly from the small Life Insurance that our son Ray had the wisdom to provide. He knew that aviation had more dangers than normal life, so he provided for his wife, which passed on to us since all the family perished in the plane crash. That Life Insurance is just about consumed. What happens next is up to the Master, our Commanding Officer, who does not send His troops into battle alone but leads them, provides for them, and is with them always.

Ariel and Yo'el Berkowitz will be coming to the Philippines to teach for an Area APMF Bible Conference in Banaue, Ifugao, the last week of December 2005. We will be there to make sure all goes well. Then they go to Japan and China to teach before coming back to do a two-week Workshop for the Wycliffe Bible Translators in the Philippines, teaching them Hebrew and proper translation procedures. Hebrew is so much different from Greek!

As for us, from Banaue, we go to Cebu City, the main city in the middle of the Philippines for a three-day Seminar on the Jewish Roots. This will be our first time to go there. Only one young lady is there who is with us in APMF, the girlfriend of Joel Cruz of Manila. They are both musicians and graduates of the University of the Philippines. Imee (Irene Marie) Alcantara helps her parents with their day-care center and gives piano lessons. We hope a couple from Mindanao, the southernmost island, will come up to join us. Vivilyn lived with us in Baguio for a couple years about 20 years ago. Her home is in Mindanao and she married a pastor from there. Both are very much interested.

The denomination they were with got heavy-handed with them, so they resigned. Solomon got a job and they studied Scripture together. Soon they came to a startling conclusion, that the fourth Commandment was to be obeyed! They started to keep the Saturday *Shabbat* with their family, and a few others joined with them. After about a year, they were thinking that they must be the only ones doing this. Maybe they should check with someone else that they could trust to see if they were ok making this change. Who would they ask? The only one they knew was Sir Walkwitz. They contacted me by email and told me their story. I replied, "Wonderful! We are doing the same!" They were overjoyed and at peace. This Seminar in Cebu City will be our first meeting with them since they made this change.

We flew into Cebu the day before the Seminar, had good fellowship with Joel and Imee, and met her parents, who were not Believers yet but were willing to host the Seminar. The next morning Joel came with us to their house. Solomon and Vivilyn Buasag were already there, having come by ship overnight. The Seminar went well the first day with a lot of students from a Bible college in town, who had a lot of questions. By evening, Solomon and Vivilyn were trying to contact their friend, Solomon's former Bible school teacher who now had a school in Cebu. Finally they made contact and went there for the night.

In the morning, Nowyn came with many of his faculty.

The Buasags had talked with him until late at night, telling him and his family how the Lord had led them. They came ready to learn more. At the end they were convinced and decided to make the change. They would become Messianic and follow the ways of Yeshua and the Apostles. Now Imee had companions to fellowship with and study with on Shabbat. Her parents sometimes joined them. Nowyn Jangad and family owned and operated Cebu Christian Institute International, an accredited private elementary and high school.

The two brothers that Tim Hegg baptized in Baguio at the 2004 Bible Conference needed some help. They live in Davao City, at the southern end of Mindanao, a large island where most of the Muslims live, almost at the southern end of the Philippines. We decided to go there for 10 days and lead a Bible Conference for any persons that they know might be interested. Their group is composed of only family and a few others. We had never been to Davao City, either, so this year we are doing some firsts. A few showed up, but most of those invited made excuses. At least Bong and Arnold showed they can set up a seminar, but getting the invitation out needs lots of help.

Next will be the 4th Annual APMF Bible Conference in Baguio April 27 – May 1, 2006, with Dr. David Friedman of the Israel College of the Bible, Jerusalem, as our teacher. Son Ron decided to give himself a vacation and flew out for two weeks to join the conference fellowship. He still has lots of friends from growing up in Baguio. With current events involving Israel heating up, we decided on a theme of Prophecy. David will teach the book of Zechariah and I will teach Bible Prophecy and Current Events.

Now I have to get busy and make my syllabus, as the participants value these for taking notes and for further study. In the past, I just teach and let them take notes, but now I am forced to provide a syllabus for each time. I am also writing this book in response to many requests for my "spiritual journey from church Tradition into Messianic understanding and practice." It is quite a journey, but Yeshua is very gracious and blesses all along the way. No problems, no complaints! Just Rejoicing that our names were written in the Lamb's Book of Life BEFORE the foundation of the world! Do you believe that? Fantastic! Check out Ephesians 1.

Oh, yes! What are we going to do for our $50^{th}$ Wedding Anniversary? Our family is so small they probably won't do anything about it, so we will plan something, whatever Naomi wants, as this is "her" anniversary! She insists it is "ours" but I always do what pleases her. Will it be Hawaii again? September 8 is a bit far off yet, so we will wait and see when the time comes closer.

And Ohhh, Yes! Guess what we are going to do this summer of 2006? Can't guess? Ok, we are going to Israel...again! Why? In our February 2006 Newsletter we asked for any invitations for ministry in the summer. The first one to reply called from Israel on March 10, to our son Ron in Florida. Miriam Munce wanted us to come to Israel to watch her house in Caesarea for the whole summer while she came to the States to see her children and grandchildren, and have some medical things taken care of. Of course the answer was, yes, but we could not go beyond the 90-day visa that Israel gives to Americans. We would use her car to keep it in condition and feed her cat. An immigrant that needs work now did the yard work.

277

## According to Roger!

This time we would have a home to which we could invite our Israeli friends to come to see us! Many of them did: Lavis, Goffers, Nirs, Solomons, Evens, Carmelis, Keidans, Pheffers, Nessims, Matalons, and some BIBAK girls working as caregivers. There are hundreds of Filipinas working as caregivers for old people in Israel. We also visited in the park in Tel Aviv near the Philippine Embassy with BIBAK girls for Bible study on their day off, as getting to Caesarea by bus was not so easy. We went to the homes of Adina Keshet in Bethlehem in Galilee with her Ifugao helper, the Avnis at their Vered Hagalil Dude Ranch, the Pfeffers, and Ellises at their Goat milk dairy, yogurt and cheese factory.

We had a wonderful summer, just living as residents in Israel with the blessing of being a blessing to others. For years, Filipinos and others were asking us to put together a Tour of Israel. OK, we will do just that. I contacted a tour guide friend as to his available dates in May 2007, and then arranged with Sar-El Tours for the details. This would be after our next APMF Annual Conference in Baguio, so that we would fly from Manila to Tel Aviv with the group.

On our way from the US to Tel Aviv for our summer in Miriam's house, we changed planes at Charles de Gaulle airport in Paris, which is totally mixed up for us. We missed our flight trying to get to a different terminal, but were able to catch another one eight hours later. Thankfully we were able to phone Miriam from Paris to let her know of the change. Miriam woke up when we arrived past midnight. The taxi from the airport cost us US$110, since it was Friday night, Shabbat, and only Arab drivers were available. At least we rode in a Mercedes Benz, a one-hour ride!

Toward the end of our summer in Israel, we met Victor Opungo from Papua New Guinea, who was studying Hebrew at Hebrew University and staying at the Home for Bible Translators, near Jerusalem. Victor and Ana, one of our BIBAK girls, are both Bible translators. She came from Thailand where she headquartered for her Bible Translation work to meet Victor again, and yes, they agreed to get married! They wanted us as part of their wedding party in Manila, but we just could not make it.

In the meantime, the Lebanon War came on! The only English news on TV was about 10 minutes at suppertime. On the radio, it was the BBC, which is always very negative about Israel. We could hear the explosions in Haifa to the north, but we had only one siren alert in Caesarea, when the Lavis were having supper with us. We decided to ignore it, as the bomb shelter was very tiny. The nearest missile landed about three miles away, but only once did they come that far south.

Miriam had some medical problems that delayed her return, but we had to leave as our visa was up. Getting an extension would be a problem. Her neighbors were very kind and helpful. George drove us to the airport on his way to work early in the morning while Mira took care of the house for a while. The family is Israeli - American except for the wife; Mira has Israeli citizenship only. The children were born in the USA. We meet so many interesting people!

APMC 1 Baguio City, Philippines 2003

Israel Ambassador Irit Ben-Abba at APMC 1

Natives resist missionary drama, APMC 1

Roger with Passover demonstration at APMC 1

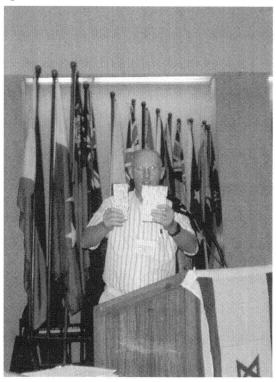

APMC 2 Tim Hegg with Baguio City Messianic Community

APMC 3
with Tim Hegg
showing his philacteries

Roger at Banaue Hotel

Welcome for Banaue Bible Conference 2005

Ariel Berkowitz
Manila Conference 2006

APMC 4
2006
Roger & David Friedman

Yeshiva 1 with John Fischer, Roger behind camera

Naomi taking John Fischer shopping in Baguio

Yeshiva Students with Forest and Iva Swineford

Roger & Dave with John Fischer for APMC 5

# CHAPTER 27

## 50<sup>th</sup> Wedding Anniv
## 5<sup>th</sup> APMF Conference & Yeshiva
## Tours of Israel, Indonesia

Arriving home from Israel after being gone for 90 days, we had cartons of mail to attend to. Bills get paid first. Personal letters get answered next. Thankfully, we had the use of Miriam's laptop for doing email in Israel. Otherwise, we would have been "in the dark" for many reasons. Our 50<sup>th</sup> Wedding Anniversary will be in less than two weeks! Randy decided to fly here to Florida and join Ron and us for a two-day celebration at a motel "on the beach" in Clearwater, Florida. We ate mostly delicious meals. September 8 was a Friday, so it was a quick weekend for Randy, but it was the best he could do.

Naomi's 75<sup>th</sup> Birthday was October 29, 2006. I decided to treat her for this and as an add-on for our 50<sup>th</sup> Anniversary, by taking her to Hawaii, her favorite destination, for a week and then pass by Glendale, Arizona to see our grandsons, son and daughter-in-law. It was a free flight, using Mileage Plus miles on United Airlines. We both have had free flights to the Philippines a couple of times in the past, using frequent flyer miles, saving us a lot of money! We arrived back from Arizona in time to vote on November 7.

My sister Mildred, at Shell Point Retirement Center in Ft. Myers, Florida, died the next day. A few months before, she had phoned to ask me if we had burial plots here. Yes we did, with Ray and family in one. She could have one of the others whenever she needed it. Her body was shipped up here and my brother Don and wife Faith arrived from Oklahoma for the burial. Then we headed south to take charge of the Memorial Service at Shell Point.

Mildred left all her assets to various Christian missions and CBC or Columbia International University. She had been single all her life, so there were no children to take care of. Earlier, she had been a missionary in Guatemala for a term, producing literacy materials, so I put "Missionary Educator" on her grave marker. There was nothing for us, which was her style. We did collect a lot of her books, which we shipped together with many of our own to the Philippines for the Libraries of several APMF related congregations. We were three siblings; now we are two.

In January 2007, I had a call from the Youth Pastor at Grace Presbyterian Church in Ocala, Florida. He had been teaching Exodus to his youth groups and thought it would be a neat thing to do a Passover for them. Would I do it for him? Certainly, as a teaching demonstration, since we would be in the Philippines on the Passover. He decided on Friday evening February 2, as we were making a free trip to Glendale, Arizona, the next week on Delta Skymiles for grandson Sam's 8th birthday.

# 50th Wedding Anniv, 5th Conf & Yeshiva, Tours of Israel, Indonesia

The pastor had a good team of adults who followed my instructions very well, preparing for the Passover Seder. Families came together, as Passover is a family-centered celebration. Many said afterward that they enjoyed it very much, the first time they had ever done that. I just wish they would catch on, that they ought to be doing Passover every year, at the Appointed Time.

Now it was time to get back to the Philippines to prepare for the 5th Annual APMF Bible Conference in Baguio City. At last, John Fischer would be the teacher. In fact, both he and his wife Patrice were coming to teach. This had been in the planning stage for several years, since John is so busy. But as head of Menorah Ministries, of which we are members, he had to come to see what we were doing!

Patrice is a teacher also, with a PhD in Linguistics, and was coming to teach a crash course in Hebrew. However, she had been out of a job for a while. Finally, a job opening at the University of South Florida opened up for her, starting in January. There was no way she could take a week off that soon to come to the Philippines, so John asked me to teach a short course to give him a break, especially since he would also be launching our Yeshiva Program. Teaching all day, for several days, is quite tiring.

Several of the young men leaders in APMF congregations are also very good Bible teachers. They have their college degrees in various disciplines and are working in their professions, but they want more solid Bible teaching for two reasons. The first is, to know a lot more for a well-rounded education in historical Bible backgrounds and interpretations in order to improve their teaching. The second is, to silence those from their former churches who claim they cannot do what they are doing without a seminary education and ordination, This is the essence of the common and abominable clergy mentality that we intend to abolish.

The criticism is not valid, but only an excuse to demoralize the young leaders and promote the clergy mentality of most church people. It will not work, because we in APMF know who we are in Yeshua. Let them talk. Why should we not provide graduate level courses for those interested, men or women, anyone in our communities? However, we will not train clergy! Those who want to be clergy can go to their seminaries and pay tuition. Our philosophy is basically "freely you have received, freely give." The cost is minimal.

So Rabbi Dr. John Fischer, head of Netzer David Yeshiva and Academic Dean of St. Petersburg Theological Seminary would teach the first two courses for APMF Yeshiva credit. The Yeshiva was scheduled to begin on March 30, 2007 and run until April 4. The Course offered was "The Gospels in Their Original Jewish Context." My co-coordinator Dave Angiwan would teach Tim Hegg's course on "Hermeneutics: Interpreting the Bible."

The Bible Conference would begin on April 4 and run until the night of April 7. The teaching was "From Messiah to Mohammed, a History of the Messianic Community during that time period." With additional reading assignments, this was also offered for credit. My course would not be for credit yet, since it was short, but could be expanded later for its importance. It was "Bible Principles of Leadership, in the home and in the congregation."

## 50th Wedding Anniv, 5th Conf & Yeshiva, Tours of Israel, Indonesia

The Memory Passage for the 5th Annual Conference in April 2007 was Isaiah 56:6-7. This passage is very significant in that we foreigners, aliens, Gentiles who have made the decision to join ourselves to the LORD (Yahweh or Yehovah) equal to accepting Yeshua HaMashiach as LORD (Yahweh or Yehovah) and Savior in the terminology of today, are fully acceptable to God, equal to Jews who do the same. But notice, that this acceptance has been from ancient times! It is not something which began when Yeshua came to earth. Gentiles who put their Trust in God have always been part of the Family of God, even though the Congregation of the LORD in the Tanach is equated to Israel.

This is also the Olive Tree Message of Romans 11, that Gentile Believers are grafted into the good olive tree together with Jewish Believers. It is also the message of Ephesians 2:8-10, where salvation has always been by the Grace of God with our Faith response. The expectation is that the newly saved person, indwelt by the Spirit, will keep Shabbat and all the rest of the Covenant responsibilities of the Torah. This validates the fact that there is only ONE Family of the LORD, Jew and Gentile together in "Israel."

The One Family of the LORD is also characterized as being made up of three or four parts, also from ancient times. Look at Psalm 115:9-13:

> "O Israel, trust thou in the LORD; he is their help and their shield. O house of Aaron, trust in the LORD; he is their help and their shield. Ye that fear the LORD, trust in the LORD; he is their help and shield. The LORD has been mindful of us; he will bless us, he will bless the house of Israel, he will bless the house of Aaron. He will bless those who fear the LORD, both small and great".

The three parts seen are: the 12 Tribes, collectively called Israel; the Tribe of Levi, headed by Aaron, the high priest; and the God Fearers, Gentiles who have joined with Israel. These God Fearers are not converts, but are those who recognize the God of Israel as the only true God, live among the Israeli people, and follow Torah as the Israelis do. God did not give any "conversion process" in the Bible. That was made up years later by rabbis of Israel to protect themselves from increasing numbers of Gentiles who wanted to convert to Judaism because they were disgusted with the paganism of their day.

Again, lets look at Psalm 118:2-4 where we find the same three divisions of Israel:

*"Let Israel now say that his mercy endures forever. Let the house of Aaron now say that his mercy endures forever. Let them now who fear the LORD say that his mercy endures forever."*

Psalm 135:19-20 lists four divisions, separating the house of Levi from the house of Aaron, but with the same God Fearers as in the previous verses:

*"Bless the LORD, O house of Israel; bless the LORD, O house of Aaron; bless the LORD, O house of Levi. Ye who fear the LORD, bless the LORD."*

There are quite a few passages that emphasize the equality between the native born Israeli and the stranger or God Fearing Gentile that lives among them, from ancient times. Here are a couple of them:

Leviticus 19:33-34. *" And if a stranger sojourn with you in your land, you shall not vex him. But the stranger that*

*dwells with you shall be unto you <u>as one born among you,</u>
and you shall love him as yourself; for you were strangers
in the land of Egypt: I am the LORD your God. "*

Numbers 15:15-16. *"One ordinance shall be both for you
of the congregation, and also for <u>the stranger who sojourns
with you,</u> an ordinance forever in your generations: as you
are, so shall the sojourner be before the LORD. <u>One law</u>
<u>(Torah)</u> and one ordinance shall be for you, and for the
stranger who sojourns with you."*

John Fischer's comments in his Menorah Ministries
Newsletter, after he got back home from the Conference
in Baguio, were quite perceptive:

"The response throughout the Yeshiva and the
Conference was overwhelmingly positive and
encouraging. Everyone was enthusiastic and very
eager to learn more. It was a group of people that was
more excited to learn, and more grateful for the
teaching they received, than could be found anywhere
in America, and in many parts of the world. And all
this, where there was virtually nothing of this sort half
a dozen years ago! God had been working; people
had been praying. After he gave the closing talk at
the conference, the people kept John for over an hour
and a half, signing books and having their picture
taken with him."

The APMF Tour of Israel was scheduled for May 3 – 15.
As happens so often, talk is big, but coming up with the
money is difficult. We had planned for a minimum of 20
persons, including ourselves. We also decided to pay our
own way to make it easier for others. Even then, we came
up with only fourteen by recruiting three friends from

Florida. We were then five Americans; one Australian, formerly of BIBAK; one Indonesian, six Filipinos; and one Filipina who was already working in Israel as a caregiver, but planned her vacation to be able to join us.

Nevertheless, it was a good tour - more intimate, with everyone learning a lot. On the last weekend, I had the Tour do the Jerusalem sites with their regular tour guide while I did a two-day Bible Conference at our hotel, for as many of the BIBAK girls working in Israel who could get one or both days off to join us. They have social fellowship with other Filipinas on their days off, but very little spiritual enrichment while in Israel.

We had hoped that our Singapore group would join us, but the dates conflicted. Filipinos are free in May as school starts in June. Singaporeans still have school in May, and vacation in June. Therefore, the Singapore group had asked me to plan a Tour of Israel exclusively for them, in June. OK, then. Their dates were June 4-17, with an extension for four of us until June 21.

It actually went a bit longer. They had heard about and wanted to see some special places, like the full-size Tabernacle set-up in the desert way down south almost to Eilat. There is not much in Eilat for a whole day's stay, so we went over to Jordan to see Petra, the rose-rock city. Other than those sites, we traveled the main spots. When I lead a Tour of Israel, I have two objectives: one, to see the historical biblical sites; and two, to see sites related to modern Israel. I leave out all the churchy stuff, which has no relevance to us unless there is ample time to check out a few that relate significantly to Messianic or church history.

## 50th Wedding Anniv, 5th Conf & Yeshiva, Tours of Israel, Indonesia

I met the Singapore group in Bangkok, Thailand. From here, we went together to Israel on El Al Israel Airlines. Their group consisted of eight families plus a few singles, making thirty six people altogether! During the Tour at different places, they had one *Bar Mitzvah* and three *Bat Mitzah* (for girls). On my return trip, I planned ahead with email contacts to stay the weekend in Bangkok to fellowship with a small Shabbat Bible study group, made up mostly of expats. It turned out well, as they were searching out their Jewish Roots and expressing their love for Israel.

As soon as I got back in Manila, I went directly to Baguio. There had been a schedule change for the afternoon lecture I was to give at the Philippine Military Academy. So the next day I went to the campus and taught on the Arab-Israel Conflict all afternoon to 300 sophomore cadets and officers. This is a course in their curriculum. In their second year, they get the historical background and current action. In their third year, they study the tactics that Israel has used to defeat their enemies, including the one that led to the Six Day War victory. I was invited to teach because of my Graduate Certificate in Middle Eastern Studies in Jerusalem and because I do not require an honorarium. External experts expect a fee, and budgets are always tight.

But also, one of our BIBAK/APMF ladies, Gladys Tamania, was on the faculty at PMA in the history department and recommended me. Two years before, she had written her doctoral dissertation on the migration of Muslims from the south of the Philippines to Baguio in the north, with the intent to make Baguio a center of Muslim culture! Actually, they are spreading all over the country as a prelude to taking over. This is a threat to the Philippines, so the government is taking notice of her dissertation and is publishing it. In fact, Muslim influence is putting pressure to have Gladys pushed out of the faculty at PMA, since she is a stalwart for Jesus and for Israel.

After my three-hour lecture, I answered questions. One Muslim Cadet commented that I seemed to portray Islam as evil. I replied that Islam portrays itself as evil before all the civilized world by its homicide bombers; the targeting of women and children; the "honor" killings of young girls who get pregnant by their brothers or fathers; the rejoicing when Israelis or Americans are killed; and so on. This kind of behavior is not seen in Western and most cultures of the world. I told the Cadet that this type of behavior speaks for itself. "If that is not the Islam you practice, then you and your fellow Muslims had better speak up and confront the radical ones, if indeed there is a difference."

For several years, three Indonesians have been coming regularly to our APMF Conferences. Each time, they'd urge us to come to Indonesia to teach. We have hesitated because it is the most populous Muslim country in the world. However, when we were at Shell Point Retirement Center for my sister's Memorial Service, we met the lady in charge there, who used to be a missionary in Indonesia. She told us it is perfectly safe in most areas of the country. Our Indonesian friends also said that we would not go to certain dangerous areas. So we agreed to go in October 2007.

We left Gainesville airport on September 29 and arrived in Jakarta on October 1 on Korean Airlines. Their schedule had us waiting in Seoul, Korea, for almost a whole day before our flight to Jakarta. So they put us up overnight in an airport hotel, for free. In Indonesia, I taught three Seminars of two days each, and one for only half-day. These were in Yogyakarta, Medan, Tarutong, and Jakarta.

A significant event happened in Yogyakarta. My teaching was to acquaint many new ones to the Hebraic Roots of biblical faith and practice, and to make firm the understanding of the older ones. While I was there, the INDONESIAN MESSIANIC FELLOWSHIP was inaugurated with "The Seven Messiah's Servants of Indonesia." Their Declaration is to merge with APMF in order to advance the Gospel throughout the islands. We accepted their Declaration and pledged to do our best to help them with our teaching and teachers as the Lord directs and enables.

Our host, Bernis Hutauruk, also took us to Bali, the tourist place, for our education! His wife, Fatimah, joined us for the trip to Sumatra island. For the seminars, they provided good translators, as the English language is not well known, even among college-educated professionals. A lot of Bible teaching is needed, so that I plan to return there as often as possible, maybe every year, jumping over from the Philippines. The Lord seems to make it clear that His area for me to serve Him is the very needy Asia Pacific region. The USA has way too much "religion," while these other countries have so little Bible Truth. Our indigenous approach on a biblical Hebraic Jewish foundation of Yeshua and the Apostles seems to be helping some get excited about this approach, further stabilizing their faith.

Since Singapore is very near Indonesia, I arranged to leave Indonesia on Friday, October 19 to go to Singapore to be with our friends there for the weekend. I did not have to do any teaching this time. I just enjoyed fellowship with them and heard some of their amazing testimonies. The

Lord brought two of their Elders out of their churches by showing them the inconsistencies between the church teachings and their Bibles. This happened totally without any contact with others outside. So they just began to study and worship at home with their families, shifting over to *Shabbat* in obedience to what they saw in Scripture. They were content to remain isolated with their families for a couple years, until they came in contact with others who had discovered the same Truth.

For Thanksgiving 2007, we decided to use Delta Sky Miles to fly Randy, Janie, Jake, and Sam to Florida for a long weekend, since Arizona schools do not have the whole week off. The weather was wonderful, we ate too much, and we enjoyed our place way out in the country. The boys enjoyed 'mowing' with our John Deere tractor, even with no grass to cut!

# CHAPTER 28

# 6th Annual Conference and 2nd Yeshiva, in Manila Dec 2007 3rd Yeshiva in Manila, Cebu, Banaue, Baguio, Nagoya, and Tokyo, March 2008

The 6th Annual APMF Bible Conference and 2nd Yeshiva (grad school) were supposed to be in the springtime. Some of the Manila groups wanted to host it there for a change in an attempt to enable more people from the Metro Manila area to benefit. Ted Franco and Joel Cruz were appointed to organize it. Their preference for a teacher was Tim Hegg, but he could not come in the springtime. The next available vacation time is the year-end Christmas time break. This time of year has many problems because it is traditionally a time when Filipino families get together. We also have the problem of trying to adjust to the different schedules of our Asia Pacific countries. However, they wanted to push through with this schedule.

Yeshiva No. 2 was December 20-25, 2007, for the course on "<u>Christology</u>", designed to make sure we understood well that Yeshua HaMashiach or Jesus The Messiah is fully God and fully man, perfect and sinless in His humanity as Adam was before he sinned. In fact, Yeshua is called the second Adam in 1 Corinthians 15. This is an area of concern because teachers of all kinds are downgrading Yeshua to someone less than God. A Messiah Redeemer who is not also God cannot make full payment for the sins of mankind. To call the Messiah Son of God must indicate that He is of the same essence as the Father. We speak of the Deity of Yeshua, since some consider divinity somewhat less than God or Deity.

Bible Conference No. 6 was December 25-28, with Tim Hegg teaching, "What's So New About the New Testament?" and "My Big Fat Greek Mind Set." Western civilization and the church are totally locked into the Greek mindset, which is not suitable to understanding the Bible. The Bible was written with a Hebrew mindset, which is quite different. To understand the Bible, we must learn to "Think Jewish, to Think like They Thought when the Texts were Written."

The Memory Passage for Conference No. 6, December 2007 was Jeremiah 31:31-34.

*"Behold the days come, says the LORD, that I will make a new (chadash =new or renewed) covenant with the house of Israel, and with the house of Judah, not according to the covenant that I made with their fathers in the day that I took them by the hand to bring them out of the land of Egypt, which, my covenant, they broke, although I was a husband to them, says the LORD; but this shall be the covenant that I will make with the house of Israel: After those days, says the LORD, I will put my law (Torah) in their inward parts, and write it in their hearts, and will be*

*their God and they shall be my people. And they shall teach no more every man his neighbor, saying, Know the LORD; for they shall all know me, from the least of them unto the greatest of them, says the LORD; for I will forgive their iniquity, and I will remember their sin no more."*

Notice carefully that the New Covenant was made with a united ISRAEL, not with the church! God works with humans only on the basis of a Covenant, the conditions of which He sets forth. Humans can accept it or reject it, but cannot change it in any way. It is a "take it or leave it" with no negotiation. God has never made any Covenant with any Gentile or church. Before Abraham, there was no distinction. God made a Covenant with Noah, which applied to all mankind. This was about behavior requirements, and did not provide for salvation from sin. With Abraham, the Covenant was for salvation from sin, by Trust in the Almighty. With Moses, the Covenant was the behavior requirements for those already saved, who had God as their husband.

Yeshiva No. 2 was well attended, while the Conference did not have as many participants as it usually did. However, there were many new attendees from the Manila churches, which lined up with the main objective for the Conference. Not many old-timers from outside the Manila area attended because the topic was somewhat a review of previous Conferences. This was just fine.

Yeshiva No. 3 was different. Naomi's companions in high school and church young people many years ago, had also retired. To make retirement more enjoyable and to satisfy a keen desire to study the Bible more practically, Forest and Iva Swineford of Ashland, Ohio constructed a scale model of The Tabernacle, using 1 inch = 1 cubit. They had been doing seminars in many churches around their area, but had run out of opportunities. So I suggested that they come to the Philippines to do the seminars there, with us. They agreed. In order to make the Yeshiva more accessible to more people, I decided to bring them to classes in six cities. Being retired, the Swinefords and we have more time to spend than our usually very busy Jewish teachers, who had time only for the Annual Conferences.

Each Yeshiva was three days. The whole title was: "EXODUS, the Establishing of the Nation of Israel: its Redemption by the Blood of the Lamb from slavery in Egypt, its Marriage to the LORD at Mt. Sinai, its Way of Life in the Ten Commandments, and its Worship in The Tabernacle, God dwelling with His people."

The Tabernacle part took 95 percent of the time. This is because the Tabernacle is the most neglected part in the usual treatment of Exodus, if Exodus is even taught at all in churches and seminaries these days. The model, about four feet by eight feet when set up from its suitcase "home," comes with a power point presentation and 64-page syllabus. To get Yeshiva credit, each student needs to attend the class, write a paper on some aspect of the Tabernacle that fascinates him, and together with his congregation, build a scale model so that he could teach it well, including the children.

We left the USA on March 12 to fly to Manila. The first Yeshiva was for the Metro Manila people on March 15-17, hosted by Ciso and Billie Padilla. Then we flew to Cebu City on the 18th and taught the Yeshiva for a large group there on March 20-22, hosted by Nowyn Jangad and Joel Cruz. The Jangad family owns and operates a Christian day school for elementary and high school students. They plan to add a college and graduate school to accommodate the APMF Yeshiva program! A few students even came from Thailand to participate in the Cebu Yeshiva!

On March 23, we flew back to Manila and took the night bus to Banaue, Ifugao Province. It was a long nine hours into the mountains! From Manila, buses only go at night, so there is no scenery to enjoy. The Yeshiva there was March 24-26. Our host, Butch Sarol, drove us to Baguio on the 27th. Again, this was a long, but this time, beautiful scenic daytime trip through the mountains. It was a first for the Swinefords. Naomi and I lived in Banaue for nine years, at the beginning of our ministry in the Philippines. We always enjoy the mountains.

The Baguio Yeshiva on March 28-29 was hosted by Nene Bowman and her sister Linda Sarda, Trustees of the University of the Cordilleras (formerly BCF). The last day, March 30, was at the Agriculture Training Institute on the campus of Benguet State University, hosted by Bernard Tad-awan, a faculty member of BSU. The 31st was a rest day, for doing some laundry. The Conference Planning Committee decided to use ATI for the 4th Yeshiva and 7th Bible Conference on April 3-12, 2009.

After having rested a bit and changed into clean clothes, we took the bus down to Manila on April 1, for a flight to Tokyo on April 2, to do shortened Seminars in Nagoya and Tokyo. In the Philippines, nearly everyone can speak English, but in Japan, we needed a translator. In order to get in on the Tabernacle Seminar, Nobuyuki Ito came to Japan to translate for us.

Nobu is a businessman working in Bangkok, Thailand, as an efficiency expert for a US company. His wife Melynda is a Filipina who teaches in a school in Japan! They have two lovely daughters in college, Sara in Japan living with her mother and Hannah in Bangkok with her father. Besides being our translator, Nobu with Melynda and Sara took excellent care of us the whole time we were in Japan, staying in their home, driving us to Nagoya for the Seminar there, back to Meiji University in Tokyo for the Seminar there, and from and to the Narita airport. Their family gets together quite often; we might say they are "frequent fliers" between Tokyo and Bangkok! We flew back home on April 7.

Now what could be so important about **The Wilderness Tabernacle** that people would be motivated to build scale models and travel around the Far East to teach it? You would not bother studying it if you believe what the *Interpreter's Bible* of the Methodist Church teaches. In Volume 1, p. 1027, it says in relation to Exodus 26:1-37, "The tabernacle here presented never actually existed. It is a product of the priestly imagination, an ideal structure. Two historical objects helped to give shape to the imaginary structure which was to illustrate a new theological conviction."

In contrast, for us who believe the Bible totally and have put our Trust in the God of the Bible, the Wilderness Tabernacle surely did exist for hundreds of years! Its importance is shown because, except for Noah' Ark, another real structure, The Tabernacle is the only structure built on earth that was designed by God and built at His command. It was His dwelling on earth among His people Israel, with a pillar of cloud over it by day and a pillar of fire at night! How can anyone calling himself a Christian and Bible believer not believe everything in the Bible, including this Tabernacle? Such is much of the church today, throwing out the Hebrew Scriptures and pretending to follow the Greek New Testament in its many different translations, which are only relatively accurate, as we will discover.

Start your study by reading Exodus 25-40. This is about the structure itself. The functions are in Leviticus, which is another study. Keeping many of the details in mind, read Hebrews chapter 9. In 9:9, the Tabernacle is called a "parable." You did not see 'parable' in your translation? Of course not, because Bible translators are sometimes dishonest when their theology conflicts with the text. The Greek word 'parabolay' is translated 'parable' in almost every other place that it occurs, except here. Why?

A parable is not the same as a figure, illustration, or symbol, as most translations use in their carelessness or attempt to deceive you. Yeshua defined a parable in Matthew 13:10-17 as a way of teaching, whereby He hides His Truth to those in the audience who have closed their eyes, ears, and heart to Him, while at the same time He reveals His Truth to those whom He has chosen, who have their eyes, ears, and heart open to Him. Yeshua speaks to the multitudes only by means of parables!

Further, in the explanation of two of the parables in Matthew 13, every part of the parable has a meaning that fits in with the overall meaning. Applying this to the Tabernacle, every color of cloth has its meaning. Each metal, each board, each post, each socket — all have their meanings which fit in with the overall meaning which is The Way to Worship God, the Way into the Presence of the Father through the Son, Yeshua HaMashiach. These symbolic meanings need to be found somewhere in Scripture, not just guessed at. This is another reason to read and re-read the whole Bible many times. Our basic clue is found in Hebrews 10:19-20:

*"Having therefore, brethren, boldness to enter into the holiest by the blood of Jesus, by a new and living way, which He has consecrated for us, through the veil, that is to say, His flesh..."*

Do you see the clue? It is that the veil in the Tabernacle that separated the Holy Place from the Holy of Holies represents the flesh of Jesus, The Messiah of Israel! That veil protected the people from the wrath of God. The high priest had to be very careful on Yom Kippur, the Day of Atonement, when he went into the Holy of Holies or he would be struck dead.

Yeshua, the Son of God, has always been The One that prevented the wrath of God from breaking out upon the people. The Temple was patterned after the Tabernacle, so this means that the veil that was torn by the Father the instant Yeshua dismissed His Spirit while on the cross, showed that the wrath of God against mankind was satisfied by Yeshua's blood sacrifice of His earthly life. Only a sinless God-man could accomplish this.

In the description in Exodus, this veil is made of distinct strips of four colors, blue, purple, scarlet, and white. This veil represents Yeshua, as we discovered above. Therefore, whenever in the Tabernacle structure, material of blue, purple, scarlet, and white occur together, that material represents Yeshua, or some aspect of who He is. Individually, blue represents the Man from heaven; white, the sinless Man from heaven; purple, the King of the Universe; and scarlet, the One who left heaven to come to earth to be born in a human body with a sinless human nature to die for our sins by shedding His blood to pay for our sins.

These four colored cloths make up the gate, the screen at

the entrance of the board structure, the inner veil as above, and the first covering over the board structure. These wide strips of cloth must be separate and distinct, but attached to each other at the edge! Models that we have seen make a serious mistake by taking four colors of yarn and weaving them together into a blur that is purplish at best. This gives no meaning at all.

The board structure has four layers covering it as a roof. The one that can be seen above when inside the Holy Place, the board structure, is made of wide strips of blue, purple, scarlet and white cloth. On top of that is a layer of goat's hair cloth, which is called the Tent. On top of the goat's hair tent is a layer of ram's skin dyed red. The top layer which is exposed to the sky is the color of the sky, a sky-blue covering of probably ram's skins dyed blue.

In your Bible, you may find that the top covering is said to be a skin of a kind of fish or an animal. But nothing is said about the color. Why? It is claimed that the Hebrew word is obscure and so each different English version has to come up with a different word for this skin. Again, Bible translators are deceiving us! With two witnesses, a testimony is accepted. And we have two witnesses: 1) The Septuagint, LXX, translates the Hebrew word with the Greek *vakinthina*, which clearly means blue. 2) Josephus, in his *Antiquities of the Jews*, p 71 says, '…sheep-skins, some of them dyed of a blue colour, and some of a scarlet.' Also on p 73 '…and great was the surprise of those who viewed these curtains at a distance, for they seemed not at all to differ from the colour of the sky.' It is totally not acceptable to us that Bible translators would not consult ancient sources, but instead put their personal or theological prejudices in their English text.

So why is it so important that the top covering be of blue skin? And why four layers over the board structure, when only one would do? The top has to be waterproof, so a skin is necessary. But notice this progression of layers and their meaning: top, the Man from heaven is the blue skin; second, who came to earth to shed His blood, scarlet skin; third, to pay for our sins, goat's hair cloth; fourth, all sins laid on Yeshua, the bottom layer, made of wide strips of blue, purple, scarlet, and white, just like the inner veil that was torn by the Father at the instant Yeshua dismissed His spirit when on the cross. The top layer must be blue, and is blue, to keep <u>the parable meaning clear</u>.

Why is the third layer of the tent, counting from the top, made of goat's hair? On Yom Kippur, only the <u>blood of a goat</u> is brought into the Holy of Holies and sprinkled on the Mercy Seat to cover the sins of the people. For the high priest, the blood of a bull is brought in first to cover his sins so he can now function for the people. The scarlet skins and the blue skins are made of rams skins.

Many people think that the blood of a lamb is brought in to cover their sins, since Yeshua is called 'the Lamb of God that takes away the sin of the world,' but the blood of a lamb is never brought in to the Mercy Seat. Remember, however, that for the original Passover, the Israelis were told they could sacrifice either a goat or a lamb. Otherwise, goats and sheep are very different kinds of animal and have very different symbolic meanings. A practical reason for goat's hair is the function of material made of goat's hair: it 'breathed' when dry but tightened up when wet to make it waterproof.

The board structure was made of 48 massive boards placed upright upon silver sockets and tied together with long horizontal poles. These 48 boards represent the Levites who lived in 48 cities scattered in Israel. The west end had six of these boards, representing the Cities of Refuge. An interesting correlation is found in Hebrews 6:18-20:

*"...that by two immutable things, in which it was impossible for God to lie, we might have a strong consolation, <u>who have fled for refuge</u> to lay hold on the hope set before us, which hope we have as an anchor of the soul, both sure and steadfast, and which enters into <u>that inside the veil</u>, where the forerunner is for us entered, even Jesus, made an high priest forever after the order of Melchizedek."*

Another interesting correlation to the board structure is found in Revelation 3:12: *"Him that overcomes will I make <u>a pillar</u> in the temple of my God..."*

The Hebrew word for board in the Tabernacle is translated as *stulos* in the LXX, Greek Septuagint. This is the same word, *stulos*, used for 'pillar' in the verse above. Both of these passages are reminding us, those who have come to Faith in Yeshua, that we are included in the Tabernacle structure, included in all of God's Plans for His people, whether Jews or Gentiles, which has always been God's ways since the beginning. These boards are also placed on sockets of silver, representing the Redemption that Yeshua purchased for us.

So, is The Tabernacle important to study, and apply? Obviously so!

# CHAPTER 29

## Discipling and Teaching in the Philippines and Thailand August 2008

Praise the LORD for email! Telephones and postal mail are still good, and we use both; but email is the basic way we keep in touch with our many disciples around the world, especially in the Asia Pacific region. However, there is nothing better than a personal visit! Sure, it costs a lot of money and takes a lot of time, but progress and growth are much accelerated by unhurried time spent together, in groups and individually.

This August trip included a lot of traveling. Naomi does not travel as well, so I let her stay home this time. However, with my Philippine cell phone activated to receive calls, and do local calling and texting, she phoned me almost every day! We do have an international calling plan, so the cost was not exorbitant, and was much cheaper than an airline ticket.

The price of airline tickets kept going up. We usually fly on Northwest Airlines since they go Manila. As a result, we have earned Gold Elite Status, which gives us some advantages and privileges. But when the difference in price was about $500 per ticket, we decided to research some more. Orbitz.com is one place to search for cheaper tickets, and Expedia.com is another.

I decided on Expedia.com this time and flew on United Airlines from Orlando to Chicago to Hong Kong, and from Hong Kong to Manila on Philippine Airlines. The one part I did not like was the leg from Chicago to Hong Kong. It was 15 ½ hours! And I do not sleep much sitting in a tight chair. Anyway, I left MCO, that's Orlando, on July 31 at 8:40am and arrived in Manila on Friday, August 1 at 8PM. That wasn't too bad given a 12-hour advance in time. Again, Arche Tubio picked me up at the airport and brought me to the Padilla's home. They want us to stay with them whenever we are in Manila and they are also in Manila. They are our age and travel a lot, but are still in the construction business.

August 2 was *Shabbat*, so I celebrated with the Metro Strata Congregation. On Sunday, I spent time at the Mount Zion Center in Quezon City to see how everything was going. On Monday, I took the Victory Liner bus to Baguio to stay again at Doane Rest, the vacation place for tired missionaries! We aren't tired, but DR makes a nice home-away-from-home for us. Jan Whetstone, the manager, does a good job of making sure everything and everyone is A-OK. A group from the LaTrinidad Bible Congregation brought supper and extra food for me so I could make breakfasts and gave a hearty "Welcome Home!"

The next nine days were mostly filled with Bible studies at the University of the Cordilleras with Bible students of Nene Bowman, the Trustee on site. I also checked out the facilities of the Agriculture Training Institute with Bernard Tad-awan, to be sure the sleeping arrangements would meet minimum standards, and met with the Conference Planning Committee to be sure each one knew his assignment. There are many willing hands in Baguio and La Trinidad; once organized, they work well as a team. Some have been with us for thirty years, and new ones keep coming.

On August 14, I took the bus back down the mountain to Manila, and the next day flew to Cagayan de Oro in the south, on the big island of Mindanao, together with an assistant, Roni Gayaman from LTBC. Colonel Oliver Enmodias met us at the airport and took me to my hotel for the three nights I would be in the area in ministry with him. Roni stayed with Oliver. Oliver is from Baguio and his family stays there. He became a disciple when he was in high school. He applied for and was accepted at the Philippine Military Academy that is based in Baguio. PMA is a very tough place for anyone, especially for a believer. We kept in touch as best we could with his tight schedule. Oliver graduated in 1990 and then was assigned here and there. So we lost contact until a couple years ago.

Early this year, 2008, he was assigned in the south, which gave opportunity for the Lord to bring Oliver back to Himself and to Messianic understanding. The evening of my arrival was Erev Shabbat, the Friday night Fellowship Meal and Bible study. Solomon and Vivilyn Buasag came from Talakag, Bukidnon, a one-hour drive away, for the evening. All of us went to their place the next morning for Shabbat Bible study. Vivilyn had studied in Baguio and lived with us for her first two years of college, so Oliver knew her back then. She and Solomon have helped Oliver a lot.

Solomon was a pastor. But he left the church when he and Vivilyn encountered too much politics in the denomination. Worshiping and studying the Bible on their own, they soon came to the conclusion that the church was partly off base, so they went back to *Shabbat* observance and biblical festivals, just like Yeshua and the Apostles.

On Sunday, August 17, Oliver drove us all to a remote tribal area in Bukidnon Province, to a congregation that wanted to hear about the real New Covenant from Jeremiah 31:31-34, in contrast to the changed New Covenant of the church. Oliver, Roni, and Solomon all gave testimonies. Solomon interpreted for us in their tribal language. The road was a terrible, dirt road with many potholes because it was the rainy season. But we and the vehicle survived.

We flew back to Manila on Monday, August 18. Roni took the bus back to Baguio while Ricky Samson picked me up at the airport and brought me to his house where I stayed for most of three days for individual discipling and teaching. Ricky had been a businessman for many years with Proctor & Gamble, a large US company. He was earning lots of money. But one day, he was born-from-above by the Holy Spirit and his life changed. He soon resigned from the company to serve the Lord, and supported himself with other endeavors.

He was instrumental, along with a few other businessmen, for establishing a mega-church in Manila with no clergy. Recently he saw the light about *Shabbat* and the false church teaching that 'the Law has been done away with in Christ.' A shock came when he read Matthew 5:17-19, a passage he had read many times before and just slid over:

> *"Think not that I am come to destroy the law, or the prophets; I am not come to destroy but to fulfill. For verily I say unto you, Till heaven and earth pass, one jot or one tittle shall in no way pass from the law, till all be fulfilled. Whosoever, therefore, shall break one of these least commandments, and shall teach men so, he shall be called the least in the kingdom of heaven; but whosoever shall do and teach them, the same shall be called great in the kingdom of heaven."*

This time, the Holy Spirit opened his eyes to what Yeshua actually said. It caused him deep repentance and regret about his past church teachings! He had many disciples. Now he needed to go back to all of them and correct his past teachings, like I had to do! Also, being an aggressive salesman, he wanted to be great in the kingdom of heaven! How to do that? He must now DO and TEACH all the Commandments, even the least one!

Yeshua did NOT come to destroy the law or the prophets! He came to fill the law full of meaning, as He continued to do in Matthew 5-7. "You have heard" referred to the common, superficial teaching of the Law of God, the Torah, so Yeshua went to the heart of the Law that He had written through Moses. Mostly the teaching and practice of that time was the Oral Torah, the *Mishnah*, the additional details that supposedly were given to Moses and which were a burden upon the people. The Torah was not and is not a burden! Rather, the Torah was and is a delight to the Believer, as Psalm 1, 19, 119 and many others attest.

315

The burden that Peter brought out at the Council in Jerusalem in Acts 15:10, the *"yoke upon the necks of the disciples, which neither our fathers nor we were able to bear"* was NOT the *Torah*, but the *Mishnah*, the Oral *Torah* of the rabbis, with its many minute details of how to obey the Law. That the Torah is not a burden is clearly illustrated in Acts 21:20 where James tells Paul, *"You see, brother, how many tens of thousands of Jews there are who believe, and they are all zealous of the law (Torah)."* The church has made a terrible mistake in twisting the teachings of Paul to say that "the law was done away with in Christ." A genuine Believer, a Disciple of Yeshua, is eager to show his love for Yeshua by obeying everything He said! That is the attitude of a *doulos*, a bond-slave, who loves his Master.

So Ricky and I spent a couple days going over all these teachings. He has many disciples in different groupings. I met with him with two of these groups. The second of these was a supper meeting in a private room at a fast food restaurant, a typical place used by businessmen. After some introductory teachings, Ricky told them that he had taught them two basic things wrong. First, there is no Old Testament and New Testament. The Word of God is one unit together and nothing was old and to be disregarded. In the past he had taught them only from the New Testament, and that was inadequate teaching without a foundation.

The second had to do with Replacement Theology. He had not used or even known the term but his teaching reflected this idea. He turned this part of the corrective teaching over to me. I did not have very much time to deal with it, but it was a start. Later, Ricky asked me if I noticed the look on the faces of these disciples. I hadn't paid much attention to that since I did not know any of them, but he said they looked shocked. Of course! It is quite shocking to realize you had believed and taught something that looked OK at one time, but turned out to be wrong upon more serious in depth study. The problem comes when starting from a wrong assumption, that the church replaced Israel, when there is no evidence whatsoever to warrant that assumption.

To show that Replacement Theology is the thought pattern of church people, whether they have heard the term or not, I sometimes use Matthew 5:13, "You are the salt of the earth," a passage nearly everyone knows. Then I ask these church people, "Who are the 'you'?" The answer is always, "Us. We are the salt of the earth." "Do you mean to say that the church is the salt of the earth?" "Yes, of course." "Did the church exist at the time Jesus spoke in Matthew?" "Well, probably not, but that is what Jesus meant." "Look at Matthew 5:1. Jesus is teaching His disciples while a multitude were gathered around. Were the disciples and the multitude Christians?" "Well, not yet, but they would be soon, once they accepted Jesus as their Lord and Savior." "But what were the disciples and the multitude before they became Christians?" "Well, I guess they were Jews." "Yes, they were Jews, all of them. Jesus is a Jew. He is telling the disciples and the multitude that they, the Jews, Israel, are the salt of the earth! Where did you get the idea that the church is the salt of the earth?" "Well, that is what our pastor has taught us." "So your pastor has taught you in a subtle way that the church has replaced Israel. He probably does not even realize that himself. So please, use this to teach others, OK?"

After this time with Ricky, he brought me back to Padilla's and joined us for a supper planning meeting with Mount Zion and Metro Strata leaders. I would be teaching an all-day Seminar hosted by Mount Zion Center that will be open to anyone, especially students from the nearby University of the Philippines. The requested portion was to be Matthew 5-7, plus anything else that comes up and some introductory foundational teachings. This Seminar will be Monday, August 25, a declared holiday.

Before that, I flew to Cebu on Friday, August 22, for teaching and fellowship with the growing congregation there, meeting at the Cebu Christian Institute International and in homes for small groups. Some special time was spent with Joel and Imee as we thought ahead to their wedding in Cebu on Sunday, December 28 this year.

A problem had developed because no one in APMF is currently licensed in the Philippines to officiate weddings. My license expired long ago, as has the license of some of the men currently in APMF. One Elder from Joel's congregation in Manila is working on his renewal and it may come through in time. The same problem exists for Keren and Richard for their wedding in Baguio on December 22. What could be done? No one wants to use any licensed clergy from their former churches, or any church person, as all had separated from the churches. Friendly relationships still exist, but there was no more working together at this point because church people are the most vocal critics.

I suggested a solution that is common in some other countries that require a civil marriage ceremony. If the couple desires an additional religious ceremony in those countries, that ceremony can be done after the civil one. We could adopt this very easily. It might be a bit cumbersome, but it will solve the legal problem until such time as leaders in APMF can qualify for licensing. Everyone in APMF wants their weddings to be really Jewish style, like as the Appointed Times celebrations. Therefore, we must do our own ceremonies and celebrations ourselves.

For Keren and Richard, they are going to arrange a visit to the office of a judge on the morning of their wedding, since they have scheduled theirs on a Monday, still a working day. For Joel and Imee, since theirs is on a Sunday, they may need to go to the office of a judge on the previous Friday, if the Elder from their congregation in Manila is not able to get his license renewed on time.

After Cebu, a very enjoyable Seminar was held at the Mount Zion Center in Manila, actually Quezon City. The place was packed full. Lunch was included. There were many good questions. A lot of theological areas were covered as we all got back on the foundation of Yeshua and His apostles. A similar Seminar is being planned for Sunday, December 7, after our trip to New Zealand.

Then it was off to Bangkok, Thailand on Friday, August 29, with another assistant, Ted Franco, our APMF Metro Manila coordinator. Melynda Ito and daughter Hannah picked us up at the airport, while Nobu finished his work for the day. We had a very nice Erev Shabbat with a small group. The Itos have guest quarters in their rented apartment so that Ted and I were comfortably billeted there.

They also have a large living room area to take care of the *Shabbat* morning Torah study and lunch, and continuing study until evening. The place was quite full with Thais, Filipinos, Australians, Japanese, and British participants. Ted brought along his laptop and Nobu brought a projector from his office. So we were very efficient in following the various Scriptures that I taught from, including the many questions that inevitably come up, and on which I enjoy teaching.

Our return flight to Manila was very late on Sunday night. Ted wanted to buy some things in town, so Nobu took us to a mall Sunday morning and then to a Thai restaurant for lunch. The menu for each selection told what blood type that dish is good for. This seems to be a new fad. Whether it has merit or not, I do not know, but it was an interesting experience. Then again we had Bible study all afternoon until 8 PM, when we had to pack up and go to the airport for our trip to Manila. This mixed group in Bangkok are just learning the changes that the church brought in over time, and adjusting to the original foundation. They are also very much interested in Israel, which is good. Several have been there more than once.

Ted left his borrowed car at the airport, so he took me to the Padilla's after our arrival at 4 AM. The security guard let me in the building and Archie let me in the apartment. I slept a bit, repacked my things, and Archie took me to the airport early the next morning, September 2, for my trip home. Ron and Naomi picked me up at the Orlando airport about 29 hours later. I now have about 2½ months to finish this book, along with many other things to do around home. A lightning strike took out our Internet satellite, my computer and related things. The septic tank drain field plugged up after many years, so we had to redo that ourselves to save money. Living way out in the countryside has its blessings and challenges, but we enjoy the fresh air and quiet.

"*Unshackled!*" Programs Nos. 3007 & 3008 were aired on radio worldwide in eight languages the first two weeks of September! It was nice to be home to hear Our Story on local radio in English. It was the request from Pacific Garden Mission in Chicago for Our Story to dramatize on their "Unshackled!" radio program that motivated me to finish writing this book. I hope the contents so far have encouraged you to read and study your Bible more and more, in order to come to the same conclusions I have — that after having first accepted Him as the Son of God and your Redeemer, Savior and Master, following in the footsteps of Yeshua, the Jewish Messiah, is the only way to live.

# CHAPTER 30

## Projecting Ahead!
## Our Story is not finished yet!

Publishing "Our Story" posthumously? No way! I am finishing this book and it will be published in time for our APMF Annual Bible Conference in April 2009. Michael Basilio of the Mount Zion Center in Manila is handling the publication. We all know that each of us is only one heartbeat away from Eternity with our LORD Yeshua, but He has also commanded us to "occupy until He Returns"! That means, Keep active!

We have been following the biblical pattern of the Book of Acts all throughout our ministry career, patterning it especially after the Apostle Paul. Therefore, since Acts Chapter 28 ends without an ending to what Yeshua has been doing through His servants, so the book According to Roger will "end" with Chapter 30, without an ending to what Yeshua will continue to do through us, His servants, forever.

Naomi and I flew out of Orlando on November 16, 2008, on United Airlines for Manila. We had 2½ days to rest up a bit from the long overnight flight with little sleep. Then on November 20, we flew on Qantas Airlines from Manila to Auckland, New Zealand, to connect with Messianic congregations there. We had never been to NZ before. We found only one functioning Messianic Congregation, the Talmidei (Disciples of) Yeshua Messianic Congregation in Auckland. The founders and leaders are Graeme and Caroline Purdie. Graeme is Jewish, and of course, both are disciples of Yeshua The Messiah. We enjoyed being with them on both Shabbats. The mornings were for the regular Torah study. After lunch, they asked me to teach and tell more about APMF. About 25 attended each week, with several young people in high school, college, or working already. NZ is far away, so we do not expect to see these lovely people very often. However, we are open to coming to do some more in-depth teaching in a Seminar or Conference as they see the need.

Monday through Friday, they had arranged a package Tour of New Zealand for us. One exciting part was meeting Georgia Kalngan, from La Trinidad Bible Congregation in the Philippines, who was working on a dairy farm in southern NZ. We were able to chat on the phone, but neither of us thought to arrange to meet somewhere along the route. But after talking, Georgia did ask her employer for time off, drove four hours to the next town we were to be in to try to find us! With no success walking around the streets of Queenstown, she went to the airport to wait for us ...and we met, and had almost an hour of good fellowship! Such perseverance is amazing!

On December 1, we flew Qantas to Brisbane, Australia, another country new to us. A family from Baguio now lives there. They hosted us and showed us some of the city. We did some Bible studies, and visited a synagogue. Australia is mostly a secular country with very little opportunity to study the Bible in a group context with good teachers. Ezra and Mordecai Tad-awan are in college in Brisbane. They and Yohanna, their mother, enjoyed being with us again and so did we being with them. She lives and teaches in Mt. Isa, a long way inland.

We arrived back in Manila on Thursday night, December 4. On Saturday, we joined the Metro Strata Messianic group in Mandaluyong. This is a new group which started mid-2007, and is growing steadily. Many months ago, I appointed three family men as a Committee to coordinate the weekly Shabbat Torah studies and other possible activities. They rotate weekly emcee responsibilities, including assigning *Torah* sections to individuals the week before to read and comment on. They have church background, so they are re-learning to do things the biblical way. It takes time to make the shift, to re-program their thinking. They are enjoying it very much, sometimes going into late afternoon as they all participate in the discussion on the Scripture of the day.

The essence of a Shabbat Messianic meeting is NOT to do "church on Saturday," which is a program with performers and spectators with the offering being a very important part. Why do most churches campaign to get more members? The more members, the bigger the offering to meet the budget, of course!

Messianics enjoy *Erev Shabbat,* which is Friday evening at home, maybe with some guests, *kiddush* wine (sanctification of the 24 hour Shabbat) and *challah* bread, followed by a festive meal. On Saturday, the focus is on reading and explaining Scripture, and the application to daily life, with everyone participating in an informal setting. Everyone enjoys singing, so of course there is a time for that.  Everyone enjoys eating, so there is a time for that also, either a light lunch or a snack, usually potluck.  Since it is Shabbat, the whole day is given over to the Lord, so there is no time pressure.  Meetings usually begin mid-morning and would end mid-to-late afternoon, sometimes going until sunset for the traditional *Havdalah*, a closing ceremony for Shabbat.  After sunset on Saturday, it is now "the first day of the week."  Biblically, "evening and morning" mark the day.

Keep that in mind when looking at certain passages that church people try to claim for "church meetings on Sunday" in Scripture.  There are none!  "Think Jewish in their day" and you will see it clearly.  In Israel, businesses close early on Friday afternoon.  Everyone wants to be home for *Erev Shabbat*.  Some entertainment businesses and eating places open after sunset on Saturday evening, but all businesses open every Sunday morning.  Don't twist Scripture to fit Traditions or prejudices!  This is still the pattern in Israel today.

Organizationally, what is a possible biblical way to set up a stable congregation?  Godly leadership is No. 1.  Who are they and how are they found?  In the Bible, they are called Elders.  Qualifications for Elders are found in 1 Timothy 3.  There are always multiple Elders in each congregation in the Bible.  There are no clergy in any congregation in the Bible except the "Nicolaitanes" in Revelation 2, which the Lord hates.  There are no "Diotrephes," those who like to be seen and heard.  Elders are always men, males; there are no female elders in the Bible.

## Projecting Ahead! Our Story is not finished yet!

Let us be sure we understand the Bible. The priests and Levites functioned at the Tabernacle and Temple for the sacrifices. They were born into that responsibility. They did not function as leaders in the Synagogues. Elders, multiple Elders, lead synagogues with a president or chairman, which usually is a rotating responsibility.

How are Elders found? Politics is to be avoided! Elders are found by each member of each congregation prayerfully seeking the guidance of the Lord to know His selection, His choice. First of all, there must be a membership. Members must be born-from-above and show a godly, Torah lifestyle, evidence of being led by the Holy Spirit. Members must commit themselves to one congregation only and be regular in attendance, taking part, and shouldering responsibilities. This is *Koinonia*, the joint participation of the Body, working together as a Team of Volunteers! After some months, even a year or more, until a level of maturity can be observed, of functioning with a regular membership and appointed committee leadership, the next step will be to see if there are any men among the membership that might be recognized as approaching the qualities of an Elder, a genuine servant of the Lord, self-supporting, an able teacher of the Bible, and so on.

To do this, the membership is informed that the next Shabbat, in the afternoon after Torah study, a meeting will be held for recognizing (not electing!) Elders. This is announced ahead, for people to be prayerfully considering the qualifications and what they know about the male members. When organizing the first membership, it would be a good practice to have each person who desires membership give his or her testimony, including a bit about themselves. As time goes on, new members would always be required to give a testimony to qualify for

327

membership. In this way, members will get to know long ahead of time the men who might qualify for Eldership.

All of the male members' names are put on the board. Each member is given a blank piece of paper. He or she is to put on that paper the names of those they feel are approaching the Bible qualifications, and that they are willing to work with those men as their leaders. Some might turn in a blank paper, or with one or more names. To be recognized as God's selection, a name must have a three-fourth approval of the membership. A unanimous approval would be ideal, but we do not want to put God to the test. If only one name is approved, then it is null and void until a later time, because there must be at least two or more Elders; the time is not yet for establishing Eldership leaders.

The membership needs to agree on a simple Statement of Faith and Practice. At first, I supply that Statement. Later on the membership might modify it, as each congregation is autonomous, but hopefully will not go astray. Then they need to agree on a certain time of year for their Annual Business Meeting. At this first Annual Business Meeting, each member must sign a commitment form for the coming year. A few weeks before the 2nd Annual Meeting, new commitment forms must be signed so that at the Annual Meeting it is known as to who is and who is not a member for the following year, and entitled to participate in the Elder selection process, which also is done each year at the Annual Meeting.

On December 7 (Pearl Harbor Day, I remember it well!), the Mount Zion folks organized with the Metro Manila folks another all day Bible Seminar. They had requested that I teach on Matthew 5-7, last August 25 on a declared holiday, which was well attended, and at which a request was made for a repeat. For this repeat, the request was to teach on the Olivet Discourse, Matthew 24-25, one of my favorite passages. After that, we took the Victory Liner bus to Baguio. We joined with La Trinidad Bible Congregation on the first Shabbat and Baguio City Messianic Congregation the next Shabbat. December 14 was the Conference Planning Committee meeting. Everything was going smoothly. Good!

Possibly the main reason for making this trip to the Philippines at this time of year was to participate in two important weddings! Keren Angiwan, whom we have known since birth, was married to Richard Nelson on December 22 in Baguio City. Richard is a Filipino from the lowlands, a graduate civil engineer and a relatively new Messianic Believer. They knew each other in high school, but then drifted apart with their different educational objectives.

Once Richard became a Believer in Yeshua and started attending Keren's congregation, the attraction started. The Angiwan family, with Richard agreeing, asked me to share the officiating with Bonifacio Doques in the Jewish Messianic style, with the canopy (*chuppah*) over them, Richard breaking the wine glass in memory of the destruction of Jerusalem and some Hebrew liturgy. They wrote out their own ceremony and vows. Since both Boni's and my licenses to officiate weddings in the Philippines had expired, Uncle Rene Daytec took Keren and Richard to the mayor of Tuba, the town next to Baguio where the Daytecs live, in the morning to do the official wedding. Boni was then assigned to be sure they showed up for the real wedding in the evening, and did not take off on their honeymoon early!

The second wedding was in Cebu City, far south of Manila

on another island. Joel Cruz married Imee (Irene Marie) Alcantara from Cebu on December 28. I again had a part by giving the message to the couple. Joel is from Manila and has been a leader in Messianic congregations for several years. Joel and Imee met at the University of the Philippines in Quezon City where both were music majors and active witnesses for Yeshua on campus.

Joel is currently employed at Cebu International School, teaching music, while Imee continues helping her mother with the family Day Care Enterprise. Together, Joel and Imee pioneered the Cebu Messianic Congregation. After a Bible Seminar with Joel and me teaching, the Jangad family "saw the light" of the Apostolic foundation and joined with them. The facilities of their Cebu Christian Institute International, currently an elementary and high school program, are used for Shabbat services. Joel and Imee also wrote their own ceremony and vows in the Jewish Messianic style. Following this wedding, we returned home to Morriston, Florida just in time to celebrate New Year's Eve.

Next in line is the 4th APMF Yeshiva and 7th APMF Bible Conference, April 5-11, 2009, to be held at the Agriculture Training Institute on the campus of the Benguet State University in LaTrinidad, Benguet Province, next to Baguio City. This year, the Yeshiva lectures and Conference teaching are combined. To get Yeshiva credit toward the Master's Degree, those attending will do additional research and writing several papers on four persons and six congregations found in Acts. The first couple of days will be a Symposium, with Position Papers being presented and discussed, and lots of interaction between attendees. This helps each to learn from the others, a step in their growth.

Projecting Ahead! Our Story is not finished yet!

Rabbi Dr. John Fischer was scheduled to come again to teach, but in January he had an emergency appendectomy. Therefore, as the usual backup for every teacher, "always ready at a moment's notice to preach, pray, or pass away," I will be the teacher. My topic is The Congregation of YHVH (the LORD), from Exodus through Revelation, concentrating on the Gospels, Great Commission, and the book of Acts.

Acts is NOT the "Birth of the Church" as the church has taught for hundreds of years, ever since the actual birth of the church at the Council of Nicea in 325. Consequently there is no "church" in the Bible, a mistranslation of the word *ekklesia*. This perverted teaching of the church is the attempt of the enemy to replace Israel in the Plan of God by something else, totally contrary to all the Promises of God. God does not lie! He always keeps His Promises, in His own time and for His own purposes. His Promises to Israel are to Israel and will always be to Israel! None are transferred to "the church."

If we accept what the church has tried to do, then all the Promises of God are not to be trusted, including Salvation and the future, and the character of God is corrupt like all the gods of the religions of the world. I totally reject all of these changes! The Creator God, the God of Abraham, Isaac, and Jacob, the God of Moses, David, Isaiah and all the Prophets is the Only God there is! He is totally what He claims for Himself, and I believe in Him totally and unconditionally. The church is wrong on many counts, beginning with this heresy that a "church" replaced Israel in the plan of God.

Following the Yeshiva and Bible Conference, I am going to China with my high school friends, Jack and Alice Fitzwilliam. Jack's parents were CIM missionaries to tribal people in

Southwest China. We will visit the area where his parents lived, taught, and began translating the New Testament, which has just been completed by others. We also will visit where Jack was born and where his father is buried. Jack was a small boy when his father died of typhus fever. We will also visit Yantai, the area where the Chefoo School for MKs was. Jack talked a lot about this place since we met in 1944. He is an only child, so I am his "brother." We served each other as best man in our weddings.

After China, there is the possibility of another trip to Israel. A friend of years ago has asked about doing a Tour again. He has eight family members that would be the core of the group. However, calculating the expense for everyone might be too much to handle. I would need a guaranteed 20 participants before I will sponsor another Tour, as too many backed out for the one in 2007. A Tour of Israel is an education, an investment in one's life, not an expense like a vacation, in our estimation.

Later, I need to make a return trip to Indonesia to continue the teaching I did in 2007, and to Bangkok, and maybe to Japan, and areas around the Philippines. Because of expense, only a limited number of the Messianic Disciples in APMF can attend the Annual Conferences. Therefore, as I am able, I want to go to their areas to teach the same things to everyone, which will reinforce the reports of those members who were privileged to attend. This of course is following Paul's itinerant discipling ministry.

The content of these regional Seminars will be a repeat of Conference No. 7 and Yeshiva No. 4, and anything else needed in each location. Acts is a basic foundational course for understanding Scripture, a connecting link between pre-Yeshua-on-earth times and after His Resurrection and return to heaven, NOT a transition from Israel to the church, from which so many false teachings have come.

Yeshiva No. 5 and Bible Conference No. 8 will probably be March 28 – April 4, 2010. Will the world situation be stable enough for APMF and us to continue this ministry? Only God knows, but He has told us to know His Prophecies and be alert to world events to see if anything fits. As Yeshua's Return comes very near, I am sure we will be able to see it and be prepared to meet Him. The first tangible sign? The return of Elijah!

*"Behold, I will send you Elijah, the prophet, before the coming of the great and terrible day of the LORD!" Malachi 4:5.*

As time runs out for this world, I hope to be active teaching and discipling until I am called Home. Will I get to see Elijah on this earth before that Call comes? I think so. In the meantime, there is no time to waste. My attitude will continue to be:

*"Therefore, my beloved brethren, be ye steadfast, unmovable, always abounding in the work of the Lord, forasmuch as you know that your labor is not in vain in the LORD." (1 Corinthians 15:58)*

# According to Roger

# CHAPTER 31

## The Best Is Yet to Come!

Significant world events are happening that motivate me to write more of what I have learned and am still learning from God's Word about what lies ahead. It is definitely not "business as usual" these days. Therefore, this Second Edition is offered to possibly help us all to see things more clearly as "The Day" approaches. These are exciting days yet cautionary, as we know very difficult times are coming, so "Prepare to meet God!"

Responses from readers of my book, According To Roger, have been very encouraging. Comments like, "I read your book in 24 hours!" and "She could not put your book down until she finished it!"and "Your book is so easy reading, it sounds just like you talking!" plus comments like these, "I learned so much from your book, lessons on trusting the Lord for everything as well as corrected Bible truth. Thanks so much!" In Jakarta recently, a doctorate in theology told me, "I learned more in the last 4 days from your teaching than I learned in 5 years in the seminary. Now I have a new paradigm to start over. Thank you very much!"

We also get encouraging comments from listeners to the Unshackled radio program that featured Our Life Story. The first segment was aired during the first week of September 2008 and the second segment during the second week. One listener emailed us from Europe after he had heard the broadcast, plus others in the USA. Since that time, listeners have found the broadcasts online at unshackled.org, the website of the Pacific Garden Mission in Chicago, Illinois that has produced these dramatized stories for radio broadcast for more than 50 years. Go to "Listen Online," click on Archives 2008, and scroll down to #3007 and #3008 for "Roger Walkwitz Part 1 and Part 2."

Listeners responding to salvation from sin offered by the Grace of God, and explained on the broadcasts, have had their lives changed forever, just like me, and hopefully you, too. This is possible because the death and resurrection of God's Son, Yeshua The Messiah, paid for those sins. Repentance and a life surrendered to God will result in being born-from-Above by God's Spirit, another soul "Unshackled" from the chains of sin.

Except for the Grace of God extended to me in 1943, I would not be writing this book. In fact, I would not even be here on earth if not for the Grace of God to bring my Mother back from a deep coma that lasted for 9 days. The newspaper dispatch in 1924, shortly after they were married, reads:

"WOMAN INJURED RIDING HORSEBACK  Mrs C A Walkwitz has shown but little improvement since she was seriously injured Friday afternoon when her horse fell on her...Mrs Walkwitz was horseback riding on the concrete road at Old Hickory (TN). As she approached the railroad tracks a train passed, frightening her horse. The horse fell over backwards, crushing Mrs. Walkwitz. The pommel of the saddle struck Mrs. Walkwitz in the chest. She also sustained a concussion of the brain. Her condition is regarded as critical, and there is only a slight chance for her recovery."

God overcame that "slight chance" and brought Mom back, to live a productive life until age 82, when a car, driven by a distraught woman, backed up and ran over my Mom, crushing her chest, while living in a retirement center. Mom came to Faith in Jesus as her Lord and Savior at the age of 46 and became an avid Bible student and witness to neighbors of her Trust in Jesus. Yeshua was the focus of life for both Mom & Dad, who also came to Faith in Jesus when he was 48 and then studied and witnessed constantly.

So I am here, and have been for 80 years, and now writing this Chapter 31, to bring you up-to-date on the Goodness of the LORD, as God is good all the time! He has His purposes, His choices, His Plans that we rarely see until after the events, sometimes, and compare them to what we find in His Bible. How wonderful to be part of God's Family!

Naomi and I are very thankful for the measure of health and strength that God has given to us to be able to continue the discipling ministry of building up the Body of Messiah in the Asia Pacific region. The developing chaos of the whole world makes us think of what might God want us to do if teaching in the Far East will no longer be possible? No significant teaching ministry in the USA has opened to us, until recently.

In January 2009, several phone calls came inviting us to

join a Shabbat Bible Study in a nearby town that had been going on for several years. It meets in their homes, alternating as circumstances warrant. We visited with them on Saturday, February 14, 2009. They study the Torah portion (3 year cycle), *Haftorah* (Prophets), and Newer Testament portions for 2 hours in the morning, and then have a delicious potluck lunch. After lunch, they study more or other topics until mid-afternoon. We offered our Guest House for the next Shabbat, and they gladly accepted, and have been coming to our GH every Shabbat when we are home! They have asked me to teach the afternoon sessions. There are about 15 participants (not just attendees!), which makes our small GH living room quite crowded, even extending into the kitchen. We had planned to build an extension on our small GH, a "family room," to accommodate more, but the zoning office is making problems for us. We live way out in the country, so what is the problem? Now a days, more "control" is what government wants, and is getting. Ridiculous security at airports – because of Islam! "Political Correctness" is destroying our country.

Does this mean we are giving up on the Asia Pacific region? Absolutely Not!! We are just preparing for any and all eventualities. In fact, our time in the AP region has become "more and more" lately! My Call from the LORD for overseas ministry was very clear, to start in Banaue, in the mountains of the Philippines. He has expanded that step by step over the years to include all of the Philippines and the other nations of the AP region, and is now expanding it to include a little bit in the USA. By email I get invitations to teach in several countries of Africa as well as South America. I probably won't go there, but it shows that some people around the world are hungry to learn the Bible on its original foundation and hopefully are eager to follow in Yeshua's footsteps.

# The Best Is Yet to Come!

Could this Bible passage be the situation that is developing worldwide?

*Amos 8:11-12 "Behold, the days are coming," declares the Lord GOD, "when I will send a famine on the land-- not a famine of bread, nor a thirst for water, but of hearing the words of the LORD. They shall wander from sea to sea, and from north to east; they shall run to and fro, to seek the word of the LORD, but they shall not find it."*

This is happening because world powers are trying to push God out of public life and substitute Humanism in its place. The ACLU (American Civil Liberties Union) in the USA can be characterized as a "Religion Exterminator." Islam is also demanding that their perverted religion and Sharia law become dominant, worldwide. What does all this mean, coupled with the economic crisis all over the world?

I was asked to deal with this during Bible Conferences and Seminars in Bangkok and Surin, Thailand in December 2009, and in Jakarta, Yogyakarta, and Medan, Indonesia in January and February 2010. The 8th Annual APMF Bible Conference in the Philippines March 30-April 3, 2010 will also try to tackle the whole world situation in relation to Bible Prophecy with the title, "As in the Days of Noah," so shall be the arrival of the Son of Man, Yeshua The Messiah! No expert Jewish Believer teacher is available, so I will be doing most of the teaching myself. No problem, as Bible prophecy has been a large and motivating part of my life since coming to know Yeshua at age 13.

Basic to all Bible prophecy is Genesis 3:15, the prediction of THE Messiah, the Seed of the woman, and the False Messiah, the seed of the serpent.

*"I will put enmity between you (serpent = Satan) and the woman (Israel), and between your offspring (Satan's son, the False Messiah) and her offspring (The Messiah, Yeshua); he shall bruise your head (fatal wound to Satan), and you shall bruise his heel (superficial wound to Yeshua)."* ESV, with mine in parentheses.

Modern skeptics question whether Satan can father a child, just like they question nearly everything in the Bible. But we believe God means exactly what He has said, and ancient history is unanimous in agreeing with God. Once God revealed His plans, Satan right away counterfeited them. We know from other Scriptures that The Messiah Yeshua will be born miraculously, from a virgin who turns out to be Miriam, descended from King David. Satan knew the same thing from the Gospel in the stars and Genesis 3:15, so he developed several religions based on a miraculous supposedly virgin-born son to confuse people. These are known popularly as the Mythologies of ancient civilizations, as if they are some kind of fairy tale. The stories are embellished, yes, but they are based on historical and biblical facts! Compare these three translations of Genesis 6:1 & 4.

*Genesis 6:1 More and more people were born, until finally they spread all over the earth. Some of their daughters were so beautiful that supernatural beings came down and married the ones they wanted.*
*Gen 6:4 The children of the supernatural beings who had married these women became famous heroes and warriors. They were called Nephilim and lived on the earth at that time and even later.*

(Contemporary English Version.)

*Genesis 6:1 When man began to multiply on the face of the land and daughters were born to them, the sons of God saw that the daughters of man were attractive. And they took as their wives any they chose.*

*Gen 6:4 The Nephilim were on the earth in those days, and also afterward, when the sons of God came in to the daughters of man and they bore children to them. These were the mighty men who were of old, the men of renown.*

(English Standard Version)

*Genesis 6:1 And it came to pass, when men began to multiply on the face of the earth, and daughters were born unto them, that the sons of God saw the daughters of men that they were fair; and they took them wives of all which they chose.*

*Gen 6:4 There were giants in the earth in those days; and also after that, when the sons of God came in unto the daughters of men, and they bare children to them, the same became mighty men, which were of old, men of renown.*

( King James Version)

These translations are faithful to the Hebrew text. In the Tanakh, the sons of God are angels, clearly identified in Job 1:6 & 2:1 as they report to God along with Satan, and in Job 38:7 when the sons of God shouted for joy at creation. (In the Apostolic Scriptures, sons of God applies to Believers.) Daughters of men are normal human women. The result of this sex between angels and human women were the *Nephilim*, translated as giants, who were mighty, famous men, who in turn became the counterfeit "virgin-born" saviors of mankind, the gods of ancient religions.

*Job 1:6 Now there was a day when the sons of God came to present themselves before the LORD, and Satan also came among them.*

*Ezekiel 8:13 But I will show you something even worse*

*than this. He took me to the north gate of the temple, where I saw women mourning for the god Tammuz. CEV*

Who is this god Tammuz that the Israeli women are mourning for? Who is the queen of heaven in Jeremiah 7 & 44 that Israelis are worshiping? Who is this Molech who requires child sacrifices? These are a few of the gods and goddesses of the pagans around Israel. Are these myths or real beings? Would a mother give her baby as a human sacrifice to a myth? NO! We dare not deny the reality of these beings, these satanic counterfeits of Bible Truth.

The original "Babylon the great, the mother of harlots" in Revelation 17 seems to be the religion developed by Nimrod and his wife, Semiramis. Nimrod was a mighty hunter against the LORD, the builder of the Tower of Babel, and the first dictator on earth. Genesis 10-11. He wanted to be worshiped, but his enemies murdered him and cut his body into pieces. Sometime later, Semiramis became pregnant, claiming that Nimrod had become a god and had come down to have sex with her, producing the miraculous son Tammuz. Based on Genesis 6, it was not Nimrod who had sex with her, but an angel who claimed to be Nimrod. Tammuz is then a Nephilim. His father was an angel and his mother was a human woman.

An unholy trinity develops, with the father being an angel-god, the mother a human woman, and the result a false virgin-born son, a redeemer of mankind. Usually the father is ignored as the mother is deified by the powers of her son, becoming a goddess and co-redeemer of mankind. Prayers are usually made to the deified mother, as she is more approachable. This mother-son religion existed all throughout ancient times: in Egypt, as Isis and

Horus; in India, as Devaki and Krishna; in Rome, as Fortuna and Jupiter; and in the Vatican system, as Mary and Jesus, who is different from the Yeshua of the Bible. Actually it is the same religious system with name changes, with the mother being called in different languages and cultures as Aphrodite, Venus, Mylitta, Cybele, Minerva, Diana, Juno, Maya, Ceres, Shing Moo.

The fallen angels who fathered these *Nephilim* are now in prison. Then who are the demons that are around, especially in Yeshua's time? I believe when the *Nephilim* died in the Flood, their spirits became the demons, who wish to inhabit a human body. Their judgment is coming yet, as one demon complained to Yeshua in Matthew 8:29.

*Matthew 8:29 And behold, they (the demons) cried out, "What have you to do with us, O Son of God? Have you come here to torment us before the time?"*

*2Peter 2:4 For if God spared not the angels that sinned, but cast them down to hell, and delivered them into chains of darkness, to be reserved unto judgment;*

*Jude 6-7 And the angels which kept not their first estate, but left their own habitation, he hath reserved in everlasting chains under darkness unto the judgment of the great day. Even as Sodom and Gomorrah...giving themselves over to fornication, and going after strange flesh, are set forth for an example, suffering the vengeance of eternal fire.*

Notice that the sin of the angels was fornication and strange flesh, sexual perversion, like Sodom and Gomorrah. Satan did not participate at that time in this ancient perversion, but he will father a son in the end times who will be The false messiah. This is the clear implication of

Genesis 3:15, the seed of the serpent. This may be part of the reason that Satan will be in prison for 1000 years. This son of Satan is described in various places as a powerful person, a true Nephilim, the beast, a giant in body and intellect, the final anti-Christ. Remember also that there is no salvation for fallen angels or *Nephilim.*

> *2Thessalonians 2:3 Let no man deceive you by any means: for that day shall not come, except there come a falling away (apostasy from Moses) first, and that man of sin be revealed, the son of perdition; who opposeth and exalteth himself above all that is called God, or that is worshipped; so that he as God sits in the temple of God, showing himself that he is God.*

> *Revelation 13:4-9 And they worshipped the dragon, which gave power unto the beast (son of Satan) and they worshipped the beast, saying, Who is like unto the beast? who is able to make war with him? And there was given unto him a mouth speaking great things and blasphemies; and power was given unto him to continue forty and two months. And he opened his mouth in blasphemy against God, to blaspheme his name, and his tabernacle, and them that dwell in heaven. And it was given unto him to make war with the saints, and to overcome them: and power was given him over all kindreds, and tongues, and nations. And all that dwell upon the earth shall worship him, whose names are not written in the book of life of the Lamb slain from the foundation of the world. If any man has an ear, let him hear!*

Four thousand years after Creation, "in the fullness of time," God brought forth His Son Yeshua, born of the virgin Miriam, the true Redeemer of mankind. For Millennia mankind has put their trust in false messiahs, false gods and goddesses, who demand much of them with no hope for the future, with some notable exceptions like Enoch, Noah, and Abraham, who represent that Remnant that had eyes to see and ears to hear that still, small voice of God and responded to Him.

Earlier I mentioned the Gospel in the stars. This is the revelation given by God to Adam & Havah and apparently was well known even to the time of David, who wrote:

*Psalm 19:1-4 How clearly the sky reveals God's glory! How plainly it shows what he has done! Each day announces it to the following day; each night repeats it to the next. No speech or words are used, no sound is heard; yet their message goes out to all the world and is heard to the ends of the earth. GNB*

*Psalm 147:4 He has decided the number of the stars and calls each one by name.*

*Job 9:9 Who makes Arcturus, Orion, and Pleiades, and the chambers of the south*

*Job 38:31 "Can you bind the chains of the Pleiades or loose the cords of Orion? Can you lead forth the Mazzaroth (Zodiac) in their season, or can you guide the Bear with its children?"*

We are talking about the legitimate science of astronomy, not the satanic counterfeit of astrology! God placed all the stars where He wanted them and gave a name to each one. These names have mostly passed down to us today with their meanings intact, which tell us the Gospel. On the 4th day of Creation, God put a beam of light from each star to the earth so that the light we see today from that distant star may not be the light produced by that star. On Day 1 of Creation, God said, "Let there be light!" and there was light. This light came from God Himself until the sun, moon, and stars were created on Day 4. In the New Heavens and New Earth, God Himself will again be the light.

*Revelation 21:23 And the city has no need of sun or moon to shine on it, for the glory of God gives it light, and its lamp is the Lamb.*

*Revelation 22:5 And night will be no more. They will need no light of lamp or sun, for the Lord God will be their light, and they will reign forever and ever.*

Now lets look carefully at Day 4 of Creation when the sun, moon, and stars were created. There is no need to compromise with the speculations of evolution, which is a lie, a huge hoax perpetrated by those who want no accountability to God. The observable evidence in nature, of true science, can readily be understood in accord with Bible statements. God created everything in a mature state, fully functioning, with the appearance of age. The chicken came first, ready to lay the first egg.

*Genesis 1:14 And God said, "Let there be lights in the expanse of the heavens to separate the day from the night. And let them be for signs and for seasons, and for days and years,*

"Seasons" is the Hebrew moadim, the Appointed Times of the LORD, summarized in Leviticus 23. The sun and moon help to regulate these times, the annual Festivals. The weekly Shabbat cannot be determined from the sun and moon, but is a fact given directly from God. No ancient culture learned the 7-day week unless they got it from Israel. As for "signs," we know that every sign has a message. The stars are to carry The message of the Gospel, starting with Virgo, the virgin conception and birth of The Messiah, and annually on through the rest of the 12 signs of the Zodiac to Leo the Lion of the tribe of Judah, pouncing on the head of the fleeing serpent, Hydra.

Connecting the stars with lines will not give the Constellations, except the Big and Little Dippers which historically were known as Arcturus or the Bear and his sons. God gave the figure for each Constellation to Adam & Havah, who passed it on to those interested. We found earlier that the heavens declare the Glory of God, and the focus of it all is Yeshua the Messiah. Is there anything else that the heavens declare? Yes, God's wrath!

*Romans 1:18-20 For the wrath of God is revealed from heaven against all ungodliness and unrighteousness of men, who by their unrighteousness suppress the truth. For what can be known about God is plain to them, because God has shown it to them. For his invisible attributes, namely, his eternal power and divine nature have been clearly perceived, ever since the creation of the world, in the things that have been made. So they are without excuse.*

The wrath of God is revealed in many of the Constellations, along with the Glory of God as He punishes His adversary in his various forms. In addition to Leo the Lion, there is Orion, the mighty one, also stomping on the head of a serpent, Eridanus, with the bright star Rigel in his foot, meaning "the foot that crushes" from Genesis 3:15. Orion also has in his hand the head of the "roaring lion that goes about to destroy us." Hercules (not the original name from God!) also shows clearly Gen 3:15, as his foot is ready to crush the head of the serpent Draco, and the tongue of Draco reaching out for his heel. In Virgo, the star in her left hand, Al Zimach (from the Hebrew *tsemach*), meaning "the branch," shines brightly, a title given to the Messiah several times. These pictures are given in the appendix.

So in summary, God laid out His Plan for Yeshua the Messiah with the Constellations in the sky and added to it His statement to Satan in Genesis 3:15, with Adam and Havah listening. Satan then got a bunch of rebellious angels to go down to earth, take on a human form in which they can function sexually (in heaven they cannot or do not, Mark 12:25, probably because there are no female angels?), grab all the beautiful girls on earth that they want and have sex with them, producing Nephilim, a being part angel and part human, wicked in all their dealings and terrifying the people on earth by their size and powers. God destroys the Nephilim in the Flood and their spirits become the demons.

This unholy trinity of angel, mother, and son form all the ancient religions, as all three become "gods" with supernatural powers. Sometimes they function together and other times as mother & son, and many times individually as fertility gods and goddesses. Their exploits are embellished in the stories called Mythology, but there is reality behind each one, and fear in those who worship them.

This same situation will prevail in the End Times!! Satan should have already fathered his son by now, 2010, ready to reveal him very soon! This son is the "seed of the serpent," the false messiah, the beast, the so-called anti-Christ, although the term "anti-christ" is used of many people and only in 1 & 2 John. To imitate Yeshua, this son of Satan should begin his "ministry" about the age of 30!

Another "same situation" will prevail in the End Times, the attempt by Satan to destroy all the Jewish people. Read the book of Esther and notice the attempt by Haman to destroy all the Jewish people in the entire Persian Empire of 127 provinces, from India to Ethiopia, which might have contained most of the Jewish people. Haman is a preview of Satan's son. Just as God worked behind the scenes to not only preserve His people, but even advance them, so God in the upcoming End Times will preserve Israel and make Israel the head of all the nations. There is good reason to celebrate Purim for the many lessons to be learned, especially that God always looks after His people, even behind the scenes. And remember, too, that Gentile Believers are together with Jewish Believers in the Good Olive Tree. God watches over ALL His children, but also over Israel as a nation including those who do not believe, as His plans are through Israel.

*Psalm 121:4 Behold, he who keeps Israel will neither slumber nor sleep.*

# According to Roger

# CHAPTER 32

## The Final
## One World Government
## and Daniel's 70 Weeks

While we watch for the emergence of the false messiah, who we identified as another *Nephilim* and son of Satan, we need to search Scripture to find out what and where his government will be. Prophecy teachers have taught for years that the anti-Christ government will be a revived Roman Empire, and they have been so excited about the Treaty of Rome and the development of the European Union. We have never accepted that, as we see a different empire.

In Daniel 2, God gave His forecast of the future empires, beginning with Babylon as the head of gold in the colossal statue that Nebuchadnezzar saw in his dream that Daniel was able to know and interpret. After Babylon, the Medo-Persian Empire, the chest of silver, swallowed Babylon, which in turn was conquered by Macedonia-Greece, the belly of brass, by Alexander the Great. Rome, the legs of iron and feet of iron and clay, was the last empire in this sequence.

Prophecy teachers tried to couple this Rome with the prophecies in Daniel 9, which is a very difficult passage, even for Hebrew scholars. Some of it was fulfilled in past time with the first coming of Yeshua. The rest of it must be fulfilled with Yeshua's Return. A total of 70 "weeks" deal with Israel and Jerusalem. Dispensational Theology set Israel aside in favor of the Church, so their analysis was 69 weeks-of-years, or 483 years, applied to Israel from the Commandment to rebuild Jerusalem issued by Artaxerxes (444BCE) to Nehemiah unto the Messiah. Then Israel is set aside and the "Church Age" begins. The Church Age ends with the Pre-Tribulation Rapture of the Church and then Israel gets its final week of 7 years of terrible Tribulation, with Yeshua returning after the 7 years. I concluded that this is anti-Israel, bordering on anti-Semitism, as well as having contradictions to several Scriptures. However, Daniel 9 is a strategic passage.

*Daniel 9:24-27 Seventy weeks are decreed as to your people, and as to your holy city, to finish the transgression, and to make an end of sins, and to make atonement for iniquity, and to bring in everlasting righteousness, and to seal up the vision and prophecy, and to anoint the Most Holy. Know, then, and understand that from the going out of a word to restore and to rebuild Jerusalem, to Messiah the Prince, shall be seven weeks and sixty-two weeks. The street shall be built again, and the wall, even in times of affliction. And after sixty-two weeks, Messiah shall be cut off, but not for Himself. And the people of a coming ruler shall destroy the city and the sanctuary. And its end shall be with the flood, and ruins are determined, and war shall be until the end. And he shall confirm a covenant with the many for one week. And in the middle of the week he shall cause the sacrifice and the offering to cease. And on a corner of the altar will be abominations that desolate, even until the end. And that which was decreed shall pour out on the desolator. LITV*

## The Final One World Government and
## Daniel's 70 Weeks

Keep all of this Daniel 9 passage in mind as we go back to Daniel 2. Remember that the ancient empires succeeded the ones before it, so that only one empire was functioning at any one time. Rome was not conquered but disintegrated and the Vatican took over.

*Daniel 2:35 Then the iron, the clay, the bronze, the silver, and the gold, all together were broken in pieces ....*

*Daniel 2:44 And in the days of those kings (Babylon, Persia, Greece, and Rome, not just the last king, Rome) the God of heaven will set up a kingdom (Israel) that shall never be destroyed....*

Significant clues are given in these two verses, 1) that all four kingdoms must be present at the same time, not successively as in ancient history, so that all four will be broken in pieces together, and 2) that when all four exist independently as "in the days of those kings (plural!)," only then will God establish His kingdom Israel which will last forever. Attempts have been made in past time to re-establish Israel, notably Napoleon (1799), but none were successful because God stated through Daniel that He would re-establish Israel only when all four kingdoms had "come back to life" as independent nations.

So in essence there will be two statues, one completed in past time with the disintegration of Rome, and the second one reconstituted in recent time in order to completely fulfill all the rest of the prophecies about Yeshua that were not fulfilled at His first coming. To identify these, we need to look at Daniel 7 and Revelation 17 and 13.

*Daniel 7:3-7 And four great beasts came up out of the sea, different from one another. The first was like a lion and had eagles' wings.... And behold, another beast, a second one, like a bear....After this I looked, and behold, another, like a leopard....After this I saw in the night visions, and behold, a fourth beast, terrifying and dreadful and exceedingly strong.*

This vision is given to Daniel many years after the one to Nebuchadnezzar. It has the same meaning as the first, but with carnivorous animals representing the kingdoms rather than metals. The gold head is now like a lion; the silver chest is now like a bear, the brass hips are now like a leopard, and the iron legs are terrifying and dreadful as Daniel could not compare it to any known animal. We know this is the case from the quote below. Keep these 4 animals in mind, as symbols in the Bible are used consistently, even between Tanakh and Newer Testament, as the 66 books are a unit.

*Daniel 7:16-17 I approached one of those who stood there and asked him the truth concerning all this. So he told me and made known to me the interpretation of the things. 'These four great beasts are four kings who shall arise out of the earth."*

Now we go to Revelation 17. There is much in the Daniel chapters and in Revelation that I would explain in a class setting, filling in the historical data and completing the picture, but for now, I will insert explanations in this long passage so that we can come to our conclusion of what and where the final one world empire will be.

*Revelation 17:4-11 The woman* (representing religion) *was arrayed in purple and scarlet, and adorned with gold and jewels and pearls, holding in her hand a golden cup full of abominations and the impurities of her sexual immorality* (religion and government together to enslave the people).

## The Final One World Government and Daniel's 70 Weeks

*And on her forehead was written a name of mystery:* "*Babylon the great* (Nimrod's kingdom), *mother* (original unholy trinity) *of prostitutes* (all the religions that came from the original) *and of earth's abominations.*" *And I saw the woman, drunk with the blood of the saints (Tanakh* time), *and the blood of the martyrs of Jesus* (NT time). *When I saw her, I marveled greatly. But the angel said to me, "Why do you marvel? I will tell you the mystery of the woman* (religions), *and of the beast* (the political powers) *with seven heads and ten horns that carries her* (using religion to accomplish political ends). *The beast that you saw was* (Nimrod's kingdom), *and is not* (in John's time), *and is about to rise from the bottomless pit* (to challenge Israel at Yeshua's Return) *and go to destruction. And the dwellers on earth whose names have not been written in the book of life from the foundation of the world will marvel to see the beast, because it was and is not and is yet to come. This calls for a mind with wisdom: the seven heads are seven mountains* (not Rome, like many teach!) *on which the woman is seated* (successively); *they are also seven kings, five of whom have fallen* (Egypt, Assyria, Babylon, Persia, Greece) *one is* (Rome), *the other has not yet come* (the Vatican that took over Rome), *and when he does come he must remain only a little while. As for the beast that was and is not, it is an eighth but it belongs to the seven* (a composite), *and it goes to destruction.*

The eighth world power is what we are primarily interested in. It is the beast that existed in past time but not in John's time, and which will return "from the abyss or bottomless pit," indicating a very evil empire. It will not be something new, but will be a composite out of some of the previous seven. Notice that Egypt and Assyria have been added to the kingdoms portrayed by the statue in Daniel 2, as these existed prior to Nebuchadnezzar's Babylon. Notice also that Nebuchadnezzar's Babylon can be termed neo-Babylon, as Nimrod's was the first and also will be the last Babylon, religion and government combined.

Finally we need to look at Revelation 13 to complete the identification.

*Revelation 13:1-2 And I saw a beast* (the final world government and ruler) *rising out of the sea* (the mass of humanity), *with ten horns and seven heads, with ten diadems on its horns and blasphemous names on its heads. And the beast that I saw was like a leopard; its feet were like a bear's, and its mouth was like a lion's mouth. And to it the dragon* (Satan) *gave his power and his throne and great authority.*

Remember the animal designations given to Daniel in his chapter 7? Symbols are and must be used consistently throughout Scripture. Some say the bear represents Russia as it does today and the lion represents England as it does today, but NO! God does not change His symbols. The body of the beast is like a leopard, referring to the area of Alexander the Great's kingdom, which spread from Macedonia and Greece all the way east to the border of India. The feet of a bear refers to the area of Persia in ancient times, and also indicates the strength of this end time kingdom, as an athlete or warrior depends on his feet and legs. The mouth of a lion refers to the area of Nebuchadnezzar's Babylon and also indicates that the dictates and pronouncements of this kingdom will come from there. There is the "Babylon" chart in the Appendix that shows this.

## The Final One World Government and
## Daniel's 70 Weeks

Now, remember what was said in Daniel 2:35 and 2:44, that all 4 kingdoms had to be destroyed at the same time (by His stone kingdom Israel) and that it would be when all 4 had "come back to life"? All 4 had disappeared from history as independent nations long, long ago, with Babylon, Persia, and Greece disappearing before the time of Yeshua, and Rome a few hundred years later. And remember that God would not cut His stone kingdom, Israel, out of a mountain until these 4 had been restored? I find it fascinating to watch God work in current events to accomplish His purposes, which most of mankind is blind and oblivious to.

Rome came "back to life" as Italy in 1870 as Geribaldi and his warriors defeated the armies of the Vatican, reclaiming the Papal States that the Vatican had set up all through the peninsula, and drove the Pope back into Vatican City. A treaty in 1929 confirmed Vatican City as an independent nation and the Pope as the sovereign. The Turkish Ottoman Empire occupied southeastern Europe and the Near East for 400 years, from 1517 to 1917. Turkey and Germany lost their bid for world power in defeat by the Allies in November 1917. As a result, England was given the Mandate by the League of Nations to divide up Turkey's Empire into independent states, including one for Israel. England betrayed Israel, but did set up Iraq in 1932 in the area that was Babylon, and did set up Iran in 1942 in the area that was Persia. Greece finally became independent in 1944. Now the stage is set for the re-birth of Israel on May 14, 1948! Imagine, if England had kept its promise in the Balfour Declaration in November 1917 to make a homeland for the Jews, the Holocaust might not have happened. The Jews could have fled to their own country, as only few nations would accept them as they fled from Hitler and Germany. England bears a lot of responsibility toward God for their anti-Semitism.

What is characteristic today about the territory that comprised the empire of Alexander the Great, from Macedonia/Greece to the border of India? It is nearly all Muslim or Islamic! Therefore, we conclude that Islam is the heart of the 8th and last world power. The strength of Islam will come from Iran, the feet of a bear, and the leadership will be based in Iraq, the mouth of a lion. Is it any wonder that Iran wants nuclear weapons and states publicly their aim to destroy Israel? The leader of this empire will have the cooperation of all the nations in the world in his attempt to destroy Israel. This leader will also be the son of Satan, a Nephilim with amazing powers.

What about the timing of this End Time scenario? We have to refer back to Daniel 9 and the "Seventy weeks are decreed as to your people, and as to your holy city." The word translated as "weeks" is the Hebrew shavua, which can mean any grouping of seven. If we assume it can mean Shavuot, the Appointed Time also called Pentecost, which occurs once a year, then we can interpret 70 weeks/ shavua to be equal to 70 years. Daniel 9 also said, "from the going out of a word to restore and to rebuild Jerusalem, to Messiah the Prince, shall be seven weeks and sixty-two weeks (69 years)." When in recent history has there been a word to restore and rebuild Jerusalem? This must be our starting point!

There might be two possibilities. 1) The United Nations Resolution 181 of November 29, 1947 that authorized the establishment of a state for Israel and a state for the Arabs in the land west of the Jordan River. Israel reluctantly accepted while the Arabs rejected and soon went to war, thereby forfeiting all rights to any of the land by International Law. England had already taken away land on the east side of the Jordan River that had been promised to Israel and made Transjordan. 2) The result of the 6-Day War of 1967 when Jerusalem was retaken from Jordan.

If 1) is the right starting point, then the Kingdom Age (Millennium) begins with Yeshua the Messiah in 2017, 70 years from 1947. If 2) is the right starting point, then the Kingdom Age begins with Yeshua the Messiah in 2037, 70 years after 1967. Which is correct, or is there another possibility? There are many things that need to happen prior to either of these end points, some in progress right now and most yet to come.

One more important factor to consider is the Appointed Times of the LORD. These moedim have a historical beginning, a perpetual celebration to "remember" them, and a prophetic aspect related to Yeshua. The first 4, Passover, Unleavened Bread (the sinless sacrifice of Yeshua), First Fruits (Yeshua's Resurrection), and Shavuot/Pentecost (the launching of the Great Commission of the completed Gospel to all the world) had their prophetic aspect fulfilled right on the exact time specified for each one, at the time of Yeshua's first coming to earth in His human body.

The remaining 3 moedim, *Yom Teruah*/Blowing of Trumpets/*Rosh HaShanah*, *Yom Kippur*/Day of Atonement, and *Sukkot*/Feast of Tabernacles should therefore also have their prophetic aspect fulfilled at the exact time specified for each one. This is using logic, but we believe this is the only way to consider it. These moedim are scheduled for *Tishrei 1*, *Tishrei* 10, and *Tishrei* 15-22, or to *Tishrei* 23 to include *Simchat*

*Torah,* the Joy of the Torah, which was added later. These days correspond to dates in September and October. What year we do not know, but if 1) or 2) above are true, then Yeshua's Return will be 69 years from the starting point, either 2016 or 2036, and in the Fall.

"And he (Satan's son) shall confirm a covenant with the many for one week (could this be one year or might it be 7 years?). And in the middle of the week he shall cause the sacrifice and the offering to cease." Since a "3½" year period is mentioned several times, I tend to think this "week" would be 7 years, so that in the middle of it, Satan's son will cause the sacrifice and offering to stop while he goes into the rebuilt Temple in Jerusalem to be worshiped directly.

It seems that since we are so close to The End, I wanted to share my thoughts with you. If they are helpful and come to pass, that will be wonderful. If some significant things do not happen soon to validate these suggested dates, then we have to study some more. For sure, those of us who know God personally and intimately should NOT be caught as by a thief in the night! That is for the outsiders who care not for God and His Word.

> *1Thessalonians 5:1-6 Now concerning the times and the seasons* (moedim), *brothers, you have no need to have anything written to you. For you yourselves are fully aware that the day of the Lord will come like a thief in the night. While people are saying, "There is peace and security," then sudden destruction will come upon them as labor pains come upon a pregnant woman, and they will not escape. But you are not in darkness, brothers, for that day to surprise you like a thief. For*

*you are all children of light, children of the day. We are not of the night or of the darkness. So then let us not sleep, as others do, but let us keep awake and be sober.*

Have I mentioned Elijah or Eliyahu? He is scheduled to come before Yeshua arrives, just like he was born before Yeshua was born, 6 months to be exact. If Elijah is one of the two witnesses in Revelation 11:3, then he will come about 3 ½ years before Yeshua. If he is not, then we might guess 6 months or more.

*Malachi 4:5-6  "Behold, I will send you Elijah the prophet before the great and awesome day of the LORD comes. And he will turn the hearts of fathers to their children and the hearts of children to their fathers, lest I come and strike the land with a decree of utter destruction."*

The False Prophet will claim that he is Elijah or greater than Elijah, because he will be able to do many big miracles including calling down fire from heaven like Elijah did.

*Revelation 13:13-14 It (the second beast or false prophet) performs great signs, even making fire come down from heaven to earth in front of people; and by the signs that it is allowed to work in the presence of the beast, it deceives those who dwell on earth.*

At this point I am not sure who this False Prophet is. My thought is, that it could be a person, maybe a Nephilim, or it could be an organization, or it could be a combination of the leader and his organization. One thought is that it might be the United Nations that will promote the beast to all the people of the earth, and the leader of the UN to be the focus of doing all these miracles. The UN certainly has a part to play in these End Time scenarios, especially because it is the agent for the Islamic agenda against Israel.

When they shall say "Peace and Security," what might this be? The only thing I can think of in today's world would be a peace treaty of some sort to temporarily solve the Arab–Israel Conflict, which is actually a war being waged by Satan through his proxy Islam and the false god Allah against Israel and The God of Abraham, Isaac, and Jacob. This would be a false "peace" treaty on the part of Islam, a trick to deceive Israel into something that would weaken them, as Islam does not negotiate honestly and does not make peace with infidels, especially Israel.

This "peace" treaty would definitely focus on Jerusalem and the Temple Mount, the place where God put His Name and Presence forever, the place to which Yeshua will return, and therefore the place most desired by Satan to thwart God's plans. Satan knows he will lose against God, but since there is no salvation for angels, he will do everything possible in his pride and hatred to inflict all the damage he can upon Israel and all Believers in Yeshua.

*2 Chronicles 7:15-16 Now my eyes will be open and my ears attentive to the prayer that is made in this place* (Solomon's Temple). *For now I have chosen and consecrated this house that my name may be there forever. My eyes and my heart will be there for all time.* (This is the reason Jews go to the Western Wall to pray; it is a special place!)

# The Final One World Government and Daniel's 70 Weeks

*Zechariah 14:4 On that day his feet (Yeshua) shall stand on the Mount of Olives that lies before Jerusalem on the east, and the Mount of Olives shall be split in two from east to west by a very wide valley, so that one half of the Mount shall move northward, and the other half southward.*

*Revelation 12:12 Therefore, rejoice, O heavens and you who dwell in them! But woe to you, O earth and sea, for the devil has come down to you in great wrath, because he knows that his time is short!" 12:17 Then the dragon became furious with the woman (Israel) and went off to make war on the rest of her offspring, on those who keep the commandments of God and hold to the testimony of Jesus.* (Those in the Good Olive Tree.)

The original UN Resolution 181 required Jerusalem to be an International City, but since the Arabs went to war against Israel, this did not happen. Jordan occupied the Old City while Israel held the newer parts of modern Jerusalem. The 6-Day War restored all of Jerusalem to Israel, but Moshe Dayan (Israel Defense Minister) gave the keys of the buildings on the Temple Mount back to the Islamic Waqf, a foolish act as he did not understand Islam nor believe God. Since then, Islam has tried to assert sovereignty over the Temple Mount, and Israel has somewhat gone along with it.

Now suppose this "peace" treaty would make Jerusalem an International City under the control of the Vatican (something the Vatican has coveted for centuries), with guarantees that all holy places of all religions would be open to all, and giving Israel the right to build their 3rd Temple up on the Temple Mount to the north of the Golden Dome where there is space and possibly the place of the Holy of Holies of the previous temples, do you think Israel would agree to this? I think they would, even though the vast majority of Israelis are secular and do not care about building the 3rd temple. If "peace" is waved in front of most Israelis, guaranteed by the UN, I think they will gladly accept it.

The Temple Institute in the Old City has already prepared everything necessary for the new temple to function, except for the building itself and possibly the red heifer, which they have been looking for. Jewish Cohanim, priests from Aaron, have been recruited and are in training to do their job. A particular DNA that distinguishes Cohanim from the tribe of Levi has been discovered so that these men are considered genuine. Another group, the Temple Mount Faithful, has already prepared the cornerstone for this new temple, and has tried each year to place it for the building but were stopped by police.

These two groups are hardly known in Israel, but quite well known among Evangelical Christians, from whom they get most of their funding. So most of "the stage is set" for this drama to begin. If our date of #1 is correct, then this "Peace Treaty" needs to be made this year, 2011, so the building of this 3rd Temple can begin, and the Abomination of Desolation set up in 3½ years. Barack Hussein Obama, can probably work this out as he knows how Islam works. Bill Clinton might help, also.

"Shofar sho good!" We are living in the End Days of human history; so lets keep our eyes and ears open, do not worry about anything, but rather Rejoice Always in Yeshua!

# The Final One World Government and Daniel's 70 Weeks

Randy & Janie Walkwitz with sons 2004

Roger & Naomi with grandson Sam 2004

Roger & Naomi in Florida office 2005

Roger's High School buddies, Jack Fitzwilliam & Harold Cook

Naomi with Lavi Family in Caesarea, Israel at house we watched

Roger with Israel Amb to Philippines Yoav Behiri in Israel 2006

Naomi & Roger with special gift from Bernis & Fatima Hutauruk,
in Sumatra, Indonesia 2007

Roger teaching Seminar in Bangkok, Thailand 2008

Roger teaching Cebu Messianic Congregation at CCII campus

Roger at Mount Zion Center in Quezon City

Roger's Tabernacle with first covering exposed.

Roger, Naomi and Ron at Pro Israel rally at UF, Gainesville, Florida

Banaue neighbors 2005

Banaue Rice Terraces

# APPENDIX A
## Hayesod Outline

The following are some of the main points in the series of 14 Lessons in the Hayesod, with some additions of my own:

1) <u>The Unified Word of God</u>. The Bible is a unit and should never have been divided into Old and New Testaments. This did not occur until about 100 years after Yeshua, when an anti-Jewish teacher taught it. There is actually continuity throughout the Hebrew and Greek Scriptures.

2) <u>The Scriptures of Israel</u>, used by Yeshua and the Apostles, were the Hebrew texts and the Septuagint (LXX), which is the Greek translation of the Hebrew texts. No one taught or preached from what is called the New Testament, as it was not in existence yet.

3) <u>Yeshua The Jewish Messiah</u> lived totally by the Law, more correctly called the Torah or the Teachings of God through Moses, and the Prophets. Yeshua is the Living Torah! Torah can be applied to the whole Bible, since it means 'teachings.'

4) <u>Our Identity in Messiah</u> now is not as "a sinner saved by grace." It <u>was</u> that at the time of salvation, but since Messiah declared us righteous, therefore in fact we are righteous, right now! We were sinners, but now we are saints who occasionally sin. The remedy for sin is 1 John 1:9.

5) God deals with humans only on the basis of a Covenant, and <u>all the Covenants are made with Israel</u>! The Abrahamic Covenant is unilateral; God does everything in salvation. The Mosaic Covenant is bilateral, for those already in the Abrahamic Covenant; God has His part and the Believer has his part. The Davidic Covenant is unilateral again; God does everything to bring about the Son of David, Yeshua, to sit on the throne of

Israel. The New Covenant has both parts: Jeremiah 31:31-34, *"Behold the days come, says the LORD, that I will make a new* (chadash = renewed*) covenant with the house of Israel and with the house of Judah…I will put my Torah in their inward parts and write it on their hearts, and I will be their God and they shall be my people…and I will forgive their iniquity and I will remember their sin no more."* God does nearly everything, but with the Torah in their hearts, the Believer is expected to obey it. This is quoted in Hebrews 8. Contrary to church Tradition, the New Covenant is <u>not</u> made with the church!

6) <u>Paul, The Misunderstood Apostle</u>, who followed Torah just like Yeshua. He did not start Christianity and he did not and could not contradict anything that Yeshua taught, even if the church claims that he did by twisting his writings.

7) <u>The Torah Community</u> = the Congregation of the LORD, the *Kahal* (Hebrew) and *Ekklesia* (Greek Septuagint and Newer Testament) throughout time, from the beginning to the end. The word "church" comes from *kuriakon* = a pagan temple in New Testament times and should never have been brought into English Bibles. Yeshua said He would continue to build up His Congregation, not abandon Israel and start something new! God keeps His Promises! It would be impossible for God to abandon Israel and replace it with the 'church'! The Congregation of the LORD can also rightly be called the Messianic Community.

8) <u>The Seasons of Our Joy</u> are the Appointed Times of the LORD, summarized in Leviticus 23: the weekly Shabbat, the annual Passover, Unleavened Bread, First Fruits, Pentecost, Trumpets, Day of Atonement, and Tabernacles. These are wrongly called Jewish Feasts. They are the LORD's Festivals or Appointments!

9) <u>How do Believing Gentiles fit into all this</u>? By being grafted into the Good Olive Tree of Romans 11 together with Jewish Believers on an equal basis. Those Jewish and Gentile branches in God's Good Olive Tree are the totality of God's Family, The Congregation of the LORD.

# APPENDIX B

## Days of Elijah
### A Bible Study on the Song Phrases

*These are the days of Elijah, Declaring the Word of the LORD.*
Eliyahu = my God is Yah.  His life record: 1 Kings 17 – 2 Kings 2:11
His return: Malachi 4:4-5.   On the mount with Yeshua and
Moses: Matthew 17:1-13; Luke 9:28-36
   John the baptizer: Luke 1:17; 3:1-6; John 1:19-23; 10:41;
Matthew 11:13-15; 16:14

*And these are the days of Your servant Moses, Righteousness being restored.*
Every revival in the Bible was a return to the Torah and a
great celebration of Passover or Sukkot (Tabernacles)!
   Moses interceding for Israel: Exodus 32:30-35.  Moses given the
Torah on Mt. Sinai. Exodus 34.
   Revival under Hezekiah: a return to Torah and celebration of
Passover in the 2nd month: 2 Chronicles 30.
   Revival under Josiah. Torah found in the Temple: 2 Chronicles
34:14.  Reforms and Passover: 2 Chronicles 34-35.
   Revival under Ezra: according to Torah, Sukkot, Temple
rebuilt, Passover. Ezra 3-6. Ezra himself  7:1-10.
   Revival under Nehemiah: prayer based on Torah. Nehemiah 1.
Walls rebuilt. Torah with Ezra at Sukkot: Nehemiah 8.
   The Song of Moses: Revelation 15:3

*And though these are days of great trials, Of famine and darkness and sword,*
   Mark 13:1-23   Matthew 24   Luke 21

*Still we are the voice in the desert shouting, "Prepare ye the way of the LORD!"*
   Acts 1:8   Matthew 28:16-20   2 Timothy 4:1-4

Chorus:
*Behold He comes, riding on the clouds, Shining like the sun at the trumpet call.*
   Matthew 24:29-31; 26:63-64

*Lift your voice, it's the year of Jubilee, Out of Zion's hill salvation comes!*
   Leviticus 25:8-55; 27:17-25    Joel 2:30-32

*And these are the days of Ezekiel, The dry bones becoming as flesh.*
   First stage in restoration of Israel: Ezekiel 37:1-8.    Second stage: Ezekiel 37:9-14.

*And these are the days of your servant David, Rebuilding a temple of praise.*
   David's life record 1 Samuel 16–1 Kings 2:11. David wrote most of the Psalms, Israel's hymnbook
   David's reorganization of the government and Temple service. 1 Chronicles 23-27 David's instruments and music used in Temple worship: 2 Chronicles 29:25-30; in laying foundation of 2nd Temple: Ezra 3:10-11; rebuilding praise after the Captivity: Nehemiah 12:24,36; and End of Days: Amos 9:11-15; Zechariah 12:7-13:1.

*And these are the days of the harvest; The fields are white in the world,*
   Now: Matthew 9:36-38; John 4:34-38.   Final: Matt 13:36-43; Revelation 14:14-20

*And we are Your laborers in Your vineyard, Declaring the Word of the LORD!*
   Matthew 28:16-20; Isaiah 6:1-8; Romans 12:1-2; Acts 8:1-4; 15:35-36;
   2 Corinthians 4:5; 2 Timothy 4:1-4

*Who was, and Who is, and Who is to come...*
   Revelation 1:4, 8; 11:15-19

# APPENDIX C
## Memory Verses
### Annual APMF Conferences

First Conference in June 2003: John 14:15 (our basic theme verse for all Conferences and put on all publications),

*"If you love Me, keep My Commandments!"* and John 14:21, *"He that has my commandments and keeps them, he is the one that loves me, and he that loves me shall be loved by my Father, and I will love him and manifest myself to him."*

Second Conference in May 2004. Joshua 1:8:

*"This book of the Law (Torah) shall not depart out of your mouth, but you shall meditate in it day and night, that you may observe to do according to all that is written in it; for then you shall make your way prosperous, and then you shall have good success."* and Psalm 1:1-2, *"Blessed is the man who walks not in the counsel of the ungodly, nor stands in the way of sinners, nor sits in the seat of the scornful. But his delight is in the Law (Torah) of the LORD; and in his Law (Torah) he meditates day and night."*

Third Conference in April 2005. Psalm 19:7-11,

*"The Law of the LORD is perfect, converting the soul; the testimony of the LORD is sure, making wise the simple. The statutes of the LORD are right, rejoicing the heart; the commandment of the LORD is pure, enlightening the eyes. The fear of the LORD is clean, enduring forever; the ordinances of the LORD are true and righteous altogether. More to be desired are they than gold, yes, than much fine gold; sweeter also than honey and the honeycomb. Moreover, by them is your servant warned; and in keeping them there is great reward."*

Fifth Conference in April 2007. Isaiah 56:6-7:

*"Also the sons of the foreigner that join themselves to the LORD, to serve him, and to love the name of the LORD, to be his servants, every one that keeps the Sabbath from polluting it, and takes hold of my*

377

covenant; even them will I bring to my holy mountain, and make them joyful in my house of prayer; their burnt offerings and their sacrifices shall be accepted upon my altar; for my house shall be called an house of prayer for all peoples."

Sixth Conference in December 2007. Jeremiah 31:31-34:
"Behold the days come, says the LORD, that I will make a new (chadash = new or renewed) covenant with the house of Israel, and with the house of Judah, not according to the covenant that I made with their fathers in the day that I took them by the hand to bring them out of the land of Egypt, which, my covenant, they broke, although I was a husband to them, says the LORD; but this shall be the covenant that I will make with the house of Israel: After those days, says the LORD, I will put my law (Torah) in their inward parts, and write it in their hearts, and will be their God and they shall be my people. And they shall teach no more every man his neighbor, saying, Know the LORD; for they shall all know me, from the least of them unto the greatest of them, says the LORD; for I will forgive their iniquity, and I will remember their sin no more."

Seventh Conference April 2009.  Matthew 28:18-20 and John 13:34-35
"Jesus came and talked with them, saying, All authority in Heaven and on earth was   given to Me.  Going therefore, disciple all nations, baptizing them into the name of the Father and of the Son and of the Holy Spirit, teaching them to observe all things, whatever I commanded you. And, behold, I myself am with you all the days until the completion of the age. Amen."

"A new commandment I give to you, that you love one another: just as I have loved you, you also are to love one another.  By this all people will know that you are my disciples, if you have love for one another."

Eighth Conference April 2010.  Hebrews 11:7
"By faith Noah, being warned by God concerning events as yet unseen, in reverent fear constructed an ark for the saving of his household. By this he condemned the world and became an heir of the righteousness that comes by faith."

378

# APPENDIX D
## Scripture References

References are usually from the King James Version and may be a quotation or only referred to in relation to the subject matter. A Glossary is not provided, as uncommon words are explained in the text or are in the Bible text already.

| Chapter 1 | Genesis 1:1; 12:3 |
|---|---|
| Chapter 2 | Revelation 2:6; Matthew 23:8; Revelation 2:15 |
| Chapter 9 | 2 Timothy 2:4 |
| Chapter 11 | Psalm 111:9 |
| Chapter 12 | Acts 19:8-10 |
| Chapter 16 | Psalm 111:9 |
| Chapter 18 | 2 Timothy 2:2; Luke 24:44-45; Acts 7:38; Luke 22:14-20 |
| Chapter 19 | 1 Kings 10:2,13; Numbers 12:1; Acts 8; Matthew 16:13-20 |
| Chapter 20 | Genesis 12:3; Revelation 7:14 & 1:9; Romans 5:3-4; 2 Corinthians 4:17; Romans 11 |
| Chapter 21 | Romans 11; Revelation 1:20 |
| Chapter 22 | 2 Corinthians 5:8; 1 John 1:9; Jeremiah 31:31-34; Hebrews 8; Leviticus 23; Romans 11 |
| Chapter 23 | Psalm 118:22; Revelation 17 & 13 |

# APPENDIX E

## Gospel in the Stars

Fig. 12

XXIX
ORION
(the Glorious One)

HERCULES

VIRGO

DRACO

HYDRA

LEO

THE FLEEING SERPENT

# APPENDIX F

## Completed Babylon Chart

A study of Satan's kingdoms that have and will persecute God's Kingdom (Israel), the stone cutout without hands, which God will make into a mountain (kingdom) to cover the earth.

*"The Beast that was"*

**NIMROD'S BABYLON - TOWER OF BABEL**

| SUCCESSIVE KINGDOMS IN DANIEL 2 | BEAST KINGDOMS IN DANIEL 7 | REV 17 | REV 13 | NAME OF NATION & YEAR OF INDEPENDENCE | | |
|---|---|---|---|---|---|---|
| EGYPT | | 1 | | Egypt | - | 1922 |
| ASSYRIA | | 2 | | Kurdistan | | |
| BABYLON | winged-lion | 3 | mouth | Iraq | - | 1932 |
| MEDO-PERSIA | bear | 4 | feet | Iran | - | 1942 |
| GREECE | leopard | 5 | body | Macedonia Greece | - | 1944 |
| ROME | terrible beast | 6 | | Italy | - | 1870 |
| | "A Stone Cut Out.." | 7 | | Vatican | - | 330 |
| | | 8 | | Islam | - | 630 |

*"The Beast that is to come"*

Thy Kingdom come; Thy will be done on earth, as it is in heaven!!!

383

Made in the USA
Charleston, SC
16 October 2013